Violence in Argentine Literature and Film
(1989–2005)

LATIN AMERICAN AND CARIBBEAN SERIES

Christon I. Archer, General Editor
ISSN 1498-2366

This series sheds light on historical and cultural topics in Latin America and the Caribbean by publishing works that challenge the canon in history, literature, and postcolonial studies. It seeks to print cutting-edge studies and research that redefine our understanding of historical and current issues in Latin America and the Caribbean.

No. 1 · **Waking the Dictator: Veracruz, the Struggle for Federalism and the Mexican Revolution** Karl B. Koth

No. 2 · **The Spirit of Hidalgo: The Mexican Revolution in Coahuila** Suzanne B. Pasztor · Copublished with Michigan State University Press

No. 3 · **Clerical Ideology in a Revolutionary Age: The Guadalajara Church and the Idea of the Mexican Nation, 1788–1853** Brian F. Connaughton, translated by Mark Allan Healey · Copublished with University Press of Colorado

No. 4 · **Monuments of Progress: Modernization and Public Health in Mexico City, 1876–1910** Claudia Agostoni · Copublished with University Press of Colorado

No. 5 · **Madness in Buenos Aires: Patients, Psychiatrists and the Argentine State, 1880–1983** Jonathan Ablard · Copublished with Ohio University Press

No. 6 · **Patrons, Partisans, and Palace Intrigues: The Court Society of Colonial Mexico, 1702–1710** Christoph Rosenmüller

No. 7 · **From Many, One: Indians, Peasants, Borders, and Education in Callista Mexico, 1924–1935** Andrae Marak

No. 8 · **Violence in Argentine Literature and Film (1989–2005)** Edited by Carolina Rocha & Elizabeth Montes Garcés

Violence in Argentine Literature and Film
(1989–2005)

Edited by
CAROLINA ROCHA AND
ELIZABETH MONTES GARCÉS

UNIVERSITY OF
CALGARY
PRESS

© 2010 Carolina Rocha and Elizabeth Montes Garcés

University of Calgary Press
2500 University Drive NW
Calgary, Alberta
Canada T2N 1N4
www.uofcpress.com

No part of this publication may be reproduced, stored in a retrieval system or transmitted, in any form or by any means, without the prior written consent of the publisher or a license from The Canadian Copyright Licensing Agency (Access Copyright). For an Access Copyright license, visit www.accesscopyright.ca or call toll free 1-800-893-5777.

LIBRARY AND ARCHIVES CANADA CATALOGUING IN PUBLICATION

Violence in Argentine literature and film (1989-2005) / edited by Carolina Rocha and Elizabeth Montes Garcés.

(Latin American and Caribbean series, 1498-2366 ; 8)
Includes bibliographical references and index.
ISBN 978-1-55238-504-3

1. Argentine literature—History and criticism. 2. Motion pictures—Argentina. 3. Politics and literature—Argentina. 4. Motion pictures—Political aspects—Argentina. 5. Literature and society—Argentina. 6. Motion pictures—Social aspects—Argentina. 7. Violence in literature. 8. Violence in motion pictures. I. Rocha, Carolina II. Montes Garcés, Elizabeth, 1962– III. Series: Latin American and Caribbean series ; 8

PQ7655.V56 2010   860.9'3556   C2010-904433-9

The University of Calgary Press acknowledges the support of the Alberta Foundation for the Arts for our publications. We acknowledge the financial support of the Government of Canada through the Canada Book Fund for our publishing activities. We acknowledge the financial support of the Canada Council for the Arts for our publishing program.

Cover image: Urban Vibe Vol 94 - #94086 (www.stockphoto.com)
Cover design by Melina Cusano
Page design and typesetting by Melina Cusano

To Armando

TABLE OF CONTENTS

Acknowledgments ... ix

Introduction ... xi

I. The Legacy of the Military Years

Torture and Abuse as a National Art Form: Gustavo Nielsen's *Auschwitz* (Fernando Reati) ... 3

Subjection and Injury in *El vuelo de la reina* by Tomás Eloy Martínez (Myriam Osorio) ... 23

Desire and Violence in Ana María Shua's *La muerte como efecto secundario* (Elizabeth Montes Garcés) ... 47

Violence and Representation: Postdictatorship Visions in Lita Stantic and Albertina Carri (Ana Forcinito) ... 67

II. Paradise Lost

Barbaric Spectacles: Masculinities in Crisis in Popular Argentine Cinema of the 1990s (Carolina Rocha) ... 93

Far from Heaven: On *El cielito*, by María Victoria Menis (Gabriela Copertari) ... 111

An Argentine Context: Civilization and Barbarism in *El aura* and *El custodio* (Beatriz Urraca) ... 125

III. The Re-Signification of Social and Geographical Spaces

Postnational Boundaries in *Bolivia* (Ignacio López-Vicuña) — 145

Contesting Spaces, Contesting Discourses in *Bolivia*, by Adrián Caetano (Natalia Jackovkis) — 163

The Violence of the Site (Zulema Moret) — 183

Projecting Buenos Aires Back to the Future: Violence in Argentine Post-Dictatorship Science Fiction Film (Victoria Ruétalo) — 203

List of Contributors — 221

Index — 225

ACKNOWLEDGMENTS

This book is the result of a collective effort, thus, the editors would like to thank all the contributors who accepted to participate in this project. It has been rewarding to work with colleagues who share our interest in the topic of violence.

We would like to extend our sincere gratitude to Paula Mae Carns, Modern Language Librarian of the University of Illinois at Urbana, for making possible the impossible, and to Rob Cagle for his help in locating sources. Thanks also to Sharon Scott for her friendship and continued support.

Elizabeth Montés Garcés is indebted to Christon Archer and the Latin American Research Centre for the fellowship on the project "Corporeal Imaginings in Latin American Female Literature," of which the article published in this collection is a part.

Carolina Rocha's essay has appeared in *Ciberletras*, and Fernando Reati's article was first published in Spanish. The editors are grateful for the permissions to reprint this article.

A number of colleagues provided helpful suggestions for the introduction. Our thanks to Zulema Moret and Fernando Reati. Santiago Juan, Dianna Niebilsky, and Norman Cheadle provided insightful comments and valuable advice. We are also grateful to Hugo Hortiguera for his suggestions. We also appreciate Adam Domskey, Talia Bugel Amanda Landa, Shawn England, and Matthew Prochenka for their editorial help. Last but not least, we would like to thank Donna Livingstone, director of the University of Calgary Press for her patience and support.

This book has been published thanks to the generous financial support of Christa Johnson, Associate Dean of Graduate Studies and Kevin Johnson, Associate Dean of Research in the College of Liberal Arts, both from Southern Illinois University Edwardsville, and Daniel Maher, Interim Dean of Humanities from the University of Calgary.

INTRODUCTION

The essays in this volume explore the representation of violence in contemporary Argentine literature and film. The interest in this topic was spurred by the social and economic tensions that developed in Argentina in the 1990s and contributed to the proliferation of narrative fiction, plays and films addressing this issue. We selected 1989 as a starting point for this examination of violence, the year when a major recession triggered a political crisis with a deep impact on Argentine society. High levels of unemployment, the devaluation of the Argentine currency, and a reduction in the level of production contributed to the abrupt end of the first democratic government during the post-military transition. Riots and popular protests accelerated the inauguration of Carlos Menem in July 1989 and highlighted the fact that even if Argentines were attempting to move away from the state-sponsored political violence that had prevailed during the military government of 1976–83, a new kind of violence was emerging, one that was the result of the new socioeconomic and political changes that were evident in the last decade of the twentieth century. These transformations provided the background from which Argentine writers, playwrights, and filmmakers deployed the topic of violence.

While the depiction and narration of crimes and acts of violence has shaped Argentine literature as a national corpus since its beginning,[1] the visual representation of violence in Argentina begins with the production of the first films in the twentieth century. A case in point is Mario

Gallo's *El fusilamiento de Dorrego* (*Dorrego's Execution*, 1908), which was followed by *Amalia* (1912), based on José Mármol's novel. These first films revisit the violent nineteenth century, a trend that continued with the arrival of sound and lasted throughout the classical period. For example, Lucas Demare's *La guerra gaucha* (*The Gaucho War*, 1942) was well received by critics and the public. During the late 1960s and early 1970s, politically committed writers and filmmakers chose to record the structural differences between social classes and the working conditions in certain trades, such as lumber and mining – Fernando Solanas' *La hora de los hornos* (*The Hour of the Furnaces*, 1973) constitutes a relevant example – so as to present hidden forms of violence. It is not surprising, then, that censorship in the early 1970s affected filmmakers and writers alike, many of whom had to exile themselves. With the return of democracy in 1983, literary and visual works shared a concern to depict, analyze, and explain the impact of seven years of military rule. After 1989, a new trend became noticeable: recent cultural production immersed audiences in the chaotic and constraining atmosphere of socioeconomic and political crisis of the last decade of the century. This trend evinces that the myths that created the nation or gave individuals a sense of identity, such as family, religion, and employment have been undermined.

In this collection of essays, we chose to focus on the visual and literary representations of violence that move audiences to question the very notions of nation and identity in a new global order. These similarities are based on the interconnections between violence, power, and social practices at play in times of late capitalism. This is so because issues such as state sovereignty, gender relations, the implementation of laws, and the "civilization versus barbarism" debate all coalesce and impinge on the images that a society has of itself, or as David Riches states,

> The expressive function of acts or images of violence capitalizes, firstly, on the visibility of violence, and secondly on the probability that all involved – however different their cultural backgrounds – are likely to draw, at the very least, some basic

common understanding from the acts or images concerned. These two properties of violence make it an excellent communicator vehicle. (1986: 12)

Thus, the essays that make up this collection seek to interpret and analyze the extent to which violence communicates structural inequalities or lines of fissure in contemporary Argentine society resulting from the transformations that the state, the economy, and society in general experienced after the first democratic government (1983–89). More specifically, when considered together, this collection attempts to answer the questions: Why has violence been a predominant topic in contemporary Argentine film and literature? What conclusions can be drawn from the dissemination of violent images and narratives that depict violence in Argentina? To understand the historical background of the period after 1989, a brief overview is presented.

HISTORICAL BACKGROUND

Carlos Menem's first term in office (1989–95) marked the beginning of a new era in Argentine life. To quickly pacify society, President Menem sought to rescue it from economic paralysis, deploying the metaphor of resurrecting the country from death. Indeed, in his July 1989 inaugural speech, President Menem called the population "to stand and walk" by taking part in the rebuilding of Argentina. Besides the "productive revolution," his political agenda consisted of implementing the policies suggested by a group of experts known as the Washington Consensus. These policies entailed the reduction of public spending through the elimination of subsidies for health and education, the opening of trade, market-adjusted interest rates, a new tax system, privatization of national assets, foreign investment, market-based exchange rates, and respect for property rights (Stark 1998: 90; based on Williamson 1990). While some of these measures helped to stabilize the economy and reduce inflation to single digits, it soon became evident that an unregulated market meant the disappearance of the welfare state and the subsequent loss of funding for health, education, and social programs.[2]

Thus, by putting an end to national-populist economic programs, President Menem was also reducing the role of the state as an arbiter among the different social classes. This decision had two noteworthy implications. First, political power sided with the upper classes that have traditionally favoured economic liberalism and have benefited the most during the years of military rule. An example of this alliance was the trust placed by President Menem on local financial groups to design and implement the liberalization of the Argentine economy (Svampa 2005: 107). Second, the interests of the middle and lower classes ceased to be the axis around which domestic policies were planned and carried out. For example, unions, which had customarily protected workers' jobs and had been a crucial player in twentieth-century Argentine politics, were unable to stop privatizations and the laying off of numerous trained workers, thus losing much of their bargaining power and centrality as political actors. Moreover, the interests of the middle class were also less crucial in policy-making.

These unexpected and radical policies altered the traditional dynamic between social classes and political actors in Argentine society. Perhaps the most ubiquitous consequence was the disappearance of many welfare and social programs, thereby leaving large sections of the population to fend for themselves without the protection or safety nets of previous years. In addition, the transformation from a welfare state to a planning one also encompassed the privatization of the bulk of state-owned companies. This transference of ownership from state-run companies to both the private sector and foreign investors had far-reaching implications for every aspect of life in Argentine society after 1989. In the years between 1989 and 1994, these policies contributed simultaneously to reversing the corrosive effects of hyperinflation and to rebuilding the domestic economy. However, in those same years, a parallel process began to take place. Alberto Barbeito and Rubén Lo Vuolo called it "exclusionary modernization," an expression that came to signify that the benefits of economic stability would be available only to a small group (1992). Indeed, after 1994, the emphasis on efficiency and high productivity along with a push for de-industrialization resulted in the downsizing of several companies, with the subsequent laying off of numerous workers. As a consequence of the implementation of this efficiency-oriented program and the resulting unemployment, a third of Argentine households were living in poverty by 1995, and by 1996 the unemployment rate had tripled in only six years: from 6 per cent in 1990 to 18.8 per cent (Svampa 2005: 35).

The deterioration of Argentines' standard of living was particularly exacerbated during President Menem's second term in office (1995–2000), during which many more jobs were lost. The ripples of two international economic crises also negatively impacted the Argentine economy, emphasizing the feeling of vulnerability of the different social classes at a time when political authorities were suspected of multiple cases of economic and judicial corruption. As a result, the concept of citizenship was devalued: as citizens were abandoned by the state, deprived of social benefits, and exposed to its excesses and abuses, many started questioning the advantages of abiding by the law.

Indeed, the concepts of citizenship and private property were greatly affected when the government of Fernando de la Rúa (term of office, 2000–2001) confiscated bank deposits and depreciated the national currency in an effort to address the issue of the national deficit. The middle class reacted by joining in *cacerolazos* (potbanging) to express their disapproval of these measures. The lower classes took part in lootings and food riots. For Argentine sociologist Javier Auyero, these acts were instances of collective violence, not only for the damage perpetrated, but also, and more importantly, for the links between looters and "third parties" (political brokers and police agents) who allowed these episodes of violence to occur (2007: 157). This social unrest prompted President de la Rúa to resign in December 2001 amid a staggering number of cases of violence that left almost three hundred stores and supermarkets looted, thirty-four people dead, and several injured (Auyero 2007).[3]

Political, social and economic instability radically affected every aspect of life in Argentina. In the days that followed de la Rúa's resignation, the country saw a succession of interim presidents until Eduardo Duhalde, former governor of Buenos Aires, was sworn in as president on January 2, 2002. President Duhalde led a transitional government also marked by a high number of social protests, especially during the year 2002. To solve the situation of those most affected by the downsizing of the state, in April 2002, the *Plan Jefas y Jefes*, a welfare program that provided a small stipend for heads of families, was approved. This plan, which still benefits 1.5 million households, was envisioned as a way to placate the urban poor. With the pacification of society, democratic continuity was ensured. In April 2003, elections took place: although former President Menem was able to garner most of the votes, the opposition actively worked to defeat him in the second round. Menem's withdrawal from the presidential race made possible the triumph of Néstor Kirchner who took over the presidency a month later.

ON OLD AND NEW TYPES OF VIOLENCE

In her introduction to *Violence: A Reader*, Catherine Besteman points to the inextricable link between power, politics, and violence. Traditional sociology shows the monopoly of physical power in modern states (Elías 1939; Weber 2002), meaning that states hold the right to sanction which types of violence are allowed within their borders. However, in post-national times or the era of globalization, a first question arises: Do nation states still monopolize physical force within their borders? The answer to this question is not simple. As states have redefined their roles in the last decades so as to adapt to new global trends, other actors, who also aspire to the monopoly of physical force, have emerged. Dissident armed groups within a state compete with the nation state for the legitimate use of physical power as a way to change policy and bring to the fore either regional demands or the rights of minority groups because of their class, race or ethnicity.

The case of Argentina is particularly complex. Political violence – military coups and civil upheavals – visibly shaped twentieth-century Argentine military history. The most recent dictatorship left an estimated 30,000 victims of state-sponsored violence. They "disappeared" – an expression that means that their whereabouts are still unknown and their remains have not been found yet. One of the priorities of President Menem in the early 1990s was to appease the Armed Forces, who in several episodes during the previous decade had resisted public scrutiny for the methods used during the Dirty War. The decrees of Full Stop and Due Obedience passed during Menem's first term in office were designed to end the inquiry into the actions taken by the Armed Forces during the 1976–83 period. Nonetheless, the controversy over events of political violence resurfaced in Argentine society in 1995 when Captain Adolfo Scilingo revealed the *modus operandi* of the Air Force to journalist Horacio Verbistky. In *El vuelo* (*The Flight*, 1995), Scilingo detailed the way drugged militants and human rights activists were thrown from airplanes into the ocean. Scilingo's confession reopened domestic as well as international interest in investigating and recording the human rights violations committed in the late 1970s and early 1980s.

This renewed interest in examining the causes and actors of the political violence of the 1970s was made evident by the publication of Marta Diana's *Mujeres guerrilleras* (*Women Fighters*, 1996) and Luis Mattini's *Hombres y mujeres del PRT-ERP. De Tucumán a La Tablada* (*Men and Women of the Workers Revolutionary Party-People's Revolutionary Army. From Tucumán to La Tablada*, 1996). Both books describe episodes of violence carried out by the armed left. As Jens Andermann et al. state:

> Since the second half of the 1990s, there has been a marked shift in intellectual and political debates on Argentina's recent past, from a discourse focused on establishing legal responsibility for human rights violations during the dictatorship, to a reconsideration of the histories of left-wing militancy and armed struggle that preceded it. (2007: 111)

Part of this attention reached and was prompted by international audiences. For example, European governments, such as those of France, Spain, and Denmark, investigated and sought to try the perpetrators of human rights abuses against their citizens who disappeared in Argentina in the late 1970s and early 1980s.

Despite the fact that human rights violations took place decades before, they are still very much part of the present. Episodes of torture and killings in which police forces abused their power are some of the legacies of the repressive apparatus. For instance, as early as December 1991, Americas Watch issued a report about human rights violations that took place in the city and province of Buenos Aires and in which the suspects were members of the police. What is more disturbing about the findings of this report is the fact that the violations of human rights occurred in the period 1986–90, that is to say, during the period of re-democratization. The report stated that at that time, "a chief problem is a continuing system of impunity for officials, familiar from the years of the dictatorship, based upon intimidation of witnesses, lawyers and officials, upon inadequate management and disciplinary methods" (1991:1). While political scientists Enrique Peruzzotti and Catalina Smulovitz have observed that the problem of impunity has affected many Latin American democracies (2006: 4), in Argentina the police force has been involved in very high-profile cases such as the murder of journalist José Luis Cabezas in 1997, the homicide of Sebastián Bordón who died in 1997 of hunger and thirst after being beaten by the police and left unconscious, and more recently in 2006, the murder of schoolteacher Carlos Fuentealba in a demonstration in the province of Santa Cruz. In addition, in March 2004, Axel Blumberg, a twenty-three-year-old student was shot by his kidnappers as a result of police intervention. The common thread in all these cases is both the abuse of power of authorities and the extreme brutality that victims endured as a result of intimidation by a force that considers itself above the law.

Another case that highlights the persistence of practices inherited from the military years is the recent disappearance of Jorge Julio López, a crucial witness in the trial of Miguel Etchecolatz, a police chief accused of torturing and murdering political dissidents during the military government of 1976–83. López disappeared on September 17, 2006, one day after testifying, and has since been unaccounted for. A telling fact about the operative of former repressors is the statement by the government of Buenos Aires that specifies that in its investigation, 549 people, among them former members of the Armed and Security Forces, both active and retired, have been under scrutiny for López's disappearance (Clarín, 18 Sept. 2007).

Since the early 1990s, a new kind of violence has become evident: violence as a result of increasing disparities within the living standards of the Argentine population. Besteman calls these disparities the "structural violence" of poverty, malnutrition, poor health, local violence and crime resulting from implicit or overt state support of hierarchies based on gender, race, sexuality, language, and class (2002: 304). In Argentina, job insecurity was one of the causes of structural violence because, as unemployment grew, work no longer occupied "the key position as basis for the construction of individual identity and peer relationships" (Grimson and Kessler 2005: 113). Unemployment was inextricably linked to the pauperization of vast sectors of the Argentine population, a circumstance that had a dramatic consequence on everyday life. Political scholars Felipe Agüero and Jeffrey Stark have used the fault-lines metaphor to refer to the situation of Latin American countries, including Argentina, in the 1990s. The fault-lines metaphor "proposes a focus on uneven development in post-authoritarian regimes" (Agüero and Stark 1998: 9). Based on geological faults, it illustrates the frictions and unresolved tensions noticeable during the 1990s in spite of democratic continuity.

In Argentina, fault-lines manifested themselves in new episodes of violence triggered as a result of the effects of structural violence. For example, laid-off workers and public employees took part in massive protests and demonstrations, which Juan Pablo Angeleone defined as "minimalist estamental" (1997: 134). In this kind of violence, the main social actors are impoverished members of the middle class who are not trying to interrupt the democratic system contrary to the case of the armed groups in the early to mid-1970s; rather, these protesters "demand that they are given what they believe they deserve" (134).[4] Argentine political scientist Adalberto Agozino also considers civil resistance a type of political violence that "attempts to introduce changes in the balance of power of a given society through coercive and non-consensual means" (2004: 21).[5] For Agozino, "social violence is being engineered by those who are excluded from the social system and who do not passively accept suffering from hunger and marginality" (2004: 28).[6] Among the different variants of civil resistance, Agozino lists *piqueteros* (picketers) – groups that organize roadblocks – , lootings and *okupas* – poor families that settle in empty houses – , all of those channels of protest of the lower classes, and potbangings and self-convocated assemblies carried out by middle-class groups. Finally, *escraches* are acts against people and institutions that participated in human rights violations.

These forms of civil resistance, manifested through political violence, are the consequence of the division of society into lower and upper classes. On one hand, upper-middle-class groups successfully adapted to the new economic order and enjoyed a good standard of living; on the other, a large proportion of the middle class lost some of their privileges and became the "new poor" who were subjected to unemployment, sub-employment, or partial unemployment. The fragmentation of society along these two distinct groups had a number of consequences that were felt throughout the different social classes. To use the words of Argentine sociologist Juan Carlos Torres, "those who won" constituted small privileged groups among masses that merely had enough to survive. The growing divide between these classes led Argentine sociologist Maristella Svampa to characterize the type of society that emerged as "exclusionary," as based on the model of limited citizenship (2005: 128). As those who were unemployed or underemployed were unable to participate effectively in the national economy, it was clear that only the upper sector could enjoy access to exclusive products and differentiating practices.

The concentration of income in the hands of a small group prompted that group to consume a wide array of products, now made available by the liberalization of trade and the reduction of import barriers. As Néstor García Canclini has indicated, the emphasis on spending gave way to changes in identity: "Today, instead, shaped by consumption, identities depend on what one owns or is capable of attaining" (2002: 16). This transformation along with the reduced role of the state in public affairs led to a de-politicization of public life. In this context, the role of consumers was emphasized in the 1990s to the detriment of public life and the exercise of a participatory style of citizenship. Those who had a lower income or no income at all were unable to effectively take part in capitalist consumption, a fact that kept them from public life.

Exclusion also resulted in higher levels of criminality in the late 1990s. Sociologist Gabriel Kessler provides indisputable data about the rise in crime during this decade: there were 560,240 reported crimes in 1990 and 1,062,241 in 1999 (2004: 22). As a result, insecurity and fear also increased. For those who could afford to leave the city, the solution entailed relocating to gated neighbourhoods, the *countries*. Those who had to remain within the city limits experienced a heightened sense of danger, which translated into a gradual abandonment of public spaces and a subsequent privatization of social life.

REVIEW OF LITERATURE

Recent publications on Latin America have thoroughly examined the topic of violence generated by changes in socioeconomic life and how these transformations influence the state's ability to sanction criminality. A case in point is *Citizens of Fear: Urban Violence in Latin America* (2002), a collection of essays edited by the late Susana Rotker that examines the social and political implications of varied forms of violence in the region. Another collection, compiled by Hugo Frühling and Joseph Tulchin,

Crime and Violence in Latin America: Citizen Security, Democracy and the State (2003), also provides insightful reflections, mostly by scholars in the political sciences, about trends in Latin America. In the same vein, focusing only on Argentina, Alejandro Isla and Daniel Miguez edited *Heridas urbanas: violencia delictiva y transformaciones sociales en los noventa* (*Urban Wounds: Criminal Violence and Social Transformations in the 1990s*, 2003), a compilation of essays analyzing violence from the point of view of sociology and anthropology.

Two frequently cited studies examine the influence of political violence on Argentina's cultural production: Fernando Reati's *Nombrar lo innombrable: violencia política y novela Argentina, 1975–1985* (*Naming the Unnamable: Political Violence and Argentine Novels, 1975–1985*, 1992) and David W. Foster's *Violence in Argentine Literature: Cultural Responses to Tyranny* (1995). These monographs assess the impact of repression primarily on the literature produced in the 1980s. Depictions of violence represented in movies have been addressed by the collection *Civilización y barbarie en el cine argentino y latinoamericano* (*Civilization and Barbarism in Argentine and Latin American Cinema*, 2005), edited by Ana Laura Lusnich. This collection covers a broad time period, surveying cinematic production since the 1930s in Argentina and Latin America.

REPRESENTATION OF VIOLENCE IN CONTEMPORARY ARGENTINE LITERATURE AND FILM

This book explores the representation of violence in Argentine literature and film over the last two decades (1989–2007). Responding to an overwhelming legacy of state repression and misogynist authoritarianism characteristic of the "dirty war" to the new forms of aggression exercised by the neoliberal policies of the nineties; the eleven articles contained in this collection engage with the question of the ethical and moral responsibility of the audience towards depictions of extreme violence, the undermining of national myths, and redefinitions of geographic and socioeconomic spaces.

In *Nombrar lo innombrable: Violencia política y novela argentina, 1975–85* (*Naming the Unnamable: Political Violence and Argentine Novels*, 1992), Fernando Reati points out that one of the prevailing tendencies of the Argentine novels of the seventies and eighties was the use of creative narrative techniques to go beyond the idealization of the victim and to look into the psychological profile of the torturer. In these narratives, readers are confronted with images that provide them with a new perspective of their own society. Authors such as Antonio Dal Masetto, Mempo Giardinelli, and Humberto Constantini were addressing a compliant civilian population that did not react against the atrocities committed either by the armed forces or the guerilla insurgents. In doing so, fiction writers of the seventies and eighties demystified the ideal of civility of Argentinian society by confronting readers with the evil within themselves.

The first four articles of the present volume focus on the legacy of the military years. Reati's analysis of the literary fiction from the previous decades can be taken one step further to examine the body as a site of torture and the role of the readers and spectators as voyeurs of those actions. His article, entitled "Torture and Abuse as a National Art Form," offers an encompassing view of violence in Gustavo Nielsen's *Auschwitz* (2004) as he traces the importance of torture and sadism in several other novels and essays, such as Alejandra Pizarnik's *La condesa sangrienta* (*The Bloody Countess*, 1965), Luis Gusman's *Villa* (1995), José Pablo Feinmann's *La crítica de las armas* (*A Critique of Weapons*, 2003), Hugo Vezzeti's *Pasado y presente* (*Past and Present*, 1985), among many others. More than merely analyzing how the characterization of the protagonist Berto works in *Auschwitz* to move the readership to become voyeurs of poignant episodes of torture, Reati encourages us to acknowledge the evil within ourselves. For Reati, Nielsen's verbalization of the atrocities committed by torturers such as Berto becomes a way to prevent them from happening again.

The combination of voyeurism and torture are also present in Tomás Eloy Martínez's *El vuelo de la reina* (2002). However, in comparison with Reati's opinion that describing torture becomes a way to exorcise violence, Myriam Osorio proposes that Tomás Eloy Martínez's novel represents the workings of an ideology that forces women to occupy a site of injury and the consequences of not embracing that site. Relying on the concept of subjectivation, a term coined by Judith Butler in her reading of Michel Foucault's *Discipline and Punish*, Osorio analyzes how Camargo, a powerful director of a Buenos Aires newspaper, attempts to control Reina Remis's body by using torture and sadism to make her comply with his idea of what a woman ought to be. The unpunished murder of Reina alludes to a culture of impunity. It also alludes to a tendency in contemporary Latin American literature to represent the excluded or marginal subjects (women, poor people, immigrants, etc.) as "fragmented and corroded body"[7]

While in the aforementioned articles, violence is perpetrated by male authoritarian figures over the bodies of children or female characters, in Ana María Shua's *La muerte como efecto secundario* (*Death as a Side Effect*, 1997), it is an authoritarian father (Gregorio Kollody) who exercises psychological violence, not only against his daughter and wife, but also against his son Ernesto. However, Gregorio is confronted with a serious disease: a tumor that blocks his intestine. He is forced into state-managed hospitals and nursing homes that profit from diseases of wealthy elderly people. In this case, the violence experienced in the sphere of the family is replicated by the state because it is the state apparatus that orchestrates a macabre plot to exercise violence against the bodies of the elderly with the only purpose of gaining profit. By using Gilles Deleuze and Félix Guattari's schizoanalysis, Elizabeth Montes Garcés explores how Ernesto (the protagonist, writer, and make-up artist of the novel) is able to expose and undermine the mechanisms of desire that are at play in an authoritarian system, which leads to violence inside and outside of the family realm.

Just as in the novels by Nielsen, Martínez, and Shua, the reader is compelled to get involved in the texts and take a different view in light of the violent images depicted in the narratives; the same effect is true in Albertina Carri's and Lita Stantic's films. According to Ana Forcinito,

Un muro de silencio (*A Wall of Silence*, 1993) and *Los rubios* (*The Blonde Ones*, 2003) place audiences in a privileged position to shift their gaze and see from a new perspective the effects of the violence in the daily lives of the sons and daughters of the disappeared and the survivors of the detention camps. Stantic and Carri develop several cinematic strategies such as the fragmentation of the narrative line, the inclusion of a film within a film, and the transformation of the gaze towards violence to bring to the fore a new project of social memory that tells the untold stories of the disappeared.

Another trait that Reati assigns to the literary fiction written in the decade of 1975–85 is the willingness to undertake the project of dismantling long-cherished national myths such as the discourse on progress and civilization as formulas to grant stability and prosperity to the nation. Therefore, the second set of articles in this collection, entitled "Paradise Lost," presents the idea of violence as a result of the undermining of the myths that gave cohesion to the idea of nation. Films produced after 1989 not only deal with longstanding myths and foundational national narratives but also, and more importantly, they re-examine and challenge the validity of those narratives. During the 1880–1930 period, the dominant national narratives stressed the idea that Argentina was an idyllic heaven where immigrants could not only prosper from the country's natural resources but also improve their lives and those of their descendants. Public schools and the university reform of 1917 granted immigrants free access to literacy and education. Free and universal education not only socialized and helped assimilate immigrants' children but it also contributed to the development of the middle class, a fact that distinguished Argentina from its Latin American neighbours. Thus, from the beginning of the twentieth century, upward social mobility helped consolidate the myth of individual progress and social integration. As domestic migrants chose cities as their places of residence, free and universal education not only socialized them in urban life but also contributed to the expansion and influence of the middle class, a proud distinction from other Latin American countries.

In the Argentina of the 1990s, the concept of civilization changed drastically as the middle class shrank numerically and lost its traditional privileges. As the state relinquished its traditional role as arbiter in social life, civilization was replaced by the law of the powerful. This shift becomes evident in Juan Bautista Stagnaro's *La furia* (*Fury*, 1997) and Marcelo Piñeyro's *Cenizas del paraíso* (*Ashes from Paradise*, 1997), which Carolina Rocha analyzes in "Barbaric Spectacles: Masculinities in Crisis in Popular Argentine Cinema of the 1990s." By relying on Sigmund Freud's and Norbert Elias' concept of civilization, Rocha examines the victimization of middle-class men at the hands of a corrupt state that fails to penalize criminal acts. This process of emasculation experienced by male victims not only challenges the concept of Argentina as a civilized society but also, and more importantly, alludes to the impact of changing socioeconomic variables on the roles that men perform in Argentine society.

If the discourse of civilization collapses in Piñeyro's and Stagnaro's films, so does the concept of progress in Gabriela Copertari's analysis of María Victoria Menis' acclaimed opera prima, *El cielito* (*Little Heaven*, 2004) the new Argentine filmmakers portrayed the reversal of that narrative of progress. As the middle classes were deeply impacted by neoliberal policies and their standard of living deteriorated, the myth of unchallenged progress and upward mobility was no longer a defining feature of Argentine society. For example, the loss of the importance of the middle class was read as a sign of the so-called Latin Americanization of Argentina (Grimson and Kessler 2005: 97) and thus an end to Argentina's long-standing exceptionalism in Latin America based on its European character and the preponderance of its middle class. As these narratives lost their efficacy, others emerged that were imbued with the disillusionment and a sense of failure that can be grouped under the term of "paradise lost."

Beatriz Urraca's study of Fabián Bielinsky's *El aura* (*The Aura*, 2005), and Rodrigo Moreno's *El custodio* (*The Bodyguard*, 2006) also goes back to Sarmiento's foundational myth of civilization and barbarism. According to Urraca, the characterization of the protagonist Rubén (the bodyguard) in *El custodio* and the unnamed taxidermist in *El aura*, the mise-en-scène, and the cinematography are still tainted by the contradictions and contested spaces created by the opposition of civilization and barbarism. Both characters, Rubén and the taxidermist, are diligent and tidy citizens but also obscure and lonely figures who are taken away to unfamiliar territories (Mar del Plata, and the untamed forests of Argentina) where the "other" within themselves takes over and makes them commit a violent act: the killing of the Minister of Planning in *El custodio*, and the Baqueano in *El aura*. Violence in this context is the result of an incontrollable act of barbarism committed by insignificant individuals to gain a moment of protagonism that will alter ordinary life forever.

While in the first part of the volume we can see the intensification of the traits identified by Fernando Reati to the literary fiction of the seventies and eighties in the filmic and literary texts produced in Argentina over the last two decades, in the second part, there is a clear departure from those premises. The four articles organized under the section entitled "The Re-signification of Social and Geographical Spaces" deal with the relationship between violence and space. To analyze this topic, we will rely on James R. Giles's study on the way spaces of violence are created in contemporary American fiction.

Drawing on Henri Lefebvre's *The Production of Space* (1974), and Edward W. Soja's *Thirdspace: Journeys to Los Angeles and Other Real-and-Imagined Places* (1996), Giles coins the term "fourthspace." In his seminal study, Lefebvre established three forms of space: the physical associated with nature, the mental, and the social. According to Giles, Lefebvre's theory owes a great deal to Foucault since the construction of mental and social spaces is strongly influenced by the violence exercised by capitalism to gain control over power and knowledge. Edward Soja posits a more positive view of a thirdspace. Rather than seeing it as an abstract space of capitalist domination, Soja builds on Lefebvre's notion of representational spaces created through language and the visual arts. For Soja the thirdspace is that of the "realimagined" that could be found in the borderline between cultures, genres, and races where resistance to diverse forms of oppression can be found. However, according to Giles, a close analysis of contemporary American fiction reveals that "systematic violence, depicted sometimes as the inevitable consequence of a male-dominated capitalism and sometimes as the expression of degraded mythologies, contributes to the varied forms of fourthspace found in these novels" (13). Thus, for Giles fictional characters are pushed to the borderline, to the margins, a fourthspace where they are incapable of resisting or counteracting the menacing effects of extreme violence.

That fourthspace where all the old mythologies that defined the nation suddenly collapse, where there is no hope for redemption, and where characters are faced with an excess of violence that seems to overflow the limits of the screen itself is what characterizes the New Argentine Cinema. In "Postnational Boundaries in *Bolivia*," Ignacio López-Vicuña analyzes how neoliberal policies imposed on Argentina undermine the very notion of nation due to the atmosphere of violence and distress that forces the characters in the film to cross the limits between law and illegality, and civilization and barbarism. By using cinematic techniques reminiscent of neo-realism such as the camera's wandering gaze, and the focalization on objects instead of events, Adrián Caetano creates disempowered characters that are helpless to change their living conditions, and whose frustration leads them to violent acts such as the killing of Freddy, a Bolivian immigrant, by Oso, a frustrated and xenophobic car driver. While in López-Vicuña's article on Adrián Caetano's *Bolivia* viewers are immersed in the fourthspace, a city of Buenos Aires that no longer fulfills their dreams, in Natalia Jacovkis's analysis of the same film the critic emphasizes the importance of the bar as a recovered space where both the discourse of modernity that created the nation and the neoliberal one fueled by globalization are being contested.

It is obvious that the city of Buenos Aires has experienced a shift in representation from being a centre of commerce, culture, and sophisticated life into a fourthspace were characters are the victims of extreme violence. That is the case in the three films analyzed by Zulema Moret:

Un día de suerte (*A Lucky Day*, 2002) by Sandra Gugliotta, *Vagón Fumador* (*Smoking Car*, 2001) by Verónica Chen, and *Hoy y Mañana* (*Today and Tomorrow*, 2003) by Alejandro Chomski. By focusing on Buenos Aires, Moret explains the way in which the city affects the life of the protagonists by uprooting them and making them victims of the violence derived from the crumbling of institutions such as the family and the workplace.[8]

While the physical space of Buenos Aires acquires a new meaning due to the deterioration of the old mythologies associated with the city in the four films discussed in the preceding paragraphs, the city is created as a merger of physical and mental spaces that transcend the present, past, and even the future in the science fiction films *Moebius* (1996), *La sonámbula* (*Sleepwalker*, 1998), and *Cóndor Crux* (*Condor Crux*, 2000). According to Victoria Ruétalo, in post-dictatorship science fiction film, violence is inflicted upon innocent civilians by medical, political, or social institutions that take away not only their bodies but also their past, present, and future. The context in which all these films are produced, and the dialogues contained within them, reflect the implementation of neoliberal policies imposed by the Menemista government that transformed the city of Buenos Aires into a violent site (or a new form of fourthspace) where there is no place for memories of the past, and where the future renders a repetition of a circular reality.

The seventeen literary and filmic texts analyzed in this collection explore the origins and ramifications of violence in Argentine society over the last two decades. By using a significant corpus of literary and cinematic techniques that range from the characterization and use of poignant descriptions of torture to the creative use of the camera's wandering gaze, filmmakers and writers manage on the one hand to compel audiences to assume the ethical dilemma of how to respond to the horrific violence perpetrated against the most vulnerable victims of society: women and children. On the other hand, in contemporary Argentine films, directors have taken advantage of cinematic techniques, such as the fragmentation of a story line, and the insertion of black and white footage, to move spectators to question the foundational myths that have created the nation, as well as to present narratives that showcase changes in family and social relations. Finally, the examples of contemporary Argentine cinema analyzed in this study display an asphyxiating fourth-space, a place where characters find no escape from the extreme violence they have to confront, and where all attempts to find redemption are brutally co-opted. Perhaps the lesson to be learned in this exploration of violence in Argentine literature and film would be to raise awareness of the pervasive effects of an ideology that uses violence as a formula to perpetuate traditional power structures and discriminatory social practices.

WORKS CITED

Agosino, Adalberto C. 2004. *Nuevas modalidades de la violencia política*. Buenos Aires: Editorial Abaco de Rodolfo Depalma.

Agüero, Felipe. 1998. "Conflicting assessments of democratization: Exploring the fault lines." In *Fault Lines of Democracy in Post-Transition Latin America*, ed. Felipe Agüero and Jeffrey Stark, 1–21. Miami: North South Press.

Americas Watch and Centro de Estudios Legales. 1991. *Police Violence in Argentina: Torture and Killings in Buenos Aires*. Americas Watch and Centro de Estudios Legales.

Andermann, Jens, Philip Derbyshire, and John Kraniauskas. 2007. "No matarás (Thou shalt not kill): An introduction." *Journal of Latin American Cultural Studies* 16, no. 2: 111–13.

Angeleone, Juan Pablo. 1997. "Levantamientos de empleados públicos provinciales. Elementos para la caracterización de un nuevo tipo de violencia en la Argentina desde la sociología política." In *Globalización, fragmentación social y violencia*, ed. Arturo Fernández and Silvia Gaveglio, 123–41. Rosario: Homo Sapiens.

Auyero, Javier. 2007. *Routine Politics and Violence in Argentina: The Gray Zone of State Power*. New York: Cambridge University Press.

Besteman, Catherine. 2002. *Violence: A Reader*. New York: Macmillan Palgrave.

Clarín. 2007. "Varias marchas reclamarán por Julio López, al cumplirse un año de su desaparición." http://www.clarin.com/diario/2007/09/18/um/m-01501713.htm (accessed Sept. 2007).

Foster, David William. 1995. *Violence in Argentine Literature: Cultural Responses to Tyranny*. Columbia: University of Missouri Press.

Frühling, Hugo, and Joseph Tulchin. 2003. *Crime and Violence in Latin America: Citizen Security, Democracy and the State*. Washington, DC: Woodrow Wilson Center Press.

García Canclini, Néstor. 2001. *Consumers and Citizens: Globalization and Multicultural Conflicts*. Minneapolis: University of Minnesota Press.

Giles, James Richard. 2006. *The Spaces of Violence*. Tuscaloosa: University of Alabama Press.

Gorelik, Adrián. 2004. *Miradas sobre Buenos Aires: Historia cultural y crítica urbana*. Buenos Aires: Siglo XXI.

Grimson, Alejandro, and Gabriel Kessler. 2005. *On Argentina and the Southern Cone: Neoliberalism and National Imaginations*. New York: Routledge.

Hortiguera, Hugo, and Carolina Rocha. 2007. *Argentinian Cultural Production during the Neoliberal Years*. Lewiston, NY: Edwin Mellen.

Isla, Alejandro, and Daniel Miguez. 2003. *Heridas urbanas: violencia delictiva y transformaciones sociales en los noventa*. Buenos Aires: Editorial de las Ciencias; FLACSO.

Kessler, Gabriel. 2004. *Sociología del delito amateur*. Buenos Aires: Paidos.

Klein, Naomi. 2007. *Shock Doctrine: The Rise of Disaster Capitalism*. New York: Metropolitan Doctrine.

Lefebvre, Henri. 1991. *The Production of Space*. Trans. Donald Nicholson-Smith. Oxford: Blackwell.

Lusnich, Ana Laura, ed. 2005. *Civilización y barbarie en el cine argentino y latinoamericano*. Buenos Aires: Biblos.

Peruzzotti, Enrique, and Catalina Smulovitz, eds. 2007. *Enforcing the Rule of Law: Social Accountability in the New Latin American Democracies*. Pittsburg: University of Pittsburg Press.

Reati, Fernando. 1992. *Nombrar lo inmobrable: Violencia política y novela argentina, 1975–1985*. Buenos Aires: Legasa.

Riches, David, ed. 1986. *The Anthropology of Violence*. Oxford: Blackwell.

Rotker, Susana. 2002. *Citizens of Fear: Urban Violence in Latin America*. New Brunswick, NJ: Rutgers University Press.

Scolum, J. David. 2001. *Violence in American Cinema*. New York: Routledge.

Soja, Edward W. 1996. *Thirdspace: Journeys to Los Angeles and Other Real-and-Imagined Places*. Cambridge, MA: Blackwell.

Svampa, Maristella. 2005. *La sociedad excluyente: La Argentina bajo el signo del neoliberalismo*. Buenos Aires: Alfaguara.

NOTES

1. Estebán Echeverría's *El matadero* (*The Slaughterhouse*, 1839), is considered to be the first Argentine short to present several acts of violence in great detail. Also Domingo F. Samiento provides an attempt to explain the sociological reasons for a violent countryside versus the more civilized urban centres.

2. For an in-depth analysis of the centrality of the market, see Hugo Hortiguera and Carolina Rocha (2007).

3. Adalberto Agozino (2004) breaks down the acts of political violence: "Si tomamos el 2001, encontramos 354 hechos de violencia política tradicional, 447 cortes de ruta y 859 'cacerolazos' – registrados sólo en trece días del mes de diciembre del 2001 (del 19 al 31/12/2001) – lo que hace un total de 1600 hechos de violencia política integral" (28). [If we take the year 2001, we find 354 episodes of traditional political violence, 447 highways interruptions and 859 'potbangings' – taken only in thirteen days from December 19th to the 31st.]

4. "Exigen que se les dé lo que creen merecer."

5. "Pretende introducir cambios en el balance de poder de una sociedad por medios coactivos y no consensuales."

6. "La violencia social está siendo motorizada por los excluidos del sistema social que no se resignan pasivamente a verse arrojados al hambre y la marginalidad."

7. In a recent article "Notes Toward an Aesthetics of Marginality in Contemporary Latin American Literature, Luz Horne and Daniel Noemi Voionmaa," published in *Latin American Studies Association FORUM* (University of Pittsburgh) 40 (2009): 36–41, the authors outline five characteristics in the treatment of marginality in current Latin American literature. Two of those characteristics are particularly interesting for this study because they link violence and marginality. The authors state that in contemporary Latin American literature there is an extreme exacerbation of violence in dealing with marginal subjects. That is quite evident in works by Paulo Lins (*Cidade de Deus* 2002), Fernando Vallejo (*La virgen de los sicarios* 1994), or César Aira (*La villa* 2001). On the other hand, there is a tendency to represent marginal subjects as completely "desubjectivized" in novels such as *Fetiche y fantoche* (1994) by Huilo Ruales and *El infarto del alma* (2002) by Diamela Eltit and Paz Errázuris, where marginal characters are depicted as only mutilated or fragmented bodies that have lost all sense of humanity.

8. For Adrián Gorelik (2004), Buenos Aires transformed itself into a Latin American city as a destiny where: "Insecurity, private protection, the disappearance of public space and the increasing poverty were particularly evident after the crisis of 2001, when

a human wave rushed to the city to look through its trash" (72). [La inseguridad, el blindaje privado, la extinción del espacio público y la miseria creciente, manifiesta plenamente a partir de la crisis del 2001, cuando una marea humana se abalanzó sobre la ciudad para revolver en sus basuras.] Gorelik analyzed the film *Mala época* (*Bad Times*, 1999) as a symptomatic representation of the disintegration of the city in times of late capitalism.

I.
THE LEGACY OF THE MILITARY YEARS

Torture and Abuse as a National Art Form: Gustavo Nielsen's *Auschwitz*[1]

FERNANDO REATI

GEORGIA STATE UNIVERSITY

Popular wisdom has it that an effective way to remove a phrase or song that is stuck in one's head is to speak the words or hum the melody to someone else. The afflicted person is then freed from the obsession, leaving the unfortunate victim now captive to it until being able to do the same thing with yet a third person. This intuitive notion that something fixated in the mind can be removed by verbalizing it appears, albeit, in a more philosophical form, in Borges' story, "El milagro secreto" ("The Secret Miracle"), when Jaromir Hladík imagines hundreds of possible deaths while he awaits, terrified, his execution by a Nazi firing squad. He understands that the best way to exorcize fear is to foresee impending horror in minute detail: "With perverse logic, he deduced that visualizing a specific situation would prevent it from happening. Adhering to this feeble magic, he made up awful things *so they would not happen* ..." (emphasis in the original; Borges: 509).[2] A comparable therapeutic practice in domestic violence or sexual abuse cases consists of verbalizing fantasies to prevent them from becoming reality. Also analogous is the Christian confession of evil thoughts, which helps cast out the sin before the sinful act occurs.

This *magic*, or suggestive power, is germane to *Auschwitz* (2004), a uniquely bizarre novel by Argentine author Gustavo Nielsen, which escapes any easy genre classification.[3] Nielsen belongs to that group of writers – among them, César Aira, Daniel Guebel, Sergio Bizzio, and Rodrigo Fresán – who opt for no referentiality in their stories. They go beyond what is plausible to the simply uproarious, as critiques of them commonly note. Nielsen writes about the alien encounter of Berto, a *porteño* (citizen of Buenos Aires), who considers himself to be "typical." The son of a Spanish father and an Italian mother, he is a chauvinistic show-off and an inveterate Don Juan, whose main agenda, at 40, is to go to bed with any woman who crosses his path. But Berto is also a "Nazi wannabe" (17). He equally despises Jews and Hindus, Paraguayans and country folk, Chinese and *"ponjas,"*[4] gays and the handicapped.[5] During one of his many nights of conquest, Berto beds a Jewish woman with the last name of Auschwitz. His sexual pleasure is heightened by his contempt for her inferior race, and the encounter, charged with his aggression and insults, becomes the stage for his hatred and prejudices. But, to his surprise, the hunter becomes the hunted when he discovers the next morning that Auschwitz has hidden the condom containing his semen in the freezer – a development that fills him with unease and humiliation. The subsequent chapters describe Berto's absurd ruminations before arriving at a surprising revelation: Auschwitz is part of an invasion by extraterrestrial beings who pilfer human sperm in order to create a mixed race – half humanoid, half alien – that will end up dominating Earth.

When Berto discovers that a strange child lives with Auschwitz, he kidnaps him to force the Jewess to return his stolen semen. The ensuing scene is of central importance to the novel, and I would therefore like to examine it in detail here. In his bachelor apartment, with the child tied to the bed, Berto quickly becomes a monster who abuses and tortures with no trace of moral restraint:

> He took two razor blades and ran them lightly over the child's body. He dug them in deeper when he came to his flat nipples, until he had gouged them out [...] He sank a fork into each wasted nipple. He twirled them round and round with both hands. He saw the two pulpy masses that were forming – his work of art [...] He positioned the steak knife over the right shoulder to saw at it [...] He began to sear his name onto the child's belly. The ember left its mark, but didn't cause the child any pain. [...] He took the scissors apart and plunged the point into different parts of the child's chest to see how the little red fountains would spurt [...] He yanked on his nasal septum with channel lock pliers until the cartilage splintered and hung there, exposed. And, since Berto did not like having things exposed, he hammered it back in. [...] Having already driven needles, window nails and broken toothpicks under the fingernails of the little hands [...] he got a jig saw, he sawed off two fingers from the child's left hand, he stuck one in the missing ear [...] He smashed a bottle with a hammer and devoted part of the night to sinking shards of glass between the fingers that were still attached.... (77–95)[6]

And so it continues, page after page in a series of morbid, horrible details that are difficult to read. The sadism of the scene is heightened even more by two additional elements that carry it to the brink of paroxysm. One of these is Berto's growing sexual excitement during the torture. He is about to rape the child when he discovers, to his surprise, that the little being from another planet has neither penis nor anus. Undaunted, and in one of the account's most horrifying scenes, Berto simply proceeds to open up a deep slit between the child's legs where his genital organs should have been. He then inserts his own penis there, and, in the words of the novel, has a "heavenly experience" of the best orgasm of his life (100). The other particular is that the child laughs and enjoys himself throughout the torture and rape, showing no sign whatsoever of pain or suffering, in a kind of sublimation of Berto's most perverse sadomasochistic fantasies.

With the torture finished, and his repertoire of abuse exhausted, Berto racks his brain for any book he has read with examples that might renew his inspiration. Slapping his forehead he recalls a well-known "manual of sadism for amateurs" (101) – *Nunca más* (*Never Again*), the report by the National Commission on the Disappearance of Persons (CONADEP) produced as proof of human rights violations in the 1985 trial against the military Juntas. Inspired by his re-reading of *Nunca más*, Berto finds himself admiring the inventiveness of professional torturers: "'*What imagination, these military guys!*' thought Berto, slapping his forehead. Not even a fifth of those things would have occurred to him" (emphasis in the original; 107).[7] He heads for his local hardware store to acquire the tools that will allow him to put the tortures outlined in the CONADEP report into practice. There, he is waited on by a knowledgeable employee who worked on a "task force" at a secret detention centre before the democracy. The scene is one of absurd, black humour – the employee confesses to Berto that you can't get real electric prods anymore, and he won't sell him his because it reminds him of the good times. But, this tone does not mask Nielsen's true intent, which is to emphasize, on the one hand, the banality of evil, as defined by Hannah Arendt in *Eichmann in Jerusalem*, and embodied in the character of the ex-torturer casually explaining to Berto how to fabricate a homemade prod, and, on the other hand, by the co-existence of victims and victimizers in a society which has yet to finish bringing the latter to justice.

How are we to interpret this veritable horror show, made harsher still by its seemingly casual, humorous treatment of the theme of torture? Perhaps its meaning begins to reveal itself when, Berto, after getting rid of the child's charred body (he had electrocuted him by torturing him with the wires of a bedside lamp) boards a commuter train. Dressed in his elegant, imported clothing, with his executive's briefcase, and surrounded by middle-class passengers like himself, he begins to ask himself whether anything about the way he looks could give him away to others as being the assassin he really is. And the answer is extremely revealing:

> Could they be reading the question in his head, like a subtitled film? How can I to go to work after having abused a little kid, after having broken his legs and arms, after having felt the crunch of that little body when I bent it double across my right knee? And the answer: Like this. The well-dressed people smiled at him. Berto felt gratified. They were saying to him, "Don't sweat it. We, too, are keeping terrible secrets and we're all packed in together, traveling in the same coach. And we put on fine clothes, and we're caring neighbours […] Let's keep on smiling, walking, working. The city awaits us. We'll leave that memory at home, hidden in the closet, stuck to the bloodstain in the bathroom sink – that stain we could never get out." (148)[8]

The contrast between the indelible stain of crime and the intent to "leave the memory at home," so that the crime might be forgotten, symbolizes what may be at the very core of the current debate in Argentina about social memory of the violent past. Deep within itself, this community experienced multiple acts of mini-complicity in the form of pretended ignorance, indifference, or even partial justification for the crimes of the dictatorship. In effect, in fiction, as well as in essays, there has been ongoing discussion for some time now about the problem of ethical and moral responsibility – if indeed, not legal – held by a large sector of the civilian population for the events of the 70s. The first years of reflection under democracy were difficult in this regard. One good measure of just how hard it was to consider the past in terms of collective responsibility was the drafting of the official theory in *Nunca más* that came to be known as the "two demons" theory. By presenting the conflict as if it were a bipolar struggle between armed forces and guerrilla insurgents, the civilian population was absolved of having to think of itself as one more agent in the violence. It is only in the past decade that the mini-complicities and mini-authoritarianisms present in Argentine society before and during the period of state terror have come under scrutiny, thus breaking down that false dichotomy between "them" and "us."

In fiction, Luis Gusmán's 1995 novel, *Villa*, was a first step in that direction. The book is about an obscure doctor from the Department of Social Welfare who, because of his extreme obsequiousness, ends up collaborating with the death squads. In a uniquely Argentine way, this illustrates the idea of the victimizer as an impersonal, mediocre bureaucrat – he could be any one of us – a concept explored by Arendt in her study of Eichmann. Another, more recent work along these lines is *La crítica de las armas* (*A Critique of Arms*) by José Pablo Feinmann (2003). His protagonist spends the years of the dictatorship waiting for that fateful knock on the door that never comes, surrounded by friends, colleagues, and neighbours who justify all that is happening around them with the proverbial, "there must be a reason." He is convinced, not only that this is "a country of cowards and accomplices" (21), but that, worse yet, he himself belongs to at least one – and possibly both – categories. *La mujer en cuestión* (*The Woman in Question*), a novel by María Teresa Andruetto (2003), is yet another example. The story revolves around a female ex-prisoner of the Perla concentration camp in Cordoba, who survives because of having sexual relations with a torturer. Her supposed betrayal pales in the face of the acts of mini-collaboration with the regime carried out by many of those same, ordinary citizens who condemn her as a traitor once democracy has returned. Among them are the fearful neighbour who wouldn't let her hide in her house, the lawyer who denounced her to the authorities, the professor who wanted her to sleep with him in exchange for information, and even her own parents, who wouldn't lend her money to flee the country.

In the field of essay and testimony, without a doubt the most powerful text is *Poder y desaparición* (*Power and Disappearance*), by Pilar Calveiro (1998). This ESMA concentration camp survivor opposes the simplistic division of captives into "heroes" or "traitors." She sheds light on the social mechanisms responsible for the ambiguous, grey-area situations camp prisoners found themselves facing on their arrival at the camps, where the line between heroism and collaboration became blurred. Independent of the prisoners' political and human particulars (ideology, personality, degree of commitment, resistance to physical pain), Calveiro demonstrates that it is important to understand the different individual survival mechanisms that come into play. These range from pretense or cooperation with regard to the small tasks necessary for the camp's functioning, to open collaboration and "switching camps" – all of which are an extension of similar social mechanisms of adaptation to overwhelming military power. According to Calveiro, "neither the guerrilla nor the men of the armed forces, and certainly not the concentration camps, constituted anything alien to society as a whole" (98).[9] On the contrary, all of these factors should be considered as a *continuum* of attitudes and ideological-psychological mechanisms: "To think of the concentration camp as a world of heroes and traitors removes it from a societal context [...] when, in fact, the hell of the camp and society belong to each other; therefore heroes and traitors, victims and victimizers are inter-connected spheres. They are components of the social framework, which includes everyone" (137).[10] What happened inside is a reflection of what happened outside; camp and society are two mirrored faces of the same, grey reality. And if there were not clearly discernible traitors or heroes in the one, it is because neither were there in the other.

A similar theme dealing with the deeply ambiguous nature of survival mechanisms within the camp, as well as in the surrounding society, emerges from *Ese infierno* (*That Hell*) (2001), a book consisting of a collection of conversations recorded over several months between Munú Actis, Cristina Aldini, Liliana Gardella, Miriam Lewin, and Elisa Tokar, five women survivors of ESMA. Along with the wish to avoid any moral judgment about individual behaviours that led, or didn't lead, to getting out alive, what comes across clearly is a tacit acknowledgment of the multiple ways in which those "on the outside," made what happened "inside" possible by their ignorance or indifference.[11] A third study confronting the difficult theme of collective responsibility, *Pasado y presente* (*Past and Present*), by Hugo Vezzetti (2002), succinctly notes that it becomes more and more evident that "a massive violation of human rights, extended over time and sustained by widespread agreement on the part of the government, as well as by sectors within the society, cannot be accomplished without the active participation of many and without agreement on the part of many others" (25).[12] This includes the majority of traditional political parties, large sectors of the church, and broad echelons of the middle class. In other words, this was a matter of a terrorized society, true, but a society that was also cautious and "prepared to survive" at any price (Vezzetti: 63).[13]

How does the gleeful tone of the narrative passages describing torture in *Auschwitz* fit within the ongoing dialogue and recent profusion of essays and fiction on collective responsibility in Argentina? What is the purpose of this apparent *aestheticization* of torture, which, along with the disappearance of persons, is most commonly associated with the memory of state terror? (And, a digression is worthwhile here: at the end of the novel, after being tortured, electrocuted and incinerated, the alien child reappears, alive and smiling – an intentional absurdity on the author's part, in a country that carries in its memory the thousands of disappeared whose bodies were never recovered.)

The portrayal of torture and sadism has a long tradition in Western literature, which has always found itself fascinated by practices that simultaneously repel and attract – much like an open abyss at our feet. Among many possible examples, *Farabeuf* (1965), that strange novel by Mexican author Salvador Elizondo, comes to mind. It contains a graphic file photograph of a Chinese subject's death by quartering for the assassination of a ruler in 1901. The title character, Farabeuf, is a surgeon who is fascinated as much by the art of dissecting cadavers as by how difficult it is to pinpoint the line between physical pain and sensual pleasure. He is supposedly both the photographer who took the picture and the author of the book, *Aspects médicaux de la torture chinoise* (*Medical Aspects of Chinese Torture*). Interest in the science of medicine, torture, and eroticism converges, not just in the novel, but, to a large extent, in Western thought, at "the horror and delight of the human body wide open to view, like the door to a magnificent house" (Elizondo: 107).[14] Thus, the description of dismemberment simultaneously compels horror and a solemn reverence in the face of the indescribable experience of the one being tortured. "Little by little they remove his clothing, and his body rises up in a nudity of flesh that is infinitely beautiful and infinitely virgin […] with his shoulders doubled back from the tight knots and his neck stretched forward; with his eyes open, open beyond pain and death. A gaze nothing can extinguish; like one might look if one could see oneself at the moment of orgasm" (132).[15] Watching oneself watching the one being tortured – we have here an essential aspect of Elizondo's disturbing novel, which forces us to think about the reader/spectator's inevitable act of voyeurism that is implicit in the reading of the book. "Disturbing hypothesis: the one being tortured is you" (143),[16] warns the narrator, after insinuating that, in some way, any one of us could be the torturer as well: "The true mechanisms of justice are, we could say, imperceptible. Who builds the gallows? Who tempers the blades on those knives? Who takes care to see that the guillotine's mechanism functions perfectly? Who oils the hinges of the garrote? The executioner's identity is as elusive as the worth of their role" (137).[17]

Closer to Argentina, *La condesa sangrienta* (*The Bloody Countess*) by Alejandra Pizarnik (1965) provokes similar disquieting thoughts. It is the poeticized story taken by Pizarnik from the novel, *La comtesse sanglante*, by the French author Valentine Penrose, of the crimes and torture perpetrated by the sadistic countess, Erzébet Báthory, in her castle. Sexual perversion, cruelty, savage eroticism and man's capacity for evil lie at the core of a story that casts the countess simultaneously as director and spectator of the *staging* that each torture of an unfortunate victim evolves into – from imprisonment by the Iron Maiden and death by freezing water, to classic forms of torment involving pliers, sharp objects, and red-hot pokers. Pizarnik's novel revolves around the countess in her attitude of the *contemplation* of horror, and words like "look," "contemplate," "eyes," and "observe" abound: "Seated on her throne, the countess watches the torture and hears the screams. Her horrid, old servants are silent figures who fetch fire, knives, needles, pokers; who torture girls, who later bury them. Like the poker or the knives, these old women are instruments of possession. This dark ceremony has only one *silent spectator*" (emphasis added; 10).[18] But alongside the countess there is another figure, unmentioned, but nevertheless implicit and omnipresent throughout the novel. It is the reader, sitting in the solitude of his room and watching the countess in the act of watching the horror. The fascination that cruelty exerted on the human body has on the countess is the same fascination that captivates the reader and won't let him put the book down, turning him into an involuntary *voyeur* of the same thing he morally condemns. There is a chapter devoted to the "great, dark mirror, the famous mirror that she, herself, had designed" (Pizarnik: 43),[19] and in which the countess spends hours watching herself between torture sessions. Isn't the novel something like the mirror the reader sees himself in, while reading about the torments taking place in the gloomy basements of the castle? Perhaps María Negroni is referring to this in her study on Pizarnik, when she cites an essay by Cristina Piña and says that the fascination this short novel compels comes from "its capacity to articulate the obscene; that is, its capacity to bring 'into our field of vision' certain parts of our experience of reality that daily life has thrust aside to some eccentric place" (102).[20] In other words, to see the countess watching and enjoying a sadistic spectacle of torture forces us to see in our own selves that which we would generally prefer to ignore.[21]

Elizondo, as well as Pizarnik – and, as might be deduced, Nielsen – illustrate something that Angela Carter holds up in her excellent study on the political significance of sexual violence and pornography in the works of the Marquis de Sade. She maintains that, just as the erotic relationship between two people mimics social relationships in the miniature, their perversions and sexual violence simply mirror, in caricature, other social perversions. Therefore, says Carter, the whip used by the Marquis to beat his victims is an extension of a greater political power: "the whip hand is always the hand with the real political power and the victim is a person who has little or no power at all" (24). Carter shows us a Marquis whose true intention is not to revel in the description of violence and evil but to make us think about what type of society would allow in its midst the existence of such practices. Thus, the act of observation inherent in the reader's voyeurism turns into an act of self-observation. The setting where evil takes place is not in some faraway space – it is a *mirror* of ourselves. Speaking about how society legitimizes evil, Diana Wang reviews the role of the German rail system in the Holocaust and puts together some hard facts: nearly a million and a half Germans worked, directly or indirectly, for the railroads that carried millions of victims in sub-human conditions to their deaths. Whether because they were obeying orders or were ignorant of what was going on, these loyal government employees registered no form of protest, renunciation, or opposition with the bureaucratic machinery running the extermination. In other words, hundreds of thousands of civil servants went about their daily routines and lived normal lives, indifferent to the evil that surrounded them. This leads Wang to a simple, but disturbing, idea: "When one thinks about evil, one always thinks of the evil in others. *The idea of our own evilness is difficult for us to assume*" (emphasis added; 97).[22]

Berto, that "typical" *porteño* with familiar, perhaps even likable, traits – his Argentine quick-wittedness and ironic sense of humour, his pointed responses to women's comments, his *macho* pride that knocks them off their feet – is a prototype of the worst of Argentina, with his homophobia, racism, and anti-immigrant xenophobia. How is it possible not to think that Berto in the 70s could have been any one of those celebrating the World Cup a few blocks from ESMA, or one of those always saying "there must be some reason" when people disappeared? And later, "they must have done something" when a disappeared person emerged from a camp alive? Berto is one of us. If the description of the tortures inflicted on the child deeply affects us, it is because of how naturally Berto invents those tortures. It is the same natural manner displayed by the ex-torturer, turned hardware store employee, when he suggests using a pillowcase instead of a hood to save a few pesos. It is even the same natural manner with which the train passengers calm Berto down, making him feel like everything is fine, that we all have terrible, hidden secrets in our past, that there's no need to worry too much about one more death. The very fact that the instruments of torture Berto uses are mundane, everyday objects that can be found in any home points to the natural, familiar nature of the evil that lurks in every human being:

> From the bathroom, he brought towels, the mop handle, a scrub brush, nail clippers, two files, razor blades, a bottle of alcohol. From the kitchen, he brought matches, another knife with a sharper point and duller edge, several forks, a skewer, a corkscrew, some glass bottles, a china plate, toothpicks. From the laundry room, which was where he kept his tools, he brought the channel lock pliers, a hammer, nails. He took a little box of pins from the sewing basket. (76)[23]

Who would not tremble with the certainty that any neighbour has similar sharp, hurtful, stabbing instruments, in his home, and that these could easily be turned into tools of horror in the wrong hands? Hence, Berto's rejoinder, when asked why he decided to torture the child, is stunning in its simplicity: "*Because I felt like it; because I guessed I would like it; because of so many things...*" (emphasis in the original; 118).[24] This is all about the banality of evil, but here, Berto is us; his evil is the evil that resides in all of us. In a country that experienced disappearances and unimaginable tortures while many remained passive or were indifferent, and where many now manifest latent hostility against foreigners and those who are different, it should come as no surprise that an extraterrestrial being might be subject to abuse by an honest citizen like Berto. Along the lines of Flaubert's famous statement that he was Madame Bovary, Nielsen is aware that he is Berto (or Berto is him, which is the same thing.) Therefore, Nielsen exorcizes such a terrifying possibility by means of the *magic* of naming evil; he spells out every imaginable torture method and despicable act, perhaps with the secret hope – as in Borges' story – that then they might not happen.

I am not presuming that *Auschwitz* is a novel solely *about* the traumatic effects of state terror in Argentina (certainly it is much more than this). But, it is possible to assert that it is *also* about this. Every society that goes through collective trauma sees each generation produce its own interpretation of it. What emerges from direct witnesses to the facts will differ from what is produced by those who lived through it indirectly or only found out about it through accounts and documents. In a discussion of the intergenerational transmission of the memories of state terror in Argentina, Elizabeth Jelin points out how important it is for such transmission to occur. She stresses also that it must not become a simple, mechanical transfer of content into the supposedly virginal vessel of the younger generation. This would have the effect of distilling the different meanings the past holds down to a single version, which could ultimately lead to saturation and rejection. It is essential for those who lived through the traumatic past in flesh and blood to pass it on, but also for those who didn't experience it to produce their own versions of its significance: "Those at the 'receiving end' should give the past its own meaning; re-interpret it, re-signify it [...] so that new generations might be able to approach the subjects and experiences of the past as 'others' – different, ready to dialogue more than to re-present it by identifying with it" (Jelin: 126).[25] In the case of Argentina, this has meant moving from the traditional methods of the human rights movements to the more original practices of H.I.J.O.S., such as *escraches* and street theater.[26] In film, there has been a movement from a more realistic presentation of horror such as in Luis Puenzo's *La historia oficial* (*The Official Story*, 1985), Marco Bechis' *Garage Olimpo* (1999), and Marcelo

Piñeyro's *Kamchatka* (2002), to the play on self-referentiality and rupture from historical verisimilitude that characterizes *Los rubios* (*The Blonde Ones*), a fictionalized documentary by the young director and daughter of disappeared parents, Albertina Carri (2003).

Auschwitz should be read from the point of view of these diverging representations of trauma, some of which accept while others question the logic behind an aesthetics based on realism and verisimilitude. The author does not belong to the same age group as those born after the dictatorship – he was born in 1962, and was 14 when the coup happened. But, neither is he part of the generation – being still very young – that actually lived through the period of state terror. Whether or not the purpose of the novel is to talk about that painful history is irrelevant. Nielsen, like all Argentines, carries a violent past within himself, and he exorcizes it in his own way, confronting the evilness inherent to all human beings by verbalizing it. This has not won him many friends in his home country, where he had difficulty finding anyone to publish his novel. He also received e-mails and telephone calls asking him to take it out of circulation. He was even accused of being racist and anti-Semitic because of the biases of his main character. In spite of all this, Nielsen faces his own human nature and recognizes himself – recognizes us – in Berto; and he chooses not to look the other way. If we are to accept popular wisdom, telling about Berto's evil allows the author to remove that evil from himself and consign it to the reader, who must now fix his scandalized (morbidly attracted?) eyes on so much immoral brutality.

Translated by Bonnie Taylor

WORKS CITED

Actis, Munú, Cristina Aldini, Liliana Gardella, Miriam Lewin, and Elisa Tokar. 2001. *Ese infierno: Conversaciones de cinco mujeres sobrevivientes de la ESMA*. Buenos Aires: Editorial Sudamericana.

Andruetto, María Teresa. 2003. *La mujer en cuestión*. Córdoba: Alción.

Arendt, Hannah. 1963. *Eichmann in Jerusalem. A Report on the Banality of Evil*. New York: Viking Press.

Borges, Jorge Luis. 1974. "El milagro secreto." *Obras completas*. Buenos Aires: Emecé.

Calveiro, Pilar. 2001. *Poder y desaparición: Los campos de concentración en Argentina*. Buenos Aires: Colihue.

Carter, Angela. 1980. *The Sadeian Woman and the Ideology of Pornography*. New York: Pantheon Books.

Elizondo, Salvador. 1992. *Farabeuf*. México: Vuelta.

Feinmann, José Pablo. 2003. *La crítica de las armas*. Buenos Aires: Norma.

Gazzera, Carlos. <YEAR?>. "Gustavo Nielsen indaga en las raíces del odio." http://www.lavozdelinterior.net/2005/0310/suplementos/cultura (accessed 10 Mar. 2005).

Gusmán, Luis. 1995. *Villa*. Buenos Aires: Alfaguara.

Jelin, Elizabeth. 2001. *Los trabajos de la memoria*. Madrid: Siglo Veintiuno.

Negroni, María. 1994. "*La condesa sangrienta*: Notas sobre un problema musical." *Hispamérica* 23, no. 68: 99–110.

Nielsen, Gustavo. 2004. *Auschwitz*. Buenos Aires: Alfaguara.

Orenstein, Eduardo. 1995. "Joel Peter Witkin. En las fronteras de lo humano." *Clarín Cultura y Nación* (19 Jan.): 4.

Pizarnik, Alejandra. 1971. *La condesa sangrienta*. Buenos Aires: Aquarius.

Vezzetti, Hugo. 2002. *Pasado y presente: Guerra, dictadura y sociedad en la Argentina*. Buenos Aires: Siglo Veintiuno.

Wang, Diana. 2002. "El Mal y su legitimación social." In *Historiografía y memoria colectiva. Tiempos y territorios*, ed. Cristina Godoy, 91–104. Buenos Aires: Miño y Dávila.

NOTES

1. A preliminary Spanish version of this article appeared as "De torturas y vejaciones como un arte nacional: *Auschwitz* de Gustavo Nielsen," in *Escribas* (Cordoba, Argentina) 3 (2006): 69–77. All translations from Spanish originals are ours.

2. "… con lógica perversa infirió que prever un detalle circunstancial es impedir que éste suceda. Fiel a esa débil magia, inventaba, *para que no sucedieran*, rasgos atroces…."

3. Writer, architect, and illustrator, he is also the author of *Playa quemada* (Burnt Beach) (stories, 1994); *La flor azteca* (*The Aztec Flower*) (novel, 1997); *El amor enfermo* (*Sick Love*) (novel, 2000); and *Marvin* (stories, 2004).

4. Translator's note: "*ponja*" (the inverted and shortened version of the word "japonés," i.e., a person from Japan) is a derogatory slang term referring to anyone of East-Asian origin.

5. In his review of the novel, Carlos Gazzera summarizes Berto as "a Nazi who hates Jews for being 'big-assed', Blacks for being 'smelly', Chinese as 'Communists', transvestites for being perverse, Bolivians and Peruvians as 'illegals', *cartoneros* [translator's note: poor people who collect garbage for sale] for being 'lice-ridden'… As you will see, it is an interesting catalogue of national intolerance." ("Un nazi que odia a las judías por 'culonas', a los negros 'por olorosos', a los chinos 'por comunistas', a los travestis por pervertidos, a los bolivianos y peruanos 'por ilegales', a los cartoneros 'por piojosos'… Como se verá, un catálogo interesante de la intolerancia nacional.")

6. "Tomó dos yilés y las paseó débilmente por el torso infantil. Las hundió más al llegar a los pezones planos, hasta extraérselos […] Le hundió un tenedor en cada pezón descarnado. Revolvió con ambas manos. Vio las dos pulpas que se estaban formando, su obra […] Con el tramontina se instaló sobre el hombro izquierdo, para aserrarlo […] Comenzó a grabar su nombre sobre la panza del niño. La brasa dejaba la marca, pero al niño no le dolía […] Desarmó la tijera y le clavó la punta en distintos lugares del pecho, para ver cómo saltaban las fuentecitas rojas […] Tiró del tabique nasal con la pinza pico de loro hasta astillar el cartílago, que quedó expuesto, y como a Berto no le gustaban las exposiciones, se lo volvió a hundir a martillazos […] Ya le había clavado agujas, clavos de vidriero y escarbadientes partidos debajo de las uñas de las manitos […] buscó una sierrita de calar, le serruchó dos dedos de la mano izquierda, le metió uno en la oreja ausente […] Rompió una botella a martillazos y dedicó parte de la noche a hundir vidrios entre los dedos que todavía se mantenían pegados..."

7. "*¡Qué imaginación, estos milicos!*, pensó Berto, mientras se palmeaba la frente. A él no se le hubieran ocurrido ni la quinta parte de las cosas".

8   "¿Estarían leyendo la pregunta en su cabeza, como en una película subtitulada? *¿Cómo empezar a trabajar después de haber vejado a un pibe, después de haberle quebrado las piernas y los brazos, después de haber sentido el crujido de ese cuerpito sobre la rodilla derecha cuando hice palanca para doblarlo al medio?* Y la respuesta: *Así*. La gente bien vestida le sonrió. Berto se sintió gratificado. Le estaban diciendo: "no te hagás problemas, nosotros también guardamos terribles secretos y viajamos apretados en el mismo vagón. Y nos ponemos ropa fina, y somos vecinos sensibles [...] a sonreír, a caminar, a trabajar de nuevo. La ciudad nos espera. Dejaremos la memoria en casa, escondida en los placares, pegoteada contra la mancha de sangre en la pileta del baño, esa mancha que nunca pudimos quitar".

9   "...ni la guerrilla ni los militares, ni por supuesto los campos de concentración constituyeron algo ajeno a la sociedad en su conjunto".

10 "Pensar el campo de concentración como un universo de héroes y traidores permite separarlo de lo social [...] Por el contrario, el infierno del campo y la sociedad se pertenecen, por eso héroes y traidores, víctimas y victimarios son también esferas interconectadas entre sí y constitutivas del entramado social, en el que todos están incluidos".

11 In *Ese infierno*, one of the ex-disappeared women relates her impressions when her captors took her out into the street in 1978, while people where celebrating the Argentine triumph in the Soccer World Cup. "It was torture! Seeing people hugging each other in the street, while I was a prisoner in a Concentration Camp, who didn't know if they were going to kill me the very next day! And I knew there were comrades being tortured at that very moment. And they took me to a pizza place on Avenida Maipú! People shouting in the street, with Argentine flags! [...] And there we were – kidnapped!" (100). ("¡Fue una tortura! Ver a la gente abrazándose en la calle, mientras que yo era una detenida en un Campo de Concentración que no sabía si iban a matarme al otro día, y que sabía que había compañeros a los que estaban torturando en ese momento. ¡Y me llevaron a una pizzería de avenida Maipú! La gente gritando en la calle, con banderas argentinas [...] ¡Y nosotros estábamos secuestrados!")

12 "...una violación masiva de los derechos humanos, extendida en el tiempo y sostenida en un amplio compromiso del Estado y de sectores de la sociedad, no puede cumplirse sin la participación activa de muchos y sin la conformidad de muchos más".

13 This is not the place for an in-depth discussion of Vezzetti's essay and his analysis of the logic of war, which permeated a large part of society. However, what is pertinent here is the distinction he makes between *criminal, political, and moral culpability*, where he takes a renewed look at Karl Jasper's thoughts on the German experience of Nazism (Vezzetti 41).

14 "...el espanto y la delicia del cuerpo humano abierto de par en par a la mirada como la puerta de una casa magnífica".

15 "Poco a poco lo despojan de sus ropas y su cuerpo se yergue en una desnudez de carne infinitamente bella e infinitamente virgen [...] con los hombros doblados hacia atrás por la tensión de las ligaduras y el cuello alargado hacia delante; con los ojos abiertos, abiertos más allá del dolor y de la muerte. Una mirada que nada puede apagar; como pudiera mirarse uno mismo en el momento del orgasmo".

16 "Hipótesis inquietante: el supliciado eres tú".

17 "Los mecanismos materiales de la justicia son, pudiéramos decir, imperceptibles. ¿Quién construye los cadalsos? ¿Quién templa la hoja de esas cuchillas? ¿Quién cuida de que el mecanismo de la guillotina funcione con toda perfección? ¿Quién acepta los goznes del garrote? La identidad de los verdugos es inasible como el mérito de sus funciones".

18 "Sentada en su trono, la condesa mira torturar y oye gritar. Sus viejas y horribles sirvientas son figuras silenciosas que traen fuego, cuchillos, agujas, atizadores; que torturan muchachas, que luego las entierran. Como el atizador o los cuchillos, esas viejas son instrumentos de una posesión. Esta sombría ceremonia tiene una sola *espectadora silenciosa*".

19 "... gran espejo sombrío, el famoso espejo cuyo modelo había diseñado ella misma".

20 "... su capacidad de articular lo obsceno, es decir, su capacidad de traer 'adentro de la escena visible' ciertas zonas de nuestra experiencia de lo real que la vida cotidiana expulsa a un lugar excéntrico".

21 *Freaks*, by Tod Browning, a film about circus freaks, is another work of art that dramatizes the strange and horrifying as a spectacle to be watched, at the same time obliging us to look at ourselves. One critic notes, "The monstrosity is not in the deformed members of this circus troupe, the monstrosity is in the soul of the perfect ones" (Orenstein: 4). ("La monstruosidad no está en los deformes integrantes de esa troupe de circo, la monstruosidad está en el alma de los perfectos").

22 "Cuando se piensa en la maldad, se piensa siempre en la del otro. *La idea de la propia maldad nos es difícil de asumir*".

23 "Del baño trajo toallas, el palo del secador, un cepillo de paja, el cortauñas, dos limas, las yiles, un frasco de alcohol. De la cocina trajo fósforos, otro cuchillo con más punta y menos filo, varios tenedores, un ensartador de brochettes, el tirabuzón, unas botellas de vidrio, un plato de loza, escarbadientes. Del lavadero, que era donde tenía sus herramientas, trajo la pinza pico de loro, un martillo, clavos. Del costurero sacó una cajita con alfileres".

24 *"Porque me dio la gana; porque supuse que me iba a gustar; por tantas cosas ..."*

25 "Que quienes 'reciben' le den su propio sentido, reinterpreten, resignifiquen [...] que las nuevas generaciones

puedan acercarse a sujetos y experiencias del pasado como 'otros', diferentes, dispuestos a dialogar más que a representar a través de la identificación".

26 *Translator's note:* H.I.J.O.S. is an Argentine group composed of sons and daughters of those killed in the 70s. *Escraches* are demonstrations or picketing by activists at the homes or workplaces of those responsible for violating human rights or engaging in corruption in the 70s, in order to "out them" and make neighbours and co-workers aware of the impunity.

Subjection and Injury in *El vuelo de la reina* by Tomás Eloy Martínez

MYRIAM OSORIO

MEMORIAL UNIVERSITY OF NEWFOUNDLAND

Journalist, professor and novelist, Tomás Eloy Martínez is known for his highly complex narrative strategies, as is perhaps best illustrated in his works *Santa Evita* (1995) and *La novela de Perón* (1997),[1] two novels that explore the union between history and fiction.[2] Intertwined to this fusion is also the novelist's deep interest in representing regimes of power. This Foucauldian notion is of crucial importance and heavily at work in Martínez's last novel, *El vuelo de la reina* (*The Flight of the Queen*), published in 2002.[3] Regimes of power dominate the narrative in two fronts: the personal lives of the main characters, in which the male seeks to subjugate and injure the female and the political arena where corruption is rampant, but unpunished.

Set in Buenos Aires between 1999 and the early twenty-first century, *El vuelo de la reina* chronicles two parallel stories: the pathological attachment of G. M. Camargo, the powerful director of a newspaper, to Reina Remis, a young and bright journalist that comes to work for him at *El diaro*,[4] and the consecutive political and economic crises that hit Argentina in 1999. Although the two stories may appear to be unconnected, they are, in fact, intrinsically linked. First, they are most obviously connected by the two principal characters, Reina and Camargo, who become romantically involved and are charged with the task of exposing the crisis through their work as editors for the newspaper. Secondly, the stories are related by the web of power relations that are made explicit through the use of surveillance in both scenarios. Indeed, surveillance serves as the driving force of the narrative in both. Camargo's obsession with exercising psychic and physical control over Reina is manifested through his constant surveillance of her. At the same time, surveillance is used to expose the secret dealings of high-level government officials. Linked to surveillance is the notion of power and the ability it may give for impunity, for control, for punishment, or for acceptance. In recreating a world that is so heavily influenced by the media, *El vuelo de la reina* portrays the intricate process by which dark, violent, and insidious stories are continuously brought to light to show the power of repeating certain stories and the sense of normalcy or impotence they create.

When it comes to the relationship between Reina and Camargo, the desire for control and punishment that he exerts produces highly problematic and dangerous behaviours that lead to Reina's destruction. While male politicians go virtually unpunished for their crimes, Camargo ensures that Reina suffers for the offences he imagines she has committed against him, through his use of denigrating language and her subjection to horrific torture. This chapter will consider the social and political implications of Camargo's behaviour by way of Judith Butler's concepts of subjection and injury. In doing so, this chapter will illustrate the extent to which power differentials are used in the novel to oppress and degrade the female.[5] Subjection inevitably produces injury and both find expresson in the novel in the language used and in the violence against the body.[6]

Drawing upon Foucault's *Discipline and Punish* (1979), Butler defines subjection as "[l]iterally, the making of a subject, the principle of regulation according to which a subject is formulated or produced. Such subjection is a kind of power that not only unilaterally acts on a given individual as a form of domination, but also activates or forms the subject" (*The Psychic Life of Power: Theories in Subjection*, 1997: 84). As Foucault argues, visual and surreptitious surveillance is of crucial importance in the process of subject formation. Surveillance is therefore used in *El vuelo de la reina* to monitor the behaviour of the female character from a distance by means of electronic equipment. In the novel, the male character's eyes act as the surveying gaze observing and describing the behaviour of a woman who becomes the surveyed. Incessant surveillance of the woman is the first step through which the male character attempts to unilaterally dominate and construct the female. In this manner, the actions of the surveyor align with Foucault's ideas that "inspection needs to be carried out ceaselessly" for effective discipline and control (*Discipline and Punishment*, 1979: 195).

Alternating between second and third person narrators, the novel begins with a scene of surveillance, in which Camargo acts – in Foucauldian terminology – as a "supervisor" operating from a "central tower" – an apartment building located in the Calle Reconquista – from which he observes the woman. The surveyed, initially referred to as *"La mujer"* (the woman)[7] by the third person narrator, is the object of intense curiosity and scrutiny for Camargo. He uses a powerful telescope to follow the woman's each and every movement in her apartment where she is always alone.[8] In the words of the narrator,

> Every night, around eleven, Camargo opens the curtains in his room on Reconquista Street, places a chair one metre away from the window, so that the shadows protect him, and waits until the woman gets into his sight. What she likes best, however, is to stop in front of the mirror in her bedroom and

very slowly undress. Camargo can then contemplate her as he pleases. (11)⁹

Clearly, through his gaze and through the details he is providing, the narrator is describing a woman over whom Camargo seeks to exert a form of domination because, from the outset, she is produced as an object for Camargo's pleasure. Besides, the readers can only see her through the narrator's visual perceptions. This represents the type of unilateral power that Butler describes, although the fact that Camargo must wait until La mujer enters in his "ángulo de mira"¹⁰ suggests that she occupies a position of object through her own volition. The woman, however, unaware that Camargo watches her each night, is unable to return the gaze or verbally question her observer. She is made the object of information but is unable to act as a subject in equal communication.

This lack of interaction is important to Camargo's heightened sense of joy, power, and control, as is effectively summarized in one the narrator's comments:

> Camargo feels insuperable happiness because the woman, when getting away from the mirror, depends exclusively on his gaze. The surrounding buildings are empty, she could die without anyone knowing, and if for even a second he would stop giving her attention, she would be an orphan within the sea of the world.¹¹

From this description it is evident that the process of subjection places the woman in a situation of radical dependency. As the Foucauldian prisoner, she is alone and isolated, moving within the confined space of her apartment and according to the narrator, dependent on some form of paternal protection. The narrator alerts the reader that Camargo's thoughts and desires veer to the perverse, as he experiences pleasure in spying on La mujer and imagining himself to hold complete power over her. Here again, Butler's analysis of subjection is a useful tool of analysis.

According to Butler, "subjection, which implies a radical dependency, takes place centrally through the body" (*The Psychic Life of Power*, 1997: 83). In *El vuelo de la reina*, both the narrator and Camargo focus attention on the sexualized portrayal of the woman's naked body. This reduces her to bodily fragments, produced by and for Camargo:

> Her thin lips are perhaps too narrow, the nose straight with a rounded tip, the chin upright and defiant. When she laughs her upper lip lifts so much that her gums are exposed. Her ankles are thick and the calves of her legs form muscles like those of a soccer player. Her breasts, too small, are, however, capable of undulating like a medusa. But her image irradiates, especially when she stands within the frame of the window, the freedom of a cat, an unconquerable indifference, something mercurial that places her far from any reach. (12)[12]

The narrative voice partitions and fragments the body of La mujer by concentrating in specific segments: the mouth, the legs, and the breasts. These separate sections do not make her body whole; on the contrary, it is an incomplete body devoid of mind, of feelings, of desires, and of will, despite the signs of strength projected by her athletic legs. This body becomes a good candidate for a regime of discipline that will attempt to produce – in Foucauldian terms – a "docile body," a body less likely to break gender rules or laws whether it is being watched or not.[13] This operation however becomes a challenge in that Reina is portrayed paradoxically and unsettlingly as someone fixed by the window frame while at the same time as possessing an animal-like freedom. This last feature further exacerbates Camargo's desire and makes him more than willing to tame this woman and foster her extreme dependency. Indeed, his primary purpose is precisely to curtail her ability and the ability of her body to evade control and to do as she pleases. As accomplices in the production of La mujer as a subjected body, the narrator and Camargo attempt not only to regulate her body's behaviour but also to damage it if it slips out of the parameters they establish. Therefore, from the beginning, they produce La mujer within the frame of their own discourse, as a body waiting to be regulated.

Their discourse advances the process of fragmenting her body when Camargo and La mujer, later introduced as Reina Remis, meet in the offices of *El diario*. Even at this first meeting, the narrator – as previously done – describes her exclusively as sexualized body parts: "In the cubicles of the Culture section, a young woman was working in front of one of the monitors.… Camargo could appreciate the rounded ass, the tits insinuating under the tight sweater" (21).[14] This time, however, there is verbal interaction between the two characters: Camargo addresses Reina in an arrogant and rude manner that is meant to instill in her a sense of fear and an appreciation of his power as an authority figure, especially among his subalterns. Reina however does not exhibit fear, but, on the contrary, responds with an unanticipated familiarity. This audacity, when later combined with Reina's ability to write, her rare knowledge of certain subjects,[15] her ability to think on her feet, awaken an intense intellectual and physical attraction within Camargo, who slowly and almost imperceptibly transforms it into abuse, subjection, and control.

Camargo therefore, acts upon this attraction by forcibly entering into Reina's private life and ordering one of his trusted employees to gather all possible information about her past. This information will allow Camargo to more effectively subject Reina to the subjection and the radical dependency discussed earlier since the more he knows about her and her body, the more power he can exercise. The following exchange illustrates this point:

> Read the results of her health exam. – Blood and urine, no problem, doctor Camargo. Only that? I want complete exams. I want to know if the people you employ have or at any time had venereal diseases, leeches, tuberculosis, irregular periods, rotten teeth, if the women are pregnant or have ever been. One must not trust women, Sicardi. (45)[16]

Despite this mistrust of women, Camargo pursues a romantic relationship with Reina, who, aware that this involvement could bring negative and unforeseen consequences, enters into the relationship nonetheless. She soon starts enjoying privileges as she ascends through the ranks of *El diario* and becomes established as a successful journalist. However, the privileges Camargo bestows upon her are overshadowed by the manifestation of his much darker and cruel side. When Camargo begins to suspect that Reina has a lover, something that she later confirms under duress, he takes audacious measures to investigate his suspicions, choosing to enter her apartment as a thief and to inspect her clothes in search of hidden secrets, papers, or any other evidence that may confirm his suspicions. The narrator suggests that Camargo's plans, however, extend beyond such an intrusion as can be seen in the narrator's second-person address to Camargo, when his rage towards Reina is mounting:

> … one more time you think about spying on her while she sleeps. You are going to do it, you are going to listen to her humidity, to hurt her thoughts, to burn her shadow, to skin the air she breathes. You are going to jump into her dreams and seize everything you find. (66)[17]

The violence of these thoughts not only signals Camargo's desire to control the exterior space surrounding Reina but also suggests that he intends to inflict psychic harm upon her. Words such as spying, hurt, burn, and skin show this man's hate and a strong desire to inflict brutal punishment. They also show his perverse desire for control through his twisted fantasies as the holder of unlimited power. He wishes to dominate Reina by abusing her to the point of perhaps brainwashing her into accepting his conceptualization of who she is, of what she wants, of what she does, of what she thinks and says, and of what she dreams. Camargo evidently will attempt to thwart Reina's concept of herself as an autonomous and free subject. She then would be totally dependent on Camargo's power to re-make her. The passage above can also be linked to

Butler's ideas on power, as she asserts that psychic life is generated by the social operation of power and that this operation of power is concealed and fortified by the psyche it produces. This is precisely what the narrator and male protagonist of *El vuelo de la reina* seek to implement. They both intently manipulate her psychic life by projecting onto her psyche their own ideas of what she should be. They seek to match their ideal submissive female subject with the woman Camargo anxiously observes every night from his dimly lit apartment. As he also drugs her, this drug stands for the social operation of power that will keep Reina asleep and unaware of her exploitation, humiliation, and abuse. The expected result is that Reina accepts the abuse and incorporates it into her normal way of life.

On one of those occasions while she is under the effect of a powerful sleeping drug, Camargo himself records a video of Reina nude. When Camargo is later watching the video alone, the narrator describes Camargo's sense of arousal and triumph in having vicariously obtained complete control of the woman and therefore in being able to unleash his desires to injure her body:

> the docility of her sleeping body is another sign of his power, he could do whatever he wants with her, and more than one time he has been tempted to tattoo her, to wound her, to inscribe on her flesh some indelible mark that tells of how many times he has been there, how many times he could come back if he felt like it to contemplate her as what she is, an object. (103)[18]

Camargo's misogynist discourse demonstrates how Reina is perceived as nothing more than an object that he can possess, thereby allowing him to justify the damage he wishes to inflict on her body. This is especially evident in the above description of Reina in her sleep, as an image in a video that – as in the beginning of the novel – frames her within a restrictive space[19] and keeps her silent, unaware, and, consequently, powerless.[20] Through his technological reduction of Reina, Camargo wants, as David Levin remarks, to "subject everyone and everything to a permanent availability and total control" (*Body's Recollection*, 1985: 133–34). This statement has troubling implications when it relates to Reina and her supposed permanent sexual availability. This expectation demeans and devalues Reina and promotes female submission. It must also be stressed that the narrator of *El vuelo de la reina* once again uses the impersonal "La mujer" suggesting that this process of submission, objectification, and devaluation can extend to any woman.[21]

Camargo's demeaning conceptualization of women is intrinsically linked to women's sexuality, as such real or imagined sexual freedom clearly poses a challenge to male possession and control. While Camargo is married and has two adolescent daughters that he never sees, Reina is supposed to be exclusively his and is not free to see or have intimate relationships with other men. In trying to establish himself as the only man in Reina's life and thus completing the process of subjection, Camargo is prepared to take radically dangerous steps that cause extreme pain and humiliation to Reina.

No other body organ, then, is as important as Reina's vagina. If her vagina is penetrated by Camargo, she is considered desirable. If, by contrast, she allows another male to penetrate her, she becomes despicable. The language used by the narrator to refer to Reina and to her vagina reveals a frighteningly misogynistic ideology. After she has supposedly had a torrid affair with a journalist in San Vicente del Caguán, Colombia, Camargo considers various sadistic forms of punishment to inflict upon her. In expressing Camargo's ideas of the necessary actions to take against Reina, the narrative voice again returns to the second person as if to suggest that Camargo was having a conversation not only with himself but also with the reader, who unwillingly becomes a sort of confidant of Camargo's sinister thoughts[22]:

> When you observe the woman through the telescope, you find it strange that her lips are broken and her chin swollen.

> You are upset that, after all, she seems happy. If someone has punished her, he has only done it half way. He would have had to take her eyes out and burn her tongue with red-hot tongs. Above all, he would have had to saw each ring of her vagina in order to extinguish the damage she has caused. (229)[23]

Although his ideas for retribution involve a hypothetical punisher, they disclose vicious violence and warn the reader of the lengths to which Camargo would go in order to castigate Reina's perceived transgression. In fact, Camargo acts in accordance with these plans of indirect punishment by hiring a destitute man named Momir to rape her. Camargo once again breaks into Reina's apartment and puts a sleeping drug in her juice, later returning with Momir to execute his horrific plan. Everything goes according to his plan, with the exception of one detail. Although Camargo has experienced pleasure and power in looking at Reina's body and movements for several weeks, he is unable to witness the act of rape. Instead, he hides in her closet and covers his face with her clothes, hearing only the screams of Momir. In contrast to her torturer, Reina is rendered completely mute and is unable to defend herself to resist the attack. She occupies the disempowering position of the victim and at the same time fulfills Camargo's fantasies for his punishing control. Unlike Camargo, who has chosen not to survey the end result of his plan, Reina's choice has been made for her: once again drugged, she is unable to look back at either of her perpetrators. This serves to reinforce the male power that is so pervasive in *El vuelo de la reina*.

As a result of this dehumanizing treatment, Reina's body becomes infected with sexual diseases. This new injury further debases her, as it will be very difficult to heal her body as well as her mind. Reina attempts to move beyond her disgrace, although without any real source of support, as she is isolated even from her mother and father. Her mother does not seem to appreciate the gravity of what has occurred. Reina visits a doctor and tries to distance herself from Camargo and El diario. She, however, never goes to the police or changes apartments. She does not seem to even consider the possibility of reporting the rape, as she has not even seen the perpetrators and will not be able to identify them.[24] As for staying in her apartment, this allows Camargo to continue to victimize her through surveillance and even through standing at her door to see her. As Reina rejects his visits, his vindictiveness leads him to use his power and influence to prevent anyone from giving her work.

Because both the narrator and Camargo inscribe Reina in their own masculine/patriarchal idea of order, Reina is thus situated within a world of power that, according to Foucauldian taxonomy is premodern and regressive. This is demonstrated by the fact that battles are fought by parties with unequal access to power; as the sovereign in the form of a lover and superior, Camargo still wields spectacular power over the Reina's body. Moreover, Camargo and the narrator reinforce the ideology that it is Reina, rather than the perpetrators of violence, who is responsible for this situation: "She could not even be sure that she had been raped. She had not seen anyone. Perhaps she should even feel guilty" (256).[25] Camargo's discrediting of his crime against Reina is further reinforced when he considers the response of Reina's Colombian lover upon being told of what had occurred. Camargo's reaction again underlines the idea that women cannot be trusted: "If Camargo were in that man's position, he would hear the story with distrust. It was idiotic to take a woman that bared her body in front of a window without curtains seriously; a woman who exposed herself to gazes and that moved her body in a provocative manner. Could one ever trust such a woman?" (256).[26]

As the archetype of an abuser, Camargo does not stop at what he has done but instead resorts to even more dangerous actions. Towards the end of the novel, Camargo follows Reina to an uninhabited area outside Buenos Aires where she goes horseback riding after having regained her strength. As she prepares to mount, an argument begins and she is shot by her ex-lover.

The tragic affair between Reina and Camargo then becomes a newspaper article, a new addition to the countless list of stories in which the jealousy and tight control of men over their lovers result in the murder of their lovers.[27] The reporting of these stories demonstrates that female abuse is a vast and insidious phenomenon and that, perhaps even more troublingly, such cases will be quickly consumed and set aside for other "more" important stories, like the corruption investigations. Although there is no apparent connection between the two, they are joined by the fact that impunity prevails, in both instances, despite the seriousness and evidence of both being crimes. The narrator conveys this message by stating: "Now it is well known that Remis' investigation on the arms trade was useless despite the evidence that Reina and Camargo gathered in the banks of Zurich" (189).[28] Reina's work is thereby rendered useless, as her efforts were futile and her body became nothing more than a disciplinary tool with which to show women the proper ways of sexual behaviour.

Reina's story also functions as a warning for other women to consider the severe consequences of breaking the patriarchal laws. It brings to the fore the power of repetition since it is, according to Butler "in the possibility of repetition that repeats against its origin that subjection might be understood to draw its inadvertently enabling power" (*The Psychic Life of Power*, 1997: 94). *El vuelo de la reina* describes such repetition in great detail. Battering and verbal and physical abuse inadvertently yet pervasively reduce Reina to a docile body that can be raped and ultimately murdered.[29] Given this reality, Camargo's desire to control Reina and her actions takes on further significance. These actions demonstrate that Camargo has internalized as well as reproduced an ideology of abuse and misogyny. At the same time, he expects Reina to conform to this ideology and to act, not in her best interest, but in the interest of her abuser.

By projecting his misogynistic beliefs onto the young and ambitious female character and by conceiving of himself as all-powerful and irresistible, Camargo reveals a contradictory relationship with his own old body, which he conceives of as extraordinarily strong but unattractive. This perception is best established as Camargo contemplates his physique in the mirror while simultaneously surveying Reina:

> A man is never the same when he is alone, and that profile is not me, repeats Camargo. He does not recognize the bulge of his abdomen, so indifferent to exercise and diets; neither does he recognize the folds of his breasts on his proud chest, or his turkey neck. The legs in the mirror are clumsy and thin, they have no harmony with his solid torso. The image in the mirror lacks dignity. What kind of dignity can a naked body have at the age of sixty three? Perhaps this question is for others to ask, but not for him. Everybody sees him as invincible; he is immune to illness or exhaustion. All the women he has been in bed with have already told him: his body is not a body; it is a force of God. (19)[30]

In the world of images that this novel creates, it is clear that Camargo is desperately trying to construct a self-image that conforms to, or even surpasses, unattainable ideals of masculinity, resulting in a number of contradictions. How can one with a "turkey neck" also be considered a force of God? This last question also develops the role of women in Camargo's magnified self-concept, as his lovers are meant to make him feel all-powerful and to reinforce his superiority and ego as a lover. His statements about his body also retain an unstinting dose of essentialism in which qualities of men (strength and masculinity) are quite clearly separated from qualities of women (passivity and femininity). Since he believes he both embodies and is perceived as the epitome of perfection, Camargo likely feels tremendous pressure to live up to these high expectations. His body, however, contradicts this idealized, masculine image. This incongruity between body and image and the resultant distance between Camargo and the ideal are symptomatic of something that has recently attracted the theoretical attention of academics: the crisis of masculinity. James Heartfield, for example, argues that the crisis of masculinity is often linked to a discourse that treats men as pathological. He adds that masculinity theories talk about this crisis in terms of loss of privilege and power.³¹ This seems to be the case with Camargo as he is feeling he is losing his body as well as his power to dominate.

Camargo's self-descrption also emphasizes the hierarchical power relationship that exists between this man, the embodiment of hegemonic masculinity, and other people, most especially women. Camargo's self-concept reinforces an extremely traditional notion of masculinity in which men, by virtue of their essentially given authority, are "naturally" supposed to inspire dread and respect. This notion is further developed through the social constructions of society, as other characters, particularly women, seem to accept and even encourage his role of dominator. The narrator's configuration of Camargo's fantasies of powerfulness fit very well with what a number of masculinist writers propound. In a chapter entitled *Theorizing Men and Masculinities*, Alsop, Fitzimons, and Lennon discuss a number of such writings, including Ben Greenstein's book *The Fragile Male* (1993). They describe how, in Greenstein's analysis, "men have evolved biologically to take a superior place in society. The challenge to male superiority in contemporary society brought about by women's increased role in the public sphere, he warns, may end in violent conflict" (*Theorizing Men and Masculinities*, 2002: 34).

Greenstein's inflammatory statement, in upholding the traditional gender roles, intensifies pressures for each to "perform" their gender under extreme concepts of masculinity and femininity. In the case of Camargo, the anxiety created by the pressures of masculinity is made clear to the reader through the distance between the image of power he seeks to project and the image of his aging body. As a result, he focuses his energies and desires on Reina, whom he considers to be the ideal means to recover his physical prowess and sense of masculinity. In fact, the narrator says that Reina was such a great lover that Camargo believed that "his body has turned young and insuperable. Sometimes he went to the bathroom after the savage love encounters and it seemed to him that his abdomen had hardened and that his hunched back returned to its straight position" (266).³²

Beyond the intimate space of the bedroom, Camargo plays a central role in the male-dominated, public world of business as the director of *El diario*. He deals with powerful government representatives and has important professional contacts with male journalists and writers in Brazil, the United States, and England. He makes the important decisions concerning which stories become headlines. In this way, Camargo incarnates the fearless journalist who unmasks government corruption and acts as a principled force in his efforts to bring crucial issues into the public's consciousness.[33] In such a critical situation, it is crucial for Camargo to have the power to look into the dark side of government corruption and relate these scandals to the public. This power allows him to influence public opinion and help construct the reality of Argentina during these times. Camargo consistently displays a great sense of arrogance in believing that he is the superior journalist and in conceiving of the other editors as incompetent and unaware. This is shown through the narrator's description of Camargo's daily routine at the newspaper headquarters, or "his kingdom" (20)[34] and through Camargo's belief that the world would be much better if he alone were to write about it. The narrative discourse suggests, then, that the exterior world becomes a malleable space ready to conform to his words and desires, in much the same way as Reina's body had been previously described.

This juxtaposition serves as a bridge between Camargo's private and public life. As a narrative strategy to get the reader to identify with him, and to offer a justification for his actions towards Reina, an entire chapter in the novel is devoted to Camargo's lonely, miserable, and motherless youth. Therefore, Camargo's sense of connectedness with his mother is seriously damaged and he begins to harbour feelings of hostility towards her. Later, when his mother leaves home to be with another man, the adolescent Camargo, unable to understand why he has been left behind, develops a deeper sense of abandonment that inflicts far more injury than his mother's previous neglect.

Camargo's father reacts very bitterly to the news of his wife's departure, "burning all the pictures, clothes and letters that his mother had left" (68)[35] and prohibiting Camargo from even saying her name. As a result, the memories of his mother rapidly fade from Camargo's mind, becoming nothing more than a "vague shadow" (68). The repression that Camargo is subjected to by his father instils in this young boy an immense resentment that he will be unable to conquer throughout his entire life. On the contrary, he nourishes this hatred, which resurfaces in several parts of the narrative. This occurs most notably when Camargo is about to kill Reina, as Reina and his mother become one entity that must be destroyed so that Camargo will not become the injured victim of abandonment once more.

This episode, exemplifies the disciplinary scene that Butler describes in her analysis of subjection and injury. Camargo's address to Reina and to his mother represents an effort to bring them back in line and to punish, or rather to injure, them for the crime of abandoning him. The effort at first fails because Reina refuses to hear Camargo and tries to escape his attempts to control her, insisting that she wants to end their relationship. She wants to move on and asks him to leave so that she can ride her horse. In doing so, she rejects her former identity as Camargo's lover and refuses to display the ideology of guilt, self-hate, and submission that Camargo expects and that the novel fuels.[36]

In addition to Reina's attempts to avoid subjection through misrecognition, she further challenges Camargo through interpellation.[37] After being shot the first time, she asks Camargo one last question: "How, Camargo?" (306). His response to the question is first to utter her name "Reina" and then to discharge a second bullet in her neck. The fact that both characters call each other by their own names at this moment of extreme tension is perhaps as melodramatic as any popular telenovela; notwithstanding, the scene describes what Jacqueline Rose has termed the "failure of identity" (*The Psychic Life of Power*, 1997: 97) because of the discrepancy between the name Reina and the person who embodies it. To utter Reina's name before her demise seems to become the ultimate weapon in the process of creating a docile body and enacting subjection and injury in terms of the unilateral power exercised on her. This power, on the other hand, serves as the force that activates the formation of Camargo as a subject.

Although the news of Reina's murder becomes headlines for *El diario*, Camargo is never charged with the crime. He, like the politicians he sought to expose, enjoys complete impunity. Reina's story, told from Camargo's perspective, shows that there is no justice for the victims; that misogyny is rampant; that society and the media are still projecting a polarized, violent, and dangerous representation of gender roles. In *El vuelo de la reina*, the mother, the wife, and the lover are vilified. Reina, who is symbolically made to stand for Camargo's mother, is murdered.

Through his attempts to dominate Reina, the male protagonist has thwarted her efforts to constitute her identity in her own terms as a queen, as an independent, high-functioning woman in a predominantly male culture. This identity is instead forcibly manipulated into a sexed and gendered body that provides visual as well as carnal pleasure to Camargo. Camargo's actions expose the destructive ways in which misogyny works socially and culturally to permeate both the body and the psyche of the female character. Although Reina attempts to show that her psyche can in a way refuse to occupy a position of subjection and injury, the end of *El vuelo de la reina* powerfully and violently indicates that there is no way out of the structure of patriarchal power that unjustly forces her to pay for this attempt with her life.[38]

WORKS CITED

Alsop, Rachel, Annette Fitzsimons, and Kathleen Lennon. 2002. *Theorizing Gender*. Cambridge: Polity Press.

Bly, Robert. 1990. *Iron John: A Book about Men*. Reading, MA: Addison-Wesley.

Butler, Judith. 1997. *The Psychic Life of Power: Theories in Subjection*. Stanford, CA: Stanford University Press.

———. 2004. *Undoing Gender*. New York: Routledge.

Calabrese, Elisa T. 1991. "Historia y Ficción: Tres Ejemplos de la Narrativa Argentina." *Rio de la Plata* 11–12: 351–60.

De Lauretis, Teresa. 1989. "The Violence of Rhetoric." In *The Violence of Representation*, ed. Nancy Armstrong and Leonard Tennenhouse, 241. London: Routledge.

Fajardo Valenzuela, Diógenes. 1993. "Procesos de (Des)mitificación en *La Novela de Perón* y *Santa Evita* de Tomás Eloy Martínez." *Verba Hispánica* 6: 23–40.

Foucault, Michel. 1988. *The Care of the Self: The History of Sexuality*, vol. 3. Trans. Robert Hurley. New York: Random House.

———. 1990. *The History of Sexuality: An Introduction*, vol. 1. Trans. Robert Hurley. New York: Random House.

———. 1995. *Discipline and Punish. The Birth of the Prison*. 2nd ed. Trans. Alan Sheridan. New York: Random House.

Ganduglia, Silvia. 1989. "La representación de la historia en *La Novela de Perón*." *Ideologies and Literature* 4, no. 1: 271–97.

Greenstein, Ben. 1994. *The Fragile Male*. Secaucus, NJ: Carol Publishing Group.

Gutiérrez Mouat, Ricardo. 1997. "Aporía y repetición en *Santa Evita*." *INTI: Revista de Literatura Hispánica* 45: 325–36.

Hartfield, James. 2002. "There is No Masculinity Crisis." *Genders* 35 http://www.genders.org/g35/g35_heartfield.html (accessed 15 Apr. 2007).

Hoff, Joan, Susan Kingsley Kent, and Caroline Ramazanoglu. 2006. "Gender as a Postmodern Category of Paralysis." In *The Feminist History Reader*, ed. Sue Morgan, 175–90. London: Routledge.

Human Rights Watch. 2007. http://www.hrw.org (accessed 2 May 2007).

Kolhatkar, Senali. 2007. *Uprising*. Radio Program. USA. http://uprisingradio.org/home/?m=20070511 (accessed 11 May 2007).

Levin, David Michael. 1985. *The Body's Recollection of Being: Phenomenological Psychology and the Deconstruction of Nihilism*. London: Routledge.

Llosa, Mario Vargas. 1996. "Placeres de la necrofilia." *La Nación*. Suplemento literario, ciencia, filosofía, historia bibliografía. Cultura: 1–2.

MacInnis, John. 2001. "The Crisis of Masculinity and the Politics of Identity." In *The Masculinities Reader*, ed. Stephen M. Whitehead and Frank J. Barret, 315. New York: Blackwell.

Martínez, Tomás Eloy. 1986. "La batalla de las versiones narrativas. Lo imaginario y la historia en la novela de los años setenta." *Boletín Cultural y Bibliográfico* 23: 21–31.

———. 2002a. *El vuelo de la reina*. Madrid: Santillana.

———. 2002b. "Periodismo y Narración: Desafíos para el siglo XXI." *Cuadernos de Literatura* 8, no. 15: 115–23.

McDuffie, Keith. 1989. *La Novela de Perón: Historia, Ficción, Testimonio*. La Historia en la Literatura Iberoamericana: Memorias del XXVI Congreso del Instituto Internacional de Literatura. Edición, Compilación y prólogo de Raquel Chang-Rodríguez y Gabriella de Beer. Inca Garcilaso Series, 1. Ediciones del Norte.

Morgan, Sue. 2006. "Introduction: Writing feminist history: theoretical debates and critical practices." In *The Feminist History Reader*, ed. Sue Morgan, 1–48. London: Routledge.

Parodi, Cristina. 1991. "Ficción y realidad en *La Novela de Perón* de Tomás Eloy Martínez." *Nuevo Texto Crítico* 4: 39–43.

Pla, Valeria Grinberg. 2005. "La Novela es un acto de libertad. Entrevista a Tomás Eloy Martínez." *Iberoamericana* 5: 155–61.

Réage, Pauline. 1965. *The Story of O*. New York: Olympia Press.

Restuccia, Frances L. 1996. "Literary Representations of Battered Women: Spectacular Domestic Punishment." In *Bodies of Writing, Bodies in Performance*, ed. Thomas Foster, Carol Siegel, and Ellen E. Berry, 42–71. New York: New York University Press.

Salem, Diana. 1999. "Historia, Memoria y Testimonio: Reflexiones Sobre la Obra de Tomás Eloy Martínez." *Alba de America* 17, no. 32: 345–52.

Zuffi, María Griselda. 1998. "Atravesando Géneros: Cuerpo y violencia en *Santa Evita*." *Romance Languages Annual* 10: 869–73.

NOTES

1. The two novels are considered remarkable attempts to reconstruct the lives of the most important figures in the history of Argentina in the twentieth century: Eva and Juan Domingo Perón.

2. See, for example, "La representación de la historia en *La novela de Perón*," by Silvia Ganduglia; "Los placeres de la necrofilia," by Mario Vargas Llosa; "Procesos de (des)mitificación en *La novela de Perón* y *Santa Evita* de Tomás Eloy Martínez," by Diógenes Fajardo; "La novela es un acto de libertad. Entrevista a Tomás Eloy Martínez," by Valeria Grinberg Pla; "Historia y ficción: Tres ejemplos de la narrativa argentina," by Elisa T. Calabrese; "Historia, memoria y testimonio: reflexiones sobre la obra de Tomás Eloy Martínez" by Diana Salem; "Ficción y realidad en *La novela de Perón* de Tomás Eloy Martínez," by Cristina Parodi; "*La novela de Perón*: Historia, ficción, testimonio," by Keith McDuffe.

3. That very same year it received the Alfaguara prize for best novel.

4. The appearance of a journalist as the main character is a feature that provides continuity to Martínez's narrative work.

5. Such linkages relate as well to the psychological and sexual tortures that women endured during the most recent dictatorship.

6. Reina's injured body can stand for the body politic, as the people of Argentina endured the vicious effects of the economic crises at the beginning of the twenty-first century.

7. Although the expression appears in small letters throughout the novel to underscore power relations, I have taken the liberty to capitalize the article, so that those power relations become more balanced. The reason for that choice has to do also with the fact that the name of the male character is always capitalized in the novel and in this study.

8. The scene, with its emphasis on the visual and the cinematographic reminds the reader of films like *Rear Window* by Alfred Hitchcock in which a man, incapacitated by a broken leg, observes his neighbours using a pair of binoculars. Among the observed is a young beautiful woman who often dances in front of her apartment window in her underwear.

9. "A eso de las once, como todas las noches, Camargo abre las cortinas de su cuarto en la calle Reconquista, dispone el sillón a un metro de distancia de la ventana para que la penumbra lo proteja, y espera a que la mujer entre en su ángulo de mira" (11). The translations of all the quotes from the novel are my own.

10. The use of "ángulo de mira" with its implications of death and shooting is unsettling as well as foreshadowing.

11 "Camargo siente una felicidad insuperable, porque la mujer al apartarse del espejo depende solo de su mirada. Los edificios alrededor están vacíos, ella podría morir sin que nadie lo supiera, y si por un instante él la desprendiera de su atención la dejaría huérfana en el océano del mundo."

12 "Tiene labios finos y tal vez demasiado estrechos, la nariz erguida hacia una punta redonda y gruesa, la barbilla enhiesta y desafiante. Cuando se ríe, alza tanto el labio superior que la franja de las encías queda a la vista. Los tobillos son gruesos y en las pantorrillas se le forman músculos de futbolista. Los pechos demasiado pequeños, son sin embargo capaces de ondulaciones de Medusa. Pero su imagen irradia, sobre todo cuando queda enmarcada por la ventana, una libertad de gata, una indiferencia inconquistable, algo mercurial que la coloca lejos de todo alcance."

13 According to Foucault, the docile body is subjected, used, transformed, and supposedly improved. After the process bad behaviours will turn into good ones.

14 "En los cubículos de la sección Cultura, una jovencita trabajaba de pie en uno de los monitores…Camargo apreció de lejos el porte airoso, el culo redondo y menudo, las tetas insinuándose bajo el suéter apretado."

15 Particularly of gnostic gospels.

16 "Léame los resultados del examen de salud.-Sangre y orina, doctor. Sin problemas. – ¿Sólo eso? Quiero exámenes completos. Quiero saber si la gente que usted contrata tiene o tuvo venéreas, ladillas, tuberculosis, reglas irregulares, muelas podridas, si las mujeres están preñadas o estuvieron alguna vez. Con las mujeres hay que desconfiar, Sicardi."

17 "Vas a hacerlo, vas a oír su humedad, a lastimar su pensamiento, a quemar su sombra, a despellejar el aire que respire. Vas a saltar dentro de su sueño y apoderarte de todo lo que encuentres."

18 "La docilidad del cuerpo dormido es otra señal de su poder, podría hacer lo que quisiera con ella, y más de una vez ha sentido la tentación de tatuarla, de herirla, de inscribir en su carne alguna marca indeleble que indique cuántas veces él ha pasado por allí, cuántas veces podría volver si le diera la gana para contemplarla como lo que es, un objeto."

19 Camargo is able to project Reina's image any time he likes on a 42-inch TV set, representing a rather dramatic form of this transformation of woman into an object of display.

20 The combination of sleep and silence brings to mind traditional fairy tales like *Sleeping Beauty*, *Snow White*, *The Little Mermaid*. It could be said that Camargo is once again enacting masculine fantasies found in those stories, as he wants to guarantee the female dependence on his male control.

21 This allows linking *El vuelo de la reina* to novels such as *The Story of O* (1955) by Pauline Réage.

22 In an interview with Juan Pablo Neyret, Tomás Eloy Martínez has indi-

cated that to get as close as possible to the character he used the second person in order to create, on the one hand, an effect of identification of the potential reader with the character. Then, the second person tries to seize the character; the interpellation has a sense of understanding as well (Internet source). I find this declaration extremely problematic because as a reader I in no way can identify with the male character that so ruthlessly vilifies and abuses her. Neither can I understand the obsession he has to denigrate and destroy her.

23 "Cuando observás a la mujer a través del telescopio, te extraña que los labios se le hayan partido y la barbilla esté hinchada. Te irrita que, a pesar de todo, parezca feliz. Si alguien la ha castigado, lo ha hecho a medias. Tendría que haberle vaciado los ojos y quemado la lengua con tenazas candentes. Sobre todo, tendría que haberle cosido cada anillo de la vagina para apagar el daño que ha causado."

24 It is widely known that most women do not report rape as doing so can have a damaging result for them in their private and public life. Furthermore, one also has to consider the mistrust that exists toward institutions like the police, which in the case of Argentina have participated in torture and disappearance.

25 "Ni siquiera podía estar segura de que la hubieran violado. No había visto a nadie. Quizás hasta se sintiera culpable."

26 "Si Camargo estuviera en el lugar de ese hombre, oiría la historia con desconfianza. Era una idiotez tomar en serio a una mujer que se desnudaba delante de una ventana sin cortinas, exponiéndose a miradas intrusas y que mecía el cuerpo de manera provocadora. ¿Se podía confiar en una mujer así?"

27 *El diario* has previously published the story of a murder extraordinarily similar to that of Reina's, as a Brazilian journalist's obsession with his lover results in his murdering her.

28 "Ahora se sabe que la minuciosa investigación de Remis sobre el contrabando de armas también quedó en nada a pesar de las pruebas que ella y Camargo recogieron en los bancos de Zurich."

29 The statistics on women murders are on the rise. The term *femicide* has gained currency to describe the frightening statistics of female homicides. Sonali Kolhatkar, the host of the radio program *Uprising*, indicates that "since the beginning of 2003, 2,300 women in Guatemala have been brutally murdered. Some of the victims are as young as seven years old." Ciudad Juarez in Mexico is well known as a place where hundreds of women have disappeared and been murdered. In Canada, aboriginal women are the victims of femicide as well. It is estimated that 500 are missing. According to Human Rights Watch, "Abuses against women are relentless, systematic, and widely tolerated, if not explicitly condoned. Violence and dis-

crimination against women are global social epidemics. We live in a world in which women do not have basic control over what happens to their bodies." See www.hrw.org.

30 "Un hombre nunca es el mismo a solas, y este perfil no soy yo, se repite Camargo. No reconoce el abultado abdomen tan indiferente a la gimnasia y a las dietas, ni los pectorales que al aflojarse, dibujan un pliegue en el pecho orgulloso, ni la membrana de pavo que le cuelga de la barbilla. La imagen del espejo tiene las piernas torpes y flacas, sin armonía con el torso macizo, y carece de dignidad. ¿Qué dignidad puede tener un cuerpo desnudo a los sesenta y tres años? Tal vez esa sea una pregunta para otros, pero no para él. A él todos lo ven como alguien invencible, inmune a las enfermedades y a la extenuación. Ya se lo han dicho las mujeres con las que se ha acostado: su cuerpo no es un cuerpo, es una fuerza de Dios."

31 Heartfield also points out that statistics in the UK show that men are more likely to commit bodily harm than women and "27 times more likely to murder." For the complete article, see http://www.genders.org/g35/g35_heartfield.html. John MacInnis states that "[T]he material and ideological legacy of millennia of patriarchy remains in the dramatic material inequality between men and women, the continued dominance of men in the public sphere, in the systemic misogyny of all kinds of mental representations of the sexes and the ubiquitous physical violence that characterize sexual relations" (*The Crisis of Masculinity and the Politics of Identity*, 2001, 315). The crisis is also connected to the crisis of capitalism, but this would require a separate analysis.

32 "lograba que Camargo creyera, al acostarse con ella que su cuerpo se había vuelto joven e insuperable. A veces iba al baño después de las salvajes funciones de amor y al observarse de reojo en el espejo, le parecía que el abdomen se le había endurecido y que la espalda … volvía a estar erguida"

33 In an article entitled "Periodismo y narración: desafíos para el siglo XXI" (Journalism and Narration: Challenges for the XXI Century), Eloy Martínez describes the role of the journalist thus: "El periodista no es un policía ni un censor ni un fiscal. El periodista es ante todo un testigo: acucioso, tenaz, incorruptible, apasionado por la verdad, pero sólo un testigo" (121). (The journalist is not a policeman, or a censor or an attorney. The journalist is above all a witness: relentless, tenacious, incorruptible, passionate to find the truth, but only a witness.) It is worth noting that Martinez's brand of journalism is highly compromised in *El vuelo de la reina*. Although Camargo in his public role as the director of *El diario* exposes the secret and corrupt dealings of the Menem government, he uses his position to pressure all the newspapers in Buenos Aires into not giving Reina a job. Besides, his role goes beyond that of a witness as he becomes the perpetrator of murder and uses that story as news for *El diario*. In his private life,

Camargo uses extremely questionable methods to control Reina. The question of whether Tomás Eloy Martínez is exposing the violence or endorsing it is a difficult one to answer. On the one hand, his novel brings back previous historical issues of tortured bodies and political and economic collapse that are still hunting the psyche of Argentina. On the other, the fact that the main male character knows that the law will not punish him for homicide seems to indicate that Eloy Martinez's postion is ambivalent.

34 "le gustaba dar vueltas por su reino desierto."

35 "encontró al padre quemando todas las fotos, las ropas y las cartas que la madre había dejado."

36 Camargo mentions films with a high content of misogyny, such as *The Night of the Hunter* (Charles Laughton, 1955.) In this film, Willa plays the role of the woman that internalizes a vision of herself as a sacrificial victim and says that she is proud of her burden. She accepts all the distorted ideas that the false preacher tells her; she changes her behaviour to fit his demands. In the end he kills her and throws her body into the river, a remarkably similar ending to the one for *El vuelo de la reina*. This alliance of the novel with the film promotes the same message of subjection and abuse.

37 I use the term *interpellation* in the Althuserian sense.

38 I would like to warmly thank Erin Aylward for all her work as a researcher for and reader of this article.

Desire and Violence in Ana María Shua's *La muerte como efecto secundario*

ELIZABETH MONTES GARCÉS

UNIVERSITY OF CALGARY

Ana María Shua was born in Buenos Aires in 1951 and has authored more than thirty books.[1] Her novel *La muerte como efecto secundario* (1997)[2] has been well received by literary critics. Specialists such as José Miguel Oviedo have focused on death as the most important topic in the novel, while others like Rhonda Buchanan have studied the importance of the epistolary structure in the development of story. Perhaps the most interesting studies that deal with the atmosphere of violence triggered by the neoliberal reforms set in motion during the Menem administration have been the articles published by Mónica Flori and Richard Young. Flori emphasizes that in *La muerte como efecto secundario*, there is a strong connection between the family crisis and the social decadence experienced in Argentine society. On the other hand, Young sees the construction of Buenos Aires as an asphyxiating urban space where extreme vigilance and terror trigger violence.

While in Flori's and Young's articles, violence is seen as the general atmosphere that surrounds the familiar and socioeconomic crises, my analysis will focus on the importance of the manipulation of desire that renders violence against the body a strategy to perpetuate capitalism and pave the way for the introduction of neoliberal reforms in Argentina. By using Gilles Deleuze and Félix Guattari's schizoanalysis, I will explore how Ernesto Kollody, the protagonist, is able to use his writing as the means to expose and undermine the mechanisms for controlling desire that are at play in an authoritarian system. The novel presents the story of Ernesto, a writer and makeup artist who tries to overcome his father's illness and the power he exercises over him by writing a letter to a woman who has been both Ernesto's and his father's lover. Ernesto's father (Gregorio Kollody) is an authoritarian man who controls everybody in his household but is also confronted with a serious disease: a tumour that blocks his intestine. Gregorio is forced into a state-run system of hospitals and nursing homes that profit from the diseases of wealthy elderly people.[3] Through his writing, Ernesto is able to reveal, not only how individuals are devoid of any desire due to the fact that their bodies are controlled by machines at the hospital, but also how his own desire has not been conquered by his father's authoritarianism, thus allowing him to be creative.

In *Anti-Oedipus: Capitalism and Schizophrenia*, Gilles Deleuze and Félix Guattari offer a critical reading of Freud's psychoanalysis of the Oedipus complex. Rather than seeing desire as stemming from the anxiety of the child to replace the father in the mother's bed, Deleuze and Guattari propose that when a child is born the social context in which he/she grows up defines his/her desire. In other words, the social has a crucial impact on the realm of the family and the individual – and not vice versa. According to Eugene Holland, in *Anti-Oedipus*,

> [Deleuze and Guattari] play Freud and Marx off against one another. […] It sets desiring-production and social-production in relation to one another […] while at the same time allowing for the historicization and critique of their separation and privatization under capitalism, thereby bringing psychoanalysis as well as political economy to the point of revolutionary autocritique. (122)

In order to associate desiring-production and social-production with each other, Deleuze and Guattari coined the term "desiring-machine" to refer to eleven "binary machines: obeying a binary law or set of rules governing associations: one machine is always coupled with another" (5). These machines refer to, but are not limited to, human organs plugged into other human organs that produce a flow. For instance, "the breast is a machine that produces milk, and the mouth is a machine coupled to it" (1). Desire is then produced by a series of flows and interruptions of the flows in a process of connective synthesis fueled by repression and permission.

Contrary to the Platonic notion of desire as lack, for Deleuze and Guattari, desire is always productive. Need stems from desire and not vice versa. Desiring-production resides in the unconscious. If desire is codified, that is, if desire is represented, then we could say that it is molar. If it is not codified, it remains in the territory of the unconscious and is molecular. Capitalism has codified desire and labeled it as merchandise. In Deleuze's words, capitalism continually deterritorializes and reterritorializes desire. Its strategy consists in interpreting desires in a given community and representing them as a piece of merchandise that will satisfy desire.[4] Desiring-machines make possible multiple connections in a process of connective syntheses that can come to a halt or an interruption in the productive process. If that occurs, there is anti-production, which causes a body that is completely devoid of desire to act on its own and produce new connections. According to Eugene Holland,

> The effect of anti-production on the connective syntheses, then, is to desexualize desire by neutralizing the organ-machine connections, and thereby constitute a surface that records networks of relations among connections, instead of producing connections themselves: it is this recording-surface that Deleuze and Guattari refer to as the body-without-organs. (28)

The recording surface or body-without-organs is nonproductive and sterile. These networks of relations among connections become a specific way to encode or territorialize desire, not allowing a free flow of desire and production. In other words, an individual whose mind and body are completely controlled by a social or political system could be considered an example of a body-without-organs. His/her body is programmed to react in predictable ways to maintain the flows and allow any institution, corporation, or government to maintain control over its members, clients, or citizens.

In the state-run system of hospitals and nursing homes ("*casas de recuperación*" [recovery homes]) described in Shua's *La muerte como efecto secundario*, the bodies of the elderly become bodies-without-organs, surfaces where a coded network of relationships are manipulated without the free will of the individual. Thus, nursing homes subsidized by the state take control of the bodies of the elderly and thereby preclude the possibility that they may express creativity. In so doing, they exercise tremendous violence against the bodies of their patients with the complacency, not only of the state, but of society at large as well. For example, they constantly check on their patients' vital signs to make sure that all the organs are functioning properly. However, they give patients skimpy dosages of painkillers to save on medication and to avoid possible side effects. When patients refuse to eat in order to protest their treatment, the nursing home personnel hook them to feeding tubes to avoid dehydration.[5] In other words, the connective synthesis between the flow of food or drink that enters into the mouth and produces pleasure is interrupted and regulated by doctors and nurses. As Ernesto explains, "In my father's room, the two beds were occupied by two elderly women hooked to several devices, and apparently in a vegetative state" (157).[6] A repressive state apparatus takes over the bodies of innocent civilians to use them as surfaces where they inscribe their own codes without allowing them any opportunity to escape or to desire on their own terms.

This is the case of Ernesto's mother. She is an elderly woman who apparently suffers from Alzheimer's disease. Due perhaps to the disease or to the enormous dosage of narcotics she is forced to take, she forgets the mechanism to swallow food. When Ernesto and his sister Cora go to visit her, they go to the cafeteria to have coffee and cookies. Cora insists to her mother the importance of feeding herself, and then Ernesto describes how their mother drinks a sip of coffee, but does not swallow it: "Mother seemed to be frozen in a liquid instant; some drops of liquid were trying to escape between her tightly closed lips and were running down her chin. […] She was not able to swallow or to spit and we had the impression that she was going to be like that forever" (125).[7] The interruption of the feeding process makes us realize how her body has lost its driving force, desire. As Ernesto says, she is like "a fragile wrinkled doll, like a piece of cloth unskillfully ironed with her yellowish complexion and her desperate eyes" (125).[8] These metaphors that equate Ernesto's mother with a surface full of marks ("wrinkled doll," "unskillfully ironed piece of cloth") suggest that her body has been programmed by the institution, redesigned and rewritten to allow the nursing home to control all her bodily and mental functions. It is indeed a body-without-organs, an unproductive encrypted surface totally emptied of desire. The treatment that Ernesto's mother receives at the state-run nursing home reminds us of the numerous torture chambers that were designed by the repressive government of the military junta during the years of "The Dirty War" (1976–83) when thousands of civilians were tortured and even killed by the military.

While Ernesto's mother seems to have lost all of her desire, his father Gregorio, a strong-willed and authoritarian man, refuses to give up the controlling role he has exercised all his life within his household and within society at large. As a wealthy individual, he is a target because his body represents valuable merchandise for the state-subsidized nursing homes. In this violent and repressive society, wealthy people (young and old) are the only ones who have a chance to survive because poor people's lives are seen as expendable. For a while, Gregorio manages to avoid living in nursing homes due to his money. However, once he develops a tumour that blocks his intestine, he has no other choice than to go to a hospital to have surgery and then be taken to the nursing home. The way the narrator describes the tumour and the place where the tumour has grown indicates a possible interruption in the desiring-machine because Gregorio's life is at risk. Ernesto explains:

> The decision to operate was not an easy one. If my father was operated on, he had little chance to survive due to his age. [...] The surgeon had to cut a piece of intestine and create an artificial anus, a tube through which all excrement would be expelled into an exterior bag that would be protruding from his stomach. [...] If everything went well, a new surgery [...] would connect the two ends of the intestine and my father would recover his sphincter (29).[9]

In other words, Gregorio is not able to fulfill his desire to eat or to defecate due to the tumour that interrupts the normal flow of food and waste. While he is at the hospital and nursing home, he loses his ability to handle his body and doctors and nurses capitalize on their desire to have direct control over Gregorio's body. Since Gregorio's own desire to recover his bodily functions is out in the open – it is a molar desire (conscious and represented) – , the nursing home has all the power to control it, to territorialize it. They will make sure that the circulation of bodily nutrients and waste keeps flowing and that the two ends of Gregorio's intestine are reconnected so that they can profit from that reconnection.

They have the power to repress the release of liquids or to let them flow as in a true capitalist enterprise.

The state-run hospitals and nursing homes in this novel are a microcosm of the Argentine nation under neoliberalism. Just as doctors and nurses use violence against bodies to keep them under control at the hospital so that the relationship between desire and production does not come to a halt, the state controls social production to keep capitalism alive and prosperous. In Deleuzian terms, the state's role is to interpret the desire of those over whom they exercise power so that it becomes conscious. Once desire is represented, then it is easy to control. In the Buenos Aires society that Shua describes, the state has been able to capitalize on citizens' fear of aging so that the state appears as if it is lifting the burden of families to take care of their elders. By doing so, they are able to keep their power, but also profit from the situation. For instance, the hospital tapes Gregorio's surgery and plays it over and over again on television and in hospital corridors for public audiences in order to praise the high efficiency of their services and the skills of their physicians. "We rushed to the projection room. [...] They had taped my father's surgery. On the screen we could see his organs, and a physician was explaining the medical procedure" (55).[10] By recording Gregorio's operation and playing the tape in public, the state manages, not only to represent the popular desire to have the elderly taken care of, but also to relieve the possible guilt that relatives might experience for leaving their aging parents and grandparents in the care of nursing homes.

In order to understand the relationship between the nursing home where Gregorio is confined and the Argentine society depicted by Shua in *La muerte como efecto secundario*, we need to explain the three different types of societies that are described in Deleuze and Guattari's *Anti-Oedipus*. According to both philosophers, there are three types of social machines: the Primitive Territorial Machine, the Barbarian Despotic Machine, and the Civilized Capitalist Machine. In the Primitive Territorial Machine, there are no written laws and societies are organized through taboo. In the Barbarian Despotic Machine, the law is written on paper, but all the members of a given society are indebted to the ones who hold power. In the Civilized Capitalist Machine, desire is privatized. In this type of society, the family is the institution that fuels capitalism by gearing desire in predictable and manageable ways. In other words, the nuclear family "is the breeding-ground for guilt and self-inhibition" and keeps the capitalist machine working.

The type of society depicted in *La muerte como efecto secundario* corresponds to two types of social bodies described by Deleuze and Guattari. On the one hand, we have a Barbaric Despotic Machine (the state-subsidized nursing homes) that exercises a violent control over every aspect of an individual's life (including his/her own body) and to whom all citizens are indebted. According to Holland, in this type of society, "rituals of cruelty and systems of inscription are instituted precisely to code all matter- and energy-flows so that they circulate throughout society and cannot escape its grasp" (71). As we have seen in the case of Gregorio, the nursing home insists on screening the film that shows the surgery performed on his intestine as a way to mark his flesh as a territory that they control. That control could be considered a form of violence exercised on the bodies of the helpless and sick individuals who are forced into nursing homes ("*casas de recuperación*"). On the other hand, we have a Capitalist Machine that uses the family to foster and reduplicate its own power strategies. In Ana María Shua's text, it is Gregorio who is, not only the victim of the manipulation of his body by a repressive and insensitive state, but also the authoritarian father figure who exercises his asphyxiating control over the members of his family. Thus, in the novel, Gregorio suffers an apparent reversal. Once the exploiter, he then becomes the exploited. However, his exploitation is short-lived because his knowledge of the state's *modus operandi* allows him to devise a way to escape to a colony of runaway men where he makes his son his slave. Therefore, he functions as a kind of hinge mechanism that permits the state apparatus to couple with the capitalist machine.

Gregorio insists on his willingness to survive his ordeal because, in comparison with others who are crippled by debt in the Buenos Aires community, he is a wealthy individual as well as a moneylender. As Ernesto recalls, "The ones who have debts, – said my father – they probably would like to die. For us lenders, life is worthwhile. We can still charge for the money they owe us" (33).[11] He is referring in particular to his son Ernesto, to whom he has lent US$10,000 so that he will take care of him. In Gregorio's eyes, Ernesto is a complete failure because he has not accumulated wealth working as a writer or a makeup artist. He knows that his son is in need, so he lends him money to have him at his service.

Gregorio has constantly exercised repressive means to control his children's behaviour, to make them feel inferior, and to show his power over them. Ernesto explains:

> Dad used all the resources at his disposal to exercise control and power over us: he tormented us with guilt, penalized us with punishment, used the power of his physical strength when we were little and his money when we were adults. He was able to combine the power of the villain and the victim. He used to control us using truth, lies, intelligence and his knowledge of our weaknesses and wishes. He also loved us passionately. (44)[12]

As Ernesto confirms, his father has ample knowledge, not only of his children's weaknesses, but also of their desires. When he is confined at the nursing home, Gregorio uses his ability to behave like the victim to convince his son that he is going to die. He pleads with Ernesto to organize his escape from the institution. Ernesto acquiesces and uses the remaining $8,000 his father has given him to pay for a private squad to rescue him. Once Gregorio is a free man, Ernesto becomes a criminal who has gone against the rules of the state and is forced to escape along with his father. They both end up at a villa on the outskirts of the city where elderly people who have escaped from nursing homes have organized their own cimarron[13] community. Gregorio has to buy his entrance into the community, and he displays no remorse in selling his son as a slave who has to work as a servant in the villa's farms in order to secure his father's status.

Following the Deleuzian model, Gregorio plays the role of the authoritarian father figure who manipulates his son's desire to save his own neck and to perpetuate his power over him by transforming him into a slave. By the same token, it is possible to draw a link between Gregorio, the father figure in Shua's novel, and Carlos Menem, the national patriarch of Argentina who marked the history of the nation with his authoritarianism and the implementation of neoliberal policies during his two presidential periods (1989–95 and 1995–99). Menem was elected president in 1989 under the promise that he was going to revive Juan Domingo Perón's economic policies. He captured the country's attention by promising that Argentina was going to become a prosperous nation. He appointed Domingo Cavallo as his economy minister to implement the swift economic reforms preached at the University of Chicago by Milton Friedman.[14] As Naomi Klein argues, "The Cavallo plan, as it came to be called, was based on the clever packaging trick that both the World Bank and the IMF had perfected: harnessing the chaos and desperation of hyperinflation crisis to pass privatization off as an integral part of the rescue mission" (198). Menem's government opened the country to foreign investment and launched a massive campaign of the privatization of all state enterprises. Initially, his policies were extremely successful and his project was seen as the ideal model for Latin America. However, once the bubble burst, it was evident that unemployment levels in Argentina had escalated to unprecedented levels, pushing more than half of the population below the poverty line. In other words, just as Gregorio in Shua's novel, Menem became a hinge mechanism who was able to exercise overwhelming power over his people due to his ability to know their most intimate desires and capitalize on them, thus allowing the capitalist machine to thrive and prosper at the expense of the lives of the Argentinian people.

Gregorio is so good at manipulating Ernesto's desire that he is able to delve into Ernesto's psyche. As Ernesto explains,

> It was impossible to hide anything from my father. He was so curious, so keen to control every aspect of our lives, even our dreams. It is impossible to keep a secret from someone that does not have scruples, from someone that does not stop at anything, from someone who is willing to open your drawers, and even your intestine. (196)[15]

Froma letter written by Ernesto to his former lover, the reader learns that Gregorio seduced his son's lover and had sex with her on a regular basis. Gregorio intervened in his son's relationship with a married woman to repress or allow desire to be consummated. However, once she discovered that she was being manipulated and having sex with both father and son, she felt horrified and stopped seeing both Ernesto and Gregorio for good. Ernesto describes her reaction when she discovered the truth,

> I wanted to tell you that I did not mind sharing you with other men, [...] that I was willing to accept anything, anything you were willing to give me. [...] But you were not willing to do it; you couldn't do it. You were crying and crying. You were horrified at what you had done. You were worried about my own dignity. [...] I was looking at you crying. (195)[16]

As Deleuze and Guattari would contend, in spite of Gregorio's efforts to control Ernesto's desire, Ernesto's willingness to continue the relationship with his lover is an indication that there could be lines-of-flight, or ways to undermine an authoritarian system that controls desire and results in violence. Gregorio's plan is to constrain and regularize desire to make it molar (conscious and represented), but there still exists the possibility of escaping the paradigm and having manifestations of the molecular, liberated desire not codified by the system. By writing a long letter to his lover, which constitutes the text of the novel that the reader has in his/her hands, Ernesto manages to make his molecular desire effective and provide for himself several lines-of-flight. He liberates himself from the guilt of being involved with a married woman and from the idea of sharing her with other men.

In the letter, Ernesto recreates the story of his encounters with his lover. Since their relationship was a forbidden one, the woman was very secretive, but her secrecy kept their passion alive and the desiring-machine at work.

> You never met any of my friends. [...] You made me sick with your secrecy.... Our relationship could have evolved into tenderness, into habit. Instead, it was kept alive thanks to your insistence in keeping it clandestine. (136)[17]

Once Ernesto isconfined to the cimarron villa where he is a peasant and a slave, he writes about the way she used to place her hand on his chest after making love: "You used to leave, and yet you were next to me, your childlike hand on my chest, and that was perhaps what I loved the most" (56).[18] The connective synthesis between her hand and his chest keeps Ernesto's desire alive, and it is productive because that event inspires him to write and keeps him away from committing parricide. By the same token, his writing brings his lover closer to him because she is the intended reader of his story. While the norm is for individuals to have just one sexual partner within the context of the nuclear family, both Ernesto and his partner have liberated themselves from a fixed idea of possessive love only possible in the realm of the nuclear family and capitalism.

Deleuze and Guattari characterize desire as nomadic, as feeding itself from fragments dispersed in the social milieu. Ernesto's relationship with his lover is kept alive because, while they are seeing each other, she insists on having him describe all the encounters he has had with other women. On those occasions, Ernesto displays his ability to tell stories, offering her all the minute details of his love affairs, even if he makes them all up:

> Some of the stories I told you were true, and others were not. [...] I would describe to you my love affairs, including all the morbid details. I used to talk to you about other women's reactions, their smell, the way they reacted to my caresses, or how my ability as a lover would make them scream, or howl when they had an orgasm. You enjoyed my stories so much that you wanted me to do to you what I had done to other women (83).[19]

Ernesto exercises his creativity to tell and make up stories, and, by doing so, he is, not only triggering desire in his partner, but also decoding molar representations of love. In many ways, Ernesto is the perfect schizophrenic. For Deleuze and Guattari, "the schizophrenic passes from one code to another, according to the questions asked him, never giving the same explanations from one day to the next, never invoking the same genealogy, never recording the same event in the same way" (15). When Ernesto tells stories to his lover, he changes the details, reorganizes the story, and makes up the most outrageous tales, which she does not believe but enjoys enormously.

Taking this argument one step further, we can also say that Ernesto, just like Ana María Shua and many other writers of her generation, are schizophrenic. They use their writing as a tool to establish contact with a wide audience as an attempt to undermine the violence and destructiveness of an authoritarian system perpetuated by figures such as Carlos Menem. According to Holland,

> The process of schizophrenia advocated by schizoanalysis is thus not about going mad or taking merely individual lines-of-flight from institutions of social repression; it is about realizing freedom in difference and through differentiation,

the principle of permanent revolution made possible in the universal history inaugurated by capitalism. (122)

That revolutionary process is accomplished in the limits of the system itself by using all of the means at the individual's disposal. In Ernesto's case, his second tool to undermine the authoritarian system is his ability as a makeup artist, a talent often disregarded because it is considered a female activity.

Ernesto is hired by Goransky, a wealthy movie director, to do the makeup of several guests that will attend a sumptuous party at the Retiro train station in Buenos Aires. The train station will be converted into the Artic and Antarctic, and all guests at the party must wear a costume appropriate for the occasion and the scenery. They can be Inuits, Patagonian Indians, good or bad spirits called Tornraks or even animals such as seals, penguins, or polar bears. Soledad Goransky, the director's wife, decides to be an Inuit girl with violet eyes to resemble the famous movie actress Elizabeth Taylor. Ernesto explains that when he works with new subjects, he must have a conversation with them to find out their wishes. As Ernesto describes,

> I was working with her [Soledad], with her face, with her personality, studying her little by little to find out up to what point she was capable of deceiving herself into thinking that she could resemble the famous actress that was once considered the most beautiful in the world. (130)[20]

Soledad's desire to resemble a famous actress makes us realize the impact of the Capitalist Machine on women. Soledad has been manipulated by capitalism to reject her own body and change her personal appearance to please the man in her life. During the rehearsal, everything goes well and the illusion is complete. However, during the party, the real features of Soledad continually reappear and Ernesto has to make repeated efforts to fix them. By constantly applying makeup on Soledad, Ernesto is reinscribing the characterization on the individual, changing the code and revealing to the audience the degree of manipulation to which she has been subjected.

Even over dead bodies, Ernesto is able to reveal the mechanisms of desire at play in the Capitalist Machine. When his neighbour's gay lover is killed in a violent attack by vandals, Ernesto offers his services to reconstruct his horribly disfigured face to prepare him for a decent burial. Alberto Romaris' partner was not a handsome man, but his body had been mutilated and his face was badly disfigured by the assassins. Ernesto starts working on the appearance of the corpse by looking for a picture or a video of the deceased:

> If one seeks an ideal face, the one the deceased would have desired for himself, the mask he would have chosen to present to the world, a photo is better: people close to us know which face we preferred. But if what's wanted is naturalness, others' view of the deceased, to recover the person not as he wanted to be seen but as the rest of the world saw him, then I prefer to work with a video. (74)[21]

In this case, Ernesto decides to work with a picture to please Romaris and give him the man he wanted to see. He even goes to the extreme of finding dentures that fit the corpse's mouth so well that when Romaris sees him, he is finally able to cry. In spite of the ephemeral nature of his work, Ernesto is able to realize Romaris's wish to see his partner as a handsome man. While the Capitalist Machine has made Romaris and his partner invisible because they were gay, Ernesto, thanks to his ability to inscribe new codes on the human skin, has been able to render Romaris and his partner visible to the world.

If, at first glance, Ernesto could be considered a failure as a writer and as a makeup artist, schizoanalysis reveals that he is indeed a true schizophrenic. By writing the letter to his lover and telling her all the stories about his affairs and sexual fantasies, he is able to trigger her desire, to counteract his father's authoritarianism and to avoid violence. His abilities as a makeup artist have allowed him to reveal to others the manipulation to which they are subjected in a capitalist society. By the end of the novel, Ernesto confesses that his new objective in life is to write:

> I am going to continue writing. I am going to write lots of letters to you. From now on, my words will be the proof that the world that I imagine is possible, and also the proof that I am still alive, orphan and light as the air. That will be my true life. (235)[22]

If doctors and nurses at the nursing homes have perpetrated overwhelming violence over the bodies there to keep desire at bay and the flow of cash feeding their bank accounts, Ernesto has discovered that the formula for liberation from oppression is to reveal the mechanisms of desire at play within capitalism and to constantly change the code. While Gregorio Kollody and the state use violent means to inscribe human bodies to control their desire and perpetuate their power, Ernesto inscribes bodies and texts creatively to let us see how human beings have been manipulated by capitalism and to allow desire to run freely.

For Deleuze and Guattari, desire is productive. It is at the heart of change and revolution. Politicians such as Carlos Menem manipulated Argentina's desire to see itself as a prosperous nation by implementing neoliberal reforms that led the country into economic crisis, violence, and extreme dependence on the IMF. Ana María Shua responded creatively by publishing *La muerte como efecto secundario*, a remarkable novel that depicts the revolutionary efforts by a writer and makeup artist to undermine an authoritarian capitalist system that controls desire and promotes violence and human destruction at the hands of corporations and corrupt state apparatuses with the sole objective to accumulate power and wealth.

WORKS CITED

Buchanan, Rhonda Dahl. 2001. "Visiones apocalípticas en una novela argentina: *La muerte como efecto secundario* de Ana María Shua." *El río de los sueños: Aproximaciones críticas a la obra de Ana María Shua*. Washington, DC: Organización de los Estados Americanos, 163–75.

Deleuze, Gilles, and Félix Guattari. 2005. *El Anti-Edipo: capitalismo y esquizofrenia*. Trad. Francisco Monge. 1ª edición argentina. Buenos Aires: Paidós.

Flori, Mónica. 2001. Familia y nación de fin de siglo: Una lectura de *La muerte como efecto secundario* de Ana María Shua. Washington, DC: Organización de los Estados Americanos. http://www.iacd.oas.org/Interamer/shua.htm (accessed 15 Nov. 2007).

García Corales, Ernesto. 2001. *El discurso finisecular en* La muerte como efecto secundario. Washington, DC: Organización de los Estados Americanos. http://www.iacd.oas.org/Interamer/shua.htm (accessed 15 Nov. 2007).

Klein, Naomi. 2007. *The Shock Doctrine: The Rise of Disaster Capitalism*. Toronto: Alfred A. Knopf.

Oviedo, José Miguel. 1998. "Una novela sobre la muerte." *Cuadernos Hispanoamericanos* 571: 153–57.

Shua, Ana María. 1997. *La muerte como efecto secundario*. Buenos Aires: Sudamericana.

Young, Richard. 2003. "Buenos Aires and the Narration of Urban Spaces and Practices." *Contemporary Latin American Cultural Studies*, ed. Stephen Hart and Richard Young, 300–311. London: Oxford University Press.

NOTES

1. Ana María Shua published her first book of poems (*El sol y yo*) when she was sixteen years old. Since then, she has published several novels, including *Soy paciente*, *Los amores de Laurita*, and *La muerte como efecto secundario*. She has also written humour books that analyze Argentinean social and cultural patterns, such as *El marido argentino promedio*, *El pueblo de los tontos*, and *Cabras, mujeres y mulas*. She has written collections of short stories, such as *Casa de Geishas*, *La sueñera*, *Viajando se conoce la gente*, and *Días de pesca*. In 1993, she received a Guggenheim fellowship and published her novel *El libro de los recuerdos*, which deals mainly with the story of her Jewish ancestors.

2. All quotations in the article are taken from the Sudamericana edition and all translations are mine.

3. According to Monica Flori, the sick body of the father represents the condition of decay of the government apparatus. However, Flori's article does not give a satisfactory explanation as to why Gregorio's sick body is almost inhumanely treated by doctors and nurses who would like only to profit from his disease.

4. For instance, water is the best liquid to calm thirst without causing an addiction. However, corporations have sold the idea that Coke is the best there is to achieve that objective. In truth, Coke makes an individual thirstier due to the amount of sugar present in the concoction, allowing the system to work by triggering consumerism. Since one Coke is probably not enough to calm one's thirst, we buy another and another, ad infinitum.

5. In many ways, the medical treatments described in Shua's novel closely resemble the torture that was inflicted on thousands of victims that were detained and disappeared during the dictatorship (1976–83).

6. "En la habitación de mi padre las camas estaban ocupadas por dos viejas esqueléticas, conectadas a diversos aparatos y, aparentemente, en estado vegetativo" (157).

7. "Pero mamá parecía congelada en un instante eterno, con los carrillos hinchados y la boca llena de líquido: algunas gotas se le escapaban entre los labios fuertemente cerrados y le corrían por la barbilla. [...] No podía escupir ni podía tragar y daba la sensación de que iba a quedarse siempre así" (125).

8. "muñeca arrugada, como un trapo mal planchado, de color amarillento y ojos desesperados" (125)

9. "La decisión de operar no era fácil. Si se operaba, tenía pocas esperanzas de sobrevivir. [...] Había que cortar un trozo de intestino y hacer un ano contra natura. Un agujero en la panza por donde brotaría la mierda mansamente, empujada por los movimientos peristálticos [...] si todo salía mejor de lo esperable, una nueva operación, [...] volvería a unir los dos extremos de

tripa que quedaban sueltos y mi padre recuperaría su esfínter" (29–30).

10. "Corrimos a la Sala de Intravideoscopia. [...] Frente a la pantalla que exhibía el funcionamiento de sus órganos, un médico disertaba" (55).

11. "Los que tienen deudas, – dijo mi padre – ésos a lo mejor querrán morirse. Para los que somos acreedores, la vida vale la pena. Yo todavía tengo mucho que cobrar" (33).

12. "Papá usó todos sus recursos para ejercer control y poder sobre nosotros: nos atormentaba con la culpa, nos penalizaba con el castigo, usaba el poder de su fuerza física cuando éramos chicos y el de su dinero cuando fuimos grandes. Era capaz de aunar el dominio del torturador y el de la víctima. Nos controlaba usando la mentira, la verdad, la inteligencia y el sabio conocimiento de nuestras debilidades y deseos. También nos quería: apasionadamente. Sólo para él" (44).

13. The term "cimarrón" is used in this context to refer to runaway men who flee the city and organized themselves in a colony in the outskirts of the city. Shua borrows the term from the colonial period in Latin America when a large amount of slaves called "cimarrones" used to flee their masters and settled in towns in the middle of the jungle called "palenques".

14. In her famous book *The Shock Doctrine: The Rise of Disaster Capitalism*, Canadian economist Naomi Klein explains how Argentina was one of the nations where the "shock doctrine" was widely implemented, first by the military junta who mounted a terror campaign to exterminate opposition to the corporate model by establishing more than three hundred torture camps where military personnel exercised torture and killed around 150,000 people. The years of repression under the military junta were followed in the 1990s by the implementation of neoliberal reforms by Domingo Cavallo and former alumni of the University of Chicago, strong believers of Milton Friedman's economic theories, to take advantage of a major economic crisis in order to privatize all state-run enterprises. For further information, see chapter 8, "Crisis Works: The Packaging of Shock Therapy" (185–201).

15. "Siempre fue difícil esconderle algo a mi padre, tan curioso, tan dispuesto a controlar incluso nuestros sueños. Es imposible ocultarle un secreto a alguien que desea saber y que no tiene ningún principio, ningún escrúpulo, nada que le impida darte vuelta y abrirte de arriba abajo para revisar tus cajones o tus tripas" (196).

16. "Hubiera querido informarte que no me importaba compartirte con cualquiera [...] que estaba dispuesto a aceptar cualquier cosa. [...] Pero no podías, no querías. Estabas horrorizada de lo que habías hecho, arrepentida. [...] Te preocupabas demasiado por mi dignidad. [...] Yo te miraba llorar" (195).

17. "Nunca conociste a mis amigos. [...] Tus preocupaciones me volvían loco... Nuestra relación podría haber evolucionado hacia la ternura, hacia

el hábito, y en cambio gracias a tu riguroso concepto de la clandestinidad, se mantuvo siempre igual" (136).

18 "Te ibas, sin dejar de estar al lado mío, tu mano de niña sobre mi pecho, y eso era quizás lo que más me fascinaba" (56)

19 "Algunas de las historias que te contaba eran ciertas, otras no. [...] Te hablaba de sus olores [...] comparaba los sonidos que mi supuesto virtuosismo extraía de ellas, las palabras inconexas que aullaban o musitaban en la recta final y no conseguía más que acentuar tu interés. [...] [M]e pedías que repitiera en tu cuerpo aquello que había hecho o fantaseado en otras" (82).

20 "Estuve trabajando con ella [Soledad], con su cara, con su personalidad, estudiándola poco a poco, para saber hasta qué punto sería capaz de engañarse a sí misma, hasta que punto podría ayudarme a hacerle creer que había comenzado a parecerse a esa mujer considerada alguna vez la más hermosa del mundo" (130).

21 "Si se busca una cara ideal, la que el muerto hubiera deseado tener, la máscara que hubiera elegido para presentarse ante el mundo, lo mejor es una foto: la gente que nos conoce bien sabe cuál era nuestra cara preferida. En cambio, si se busca naturalidad, la mirada de los otros, recuperar a la persona no como hubiera querido verse sino como la veían los demás, prefiero trabajar con un video" (74).

22 "Voy a seguir escribiendo, voy a escribirte muchas cartas, solo cartas, y mis palabras de aquí en adelante serán la prueba de que ese mundo que imagino es posible y también la prueba de que sigo en él, de que empecé por fin huérfano y liviano como el aire, mi verdadera vida" (235).

Violence and Representation: Postdictatorship Visions in Lita Stantic and Albertina Carri

ANA FORCINITO

UNIVERSITY OF MINNESOTA

With the pioneer representation of *The Official Story* (1985), most of the films related to the most recent dictatorship in Argentina (1976–83) depicted the cultural transition to democracy with the allegorical image of a secret that had to be revealed. The act of revelation, as a visual practice that invites us to see what was supposed to remain concealed, is suggesting that gazing – as a cultural practice of the redemocratization process – is inextricably linked to the construction of social memory and the new cultural significations that dislocate the totalitarian gaze and its monolithic meaning. In this process the films of the postdictatorship era in Argentina examine different ways to represent state-based violence. The violence of the past is approached from the perspective of fundamental human rights, creating a revision of the past as well as a reflection about the present.

In this essay, I will approach the representation of violence during the Argentine postdictatorship of the 1990s and the new millennium by focusing on the construction of social memories and visions in two key films: *Un muro de silencio* (1993) by Lita Stantic and *Los rubios* (2003) by Albertina Carri. The first one serves as a fictional testimonial narrative of disappearance and survival. The second one, a documentary film, uses fictionalization to challenge the testimonial format.[1] Both films emphasize that the revision of the dictatorship's violence implies the need for a deprivatization of the gaze, and a rearticulation of a public vision and the battle for its re-signification. These two films explore the relation of authoritarianism and re-representation by focusing on the metaphoric imprisonment of the ability to see as a consequence of authoritarianism. Therefore they represent the complexities and conflicts of the becoming public of a gaze that – like citizenship more generally – suffered a process of "privatization." Privatization here means a reclusion to the private sphere as opposed to the public, and the deprivation of that place from its public dimension. Argentine film during the dictatorship suffered not only from the exile of some of the directors of the New Latin American Cinema of the 1960s, but also from being deprived – by censorship – of the possibility of articulating any dissident or critical meaning. In a recent cultural study of the Argentine dictatorship, Hugo Vezzetti suggests that there was a process of privatization during the military regime that changed the very meaning of citizenship, and that this confinement of citizens to the private space was a response to the chaos of the public sphere. Further, it was also a search for shelter from the public dimension of being a citizen, and a shelter that protected a fearful Argentine population from the terror and violence exercised by the regime (51). Thus, representing past violence implies a revisioning of the nonauthoritarian gaze and the ability after the collapse of military regimes to see the human rights abuses they committed. The representation of violence raises questions about the very possibility of portraying the images that are now being remembered, and of imagining visions for those images that had disappeared.

The main concern of the two films discussed in these pages is, on the one hand, the representation of detention, death, disappearance, and survival and, on the other hand, an exploration of the legitimacy of representation itself: What is suppressed or displaced in the attempt of reconstructing the past from the cultural clues provided by the present? What is the role of interpretation in these attempts to gaze upon the unspoken violence of that past? How do these interpretations affect the present, not only because the violence of that past has remained as a ghost haunting the redemocratization process, but also because the attempt to remember that past implies the acceptance that there are unrecoverable gaps that cannot be completely restored? And, in particular, how do cinematic representations challenge, not only the dictatorial meaning of the past, but also the significations that accompanied the process of impunity during the 1990s? These ruptures of representation echo a violence that still persists in contemporary Argentine culture, not only as the effects of new forms of violence emerged with neoliberal policies, or because of the renewed forms of violence that came along with the process of impunity, but also due to the epistemological limit of the reconstruction of the past and the violence that all interpretation implies.

LITA STANTIC AND THE CLAIM OF PUBLIC GAZE[2]

Un muro de silencio (*A Wall of Silence*, 1993) – the only film directed by Stantic – explores the construction of "revisions" and new meanings. Such revisions are discussed here with Teresa de Lauretis (1984) in mind when, following Adrienne Rich, she stated: "The revision ... ('Re-vision – the act of looking back, of seeing with fresh eyes,' writes Rich, is for women 'an act of survival') refers to the project of reclaiming vision, of 'seeing difference differently'" (*Alice doesn't: Feminism, semiotics, cinema*: 297). In Stantic's film the focus of this revision challenges the possibility of reconstructing the devastated ability of the postdictatorship vision. Here a transgressive gaze is related to the opening of new spaces of vision – a direct look to the detention camp in the last scene accompanied the look towards the spectator as a possible accomplice, not only of the silence that surrounded the abuses of the military regime, but also of the paralysis that accompanies the impunity process that started in 1986.[3] It could be said that the central aspect of *Un muro de silencio* is the gaze, and furthermore the construction of a social gaze that, as memory, is still under construction.[4] As shown in the title, the film is concerned with the synchronicity between the visual (the wall) and the auditory (silence). The film circulated in international film festivals and was awarded the Glauber Rocha Prize from the foreign press in the Havana Festival and the Human Rights Award in the Florianópolis Festival (http://www.litastantic.com.ar/unmuro/index.htm). Nevertheless, its debut went almost unnoticed in Buenos Aires, and the reception outside of the Latin American festival circuit seemed to show a certain fatigue regarding the theme of the disappeared.

Un muro de silencio deals mainly with the possibility of reconstructing the history of a clandestine detention camp survivor whose husband was one of the Argentine *desaparecidos* during the military regime. This is a rather common theme in postdictatorship cinema, especially in the early years.[7] Nevertheless, the film implies a change from the interpretations of violence and terror in the 1980s. The most evident change is that the two key figures of the redemocratization process, the *desaparecidos* and the exiles, are not the main focus. This is a film about survival, and most importantly, about the difficulties of the representation of survival. The visual representation of disappearance, violence, and complicity seems to imply, as Pilar Calveiro (2005) has argued in her approach to memory, not so much the puzzle model where all pieces fit exactly in one place, but rather the kaleidoscope model and the possibility of recognizing different figures (19).

Furthermore, the film belongs to a new moment in the redemocratization process, a moment characterized by the idea that impunity was the condition for the consolidation of democracy. This re-signification of what democracy means – in particular when we consider that in the years following the end of the dictatorship the Argentine transition is understood as linked to the concept of human rights – is inextricably bound to the impunity laws that were sanctioned in 1986. The wall of silence is associated, not only with what happened in the past, but also with how the past is re-signified in the present and, in particular, the silence that impunity represents in a country where the two most important instances of redemocratization are, as Vezzetti suggested, the *Nunca Más* and the Junta Trials. The film is situated in this paradox, and if it is a film about disappearance it is not so much because it represents missing citizens but because it is pointing to the meaning that is now missing or lost when attempting to understand the past and the present. The film deals with representation itself. The (im)possibility of reconstruction is explored through the figure of an English director, Kate Benson (Vanessa Redgrave), who arrives in Buenos Aires to make a film. The other character involved in the film production is Bruno Tealdi (Lautaro Murúa), the scriptwriter and also the former professor of the story's protagonist. The film is set in 1989, the year marked by the *Indulto* (Amnesty Laws) that pardoned the military leaders put on trial in 1985.

Both gazes (Benson's and Tealdi's) are, in different ways, foreign. In the director's case, it is very clear. As Catherine Grant (1997) suggests, the film explores the possibility of the existence of a "solidarity camera" regarding a traumatic part of Argentine history through a conscious foreign collaboration within national cinema. Grant maintains that the figure of the foreigner can be thought of as a "mediator" between two cultures, even in reference to Kate's failure to know what really happened, adding: "She will presumably return home to her film project about Ireland, disillusioned by the possibilities for her Argentine film" (1997: 323). *Un muro del silencio* clearly posits the theme of foreignness, and Kate can be seen almost as a metaphor for the foreignness or distancing of many Argentines who disregard what happened during the dictatorship (authoritarianism was lived outside as well as inside the detention camp).

Kate's gaze is not the only foreign gaze; in another sense, Bruno's is just as foreign. Despite the fact that he is Argentinian and even wrote the story Kate is trying to portray in the film, he must also confront his own situation of being outside of the detention experience. Kate as well as Bruno looks through a foreign, distant, and displaced mirror: Kate as a First World woman director and Bruno as a writer – a scriptwriter – who remains outside the experience of the clandestine camp. The two have their privilege (First World/patriarchal discourse) from which they dislocate from the survivors' experience. Nevertheless, the look of Silvia Cassini, the survivor of kidnapping and detention and the widow of a *desaparecido*, represents in some way one of the two "eccentric gazes" of the film. The other is that of her daughter, also a detention camp survivor.[6] I consider the survivor's gaze as such; that is, a gaze that is displaced from the dominant forms of representation, and silenced or marginalized in some way. This evaluation seems somewhat exaggerated considering the central place that survivors have played in the Argentine transition to democracy, whether as members of the National Commission for the Disappearance of Persons (CONADEP) or testifying at the Junta Trials. Nevertheless, only recently have more openings been made for the appearance, not only of texts produced by survivors, but also of texts whose central topic is survival, given that in the first decades of redemocratization, as Vezzetti suggests, the *desaparecido* is the one who has a central place in the re-signification of the democratic process, particularly in testimonial narratives that centred around the figure of the *desaparecido*, or to the specific questions (torture, location of the detention centre, denouncing torturers) that the survivors could answer about the missing ones.[7]

Un muro de silencio elaborates upon the very difficulty of seeing what is on the other side of this metaphoric wall: the life of a survivor after liberation. There are irreconcilable visions (Bruno, Kate, Silvia). Fictional and real levels overlap (the film within the film, the directors – Stantic/Benson, the scriptwriters, the actors). Kate is repeatedly wondering how to look at these characters (especially Ana, Silvia's fictional name) and giving us spectators a fragmented narrative, which as such is proposed as a story impossible to narrate. Her vision is impertinent because the question of looking concerns the subject of the vision; as a foreigner, Kate is a subject who grapples to understand Argentine history. Her solidarity is not enough for her to find a pertinent gaze. The other subject of the gaze is Bruno, and his vision is also impertinent; it is exposed as a paternalist gaze that appropriates the right of narration.[8] While it is obvious that this gaze is not foreign to the past as is Kate's, it is impertinent nevertheless because it is both emotionally close to Silvia's story and yet epistemologically distant. Bruno also narrates from his lack of knowledge, and at the end, in his confrontation scene with Silvia, it is evident that in this past/present dichotomy, Bruno's impertinence has to do with not knowing (as Kate does not know) what Silvia wants to remember or what she wants to forget. It is the impertinence and the foreignness of these visions that triggers the question about our own impertinence, and our own foreignness as spectators, in the process of interpreting, making sense, and attempting to understand what remains behind the wall of silence.

Representing terror implies also a passage through the paths of memory. The depiction of violence, a decade after it took place, cannot be thought of outside the gaps in the recollection of that violence. The scene of the kidnapping – in Kate's film – as well as the depiction of the assassination of a human rights lawyer (right after he visits Silvia to present a writ of habeas corpus for her husband) are not about accuracy but about what Rene Jara (1986) called "the traces of the real" in reference to testimonial narrative: a reminder of that which cannot be recovered (2). A decade after democratization, it seems that the film proposes that violence is fading in the memories of the past, and even more so when translated to any means of representation: it can only be portrayed as a trace.

Consequently, one of the most revealing scenes in the film takes place near the end when Silvia and her daughter are looking at a detention centre. The climax consists not of the recuperation of the traumatic images of the past but of the image of two generations of survivors looking at a building and, simultaneously, attaching a meaning to what is seen. Silvia acquires power through her recovered gaze, a gaze that is also a memory and a question. "Didn't people know what went on in there?" asks her daughter. "They all knew," Silvia answers, while the image freezes on her child. Looking and knowing are juxtaposed in the formation of this double subjectivity: a subject in the circuits of design of meaning as a former detainee and as a witness.

Many Argentine films of the postdictatorship era include images of covered or uncovered eyes, a clear allusion to the blindfolded victims in the detention centres, and the affirmation of the eyes of the witnesses, of what they saw or heard. We can think of the image of one of the posters for María Luisa Bemberg's *Camila*, scenes from Marcos Bechis's *Garage Olimpo*, and many memory projects related to human rights in Argentina that emphasize gazing in the reconstruction of meaning after the military regime.[9] Stantic's attention to the gaze manages to recover Silvia Cassini's memories, but despite the centrality of her story, her gaze is lost in the unfolding of vision (the "historical" and the fictional character) and in the gazes of the other characters (Bruno and Kate, among others). The film proposes a change of perspective from outside the experience of the clandestine camp to one from within – that is, toward the survivor as a subject of the gaze – an eccentric gaze, as I argued earlier, because it is a way of looking that was subordinated to the dictatorial modes of representation, and then marginalized within the cultural debates of the democratic return.[10] Thus, multiple gazes (Kate's, Bruno's, Silvia's, and her daughter's) serve to disperse the possibility of a homogeneous gaze and to put forth looks of fragmentation, uncertainty, obscure areas, and unanswered questions.[11] These superimpositions construct a net of memory that seeks, not only to undo the authoritarian gaze, but also to reaffirm multiple visions in the reconstruction of what remains behind the wall of silence, the *indulto* and the official politics of oblivion that come with it. The personal stories that inhabit social memory are neither private nor secret. The film depicts a process of private accounts of what is remembered and forgotten "becoming public."

The film emphasizes survival instead of victimization, but not as a celebration. On the contrary, it explores what Elizabeth Jelin has called "the labors of mourning," which is the process of "working through the painful memories and recollections instead of reliving them and acting them out" (2003: 6). Moreover, the film shows what is lost in the representation process, not as a denial of terror or authoritarianism, but as an exploration of the effects that violence has had in representation itself. Silvia looks at the clandestine detention centre and then at her daughter at the end of the film. Finally the gaze of the daughter looks first at the centre, and then at the spectator, perhaps underlining that the process of representation does include spectatorship. What is it that the spectators see or do not see? What are their strategies in understanding the state violence of the last military regime, and in particular the possible complicities between the junta and the paralysis of a terrorized society? What are the spectator's memories and the re-signification of them? What is, after all, the spectator's own wall of silence?

ALBERTINA CARRI AND THE STRUGGLE FOR A DISPLACED GAZE

The revision of the gaze constitutes a central aspect of Albertina Carri's *Los rubios*. Her film revisits the past from the perspective of a new generation, and it poses innovative questions about the representation of violence by blurring documentary and fiction in an attempt to question the limits and the pertinences of both genres. Carri's vision attempts, not only to re-examine her identity, but also to explore it as a fiction and a construct.

Carri is herself the daughter of two *desaparecidos* (Roberto Carri and Ana María Caruso), and she witnessed the detention of her parents when she was three years old. Her gaze in a film that crosses the borders between fiction and documentary is situated almost thirty years after the beginning of the military coup, during a very different wave of redemocratization. Carri chooses to have a fictional character representing her role. At the beginning, Analía Couceyro says, "I am Analía Couceyro and I will play Albertina's Carri's role." We also see Carri, but in her role as director. In this documentary film, Carri plays with the borders of fiction and testimony to gather information about her parents, in particular the moment of their kidnapping and their experience of detention. Carri shows the process of her own search for a narrative of the past through interviews with former militants, survivors of the detention camp where her parents disappeared, and neighbours from the town where they lived before the detention.

One of the main concerns of the film is to show the process of representation itself, starting with the duplication of Carri in her fictional double, Couceyro, and continuing with the acknowledgment that Carri, as Carri, will still be present in the film, sometimes even remaking scenes, as in the moment when the film shows first Couceyro having a DNA test done, and then Carri undergoing exactly the same procedure. One of the first shots of the film brings the presence of Roberto Carri. The reading of his book *Isidro Velázquez* demonstrates that the space for the presence of the missing citizens is already there: that is the point of departure. The film is not about Carri's missing parents, however; it is much more about the search for her own process of signification. Nevertheless, the reading of a quote from Roberto Carri's book brings to the forefront the intellectual aspect of the generation of the sixties and seventies, although it does so through a displacement. The quote does not actually come from Carri's text; rather, it comes from Juan Díaz del Moral, and Martín Kohan refers to this displacement as a mark of the present absence of the father: "By force of distance and separation of the past, in the scene of the daughter reading about her father, nothing is more lacking than her father's writing" (29). An earlier scene depicts Albertina Carri saying, "Check that I'm not in this frame." Therefore, from the beginning it is clear that the film will contrast two different voices and projects: that of Carri and that of the former generation.

Carri addresses this generational conflict when she makes public the letter in which the Instituto Nacional de Cine y Artes Audiovisuales denied funding to *Los rubios*. Here the National Cinema Institute asked for "more documentary rigour," referring in part to the fact that Carri planned to represent herself through an actress (Analía Couceyro) who, from the beginning, declares her name and fictional role as that of Albertina Carri. The ambivalence of this juxtaposition of the director and actress, stressed by the fictionality of the Carri character (represented by Couceyro), and also the identification of each of them as Analía Couceyro and Albertina Carri, can also be seen in the shots during rehearsal and discussions among the filmmakers in which Carri is Carri and Couceyro is Couceyro. The scenes featuring interviews with the *compañeros* of her politically militant parents, just like the interviews with neighbours in the Matanza, also have this mark of ambivalence.

This complexity of identity and the fictionalization of the documentary as genre is what provoked the rejection of the National Cinema Institute. This was their argument:

> We believe that the project is worthy and ask in this sense that it be revised with a greater documentary rigour. The history as it is formulated poses the conflict of fictionalizing one's own experience, when pain might cloud the interpretation of lacerating facts. The claim of the protagonist over the absence of her parents, if this is the central point, requires a more demanding search for testimony that would crystallize with the participation of her parent's companions, with affinities and disagreements. Roberto Carri and Ana María Caruso were two engaged intellectuals in the seventies whose tragic destiny deserves that this project be completed.[12]

Although Couceyro's voice reads the message, Carri's voice adds to the discussion of the text in saying, "It isn't the film they needed ... as a generation." That is, the generational transgression that the film implies is brought forth, just as in the work of other producers of the new independent cinema that arose at the end of the nineties, in part because it displaces the subjects of interpretation and gaze and means of representation.[13] *Los rubios* provides an exploration of memory from another perspective, from the fragments, the rips, and the cracks of Carri's own childhood representation (Albertina Carri was three years old when her parents disappeared):

> In 1999 I began an investigation of fiction in memory (objective facts confronted by fantasy, accounts fragmented by the impossibility of remembering certain elements, and the impossibility of forgetting certain details that came at random). I submerged myself into that tunnel and that search became the first half-hour of *Los rubios*.[14]

At the same time, this fragmentation of memories is accompanied by a search for identity, as fiction, as distortion, as a project that refuses to be completed. To Regine Robin's quote, "La necesidad de construir la propia identidad se desata cuando ésta se ve amenazada, cuando no es posible la unicidad" (The need to construct your own identity is triggered when it appears to be threatened, when uniqueness is not possible), Carri adds through her "fictional" character, "En mi caso el estigma de la amenaza perdura desde aquellas épocas del terror y violencia en la que decir mi apellido implicaba peligro" (In my case the stigma of threat has endured ever since those times of terror and violence when saying my last name implied danger).[15] The question of identity cannot be detached from the debates about identity that were brought up by the organization HIJ@S and Grandmothers of the Plaza de Mayo. In fact, according to Gabriela Cerruti, the organization HIJ@S inaugurated a new moment in the construction of memory during the postdictatorship period. They are the ones who argue that memory is a construction against the interpretative rule of the late eighties and early nineties in which the official politics of memory were, as Stantic suggests in her title, a "wall of silence." Cerruti sees that the definition of the organization as "against oblivion and silence" is the key in the understanding the context in which they attempt to reconstruct memory and to promote justice. (We should add here that some of the trials of military officers after the impunity laws took place precisely because of the struggles of the *Abuelas* and HIJ@S.) Nevertheless, at this point it is also important to mention the repeated opportunities in which Carri has declared that she was not part of the organization HIJ@S. Looking from the outside at an organization centred on the children of detainees and *desaparecidos*, Carri's eyes are also attempting, like HIJ@S, to argue for the need of the reconstruction of memory and identity by her generation.

In his analysis of *Los rubios*, Kohan discusses the operations of inclusion and distancing, given that the film incorporates, on the one hand, testimony from militant companions of the parents, while, on the other hand, doing so through their displacement (we see them on the video screen that Carri/Couceyro watches while she writes notes, or while she looks at photos). It is evident that these companions do not have a central place, relegated as they are to the margins. As Kohan writes, "If she had excluded it or left it out of the film, we wouldn't see it; as she pushes it away, as she displaces it, we see the way in which this slippage applies" (28). Carri also displaces herself while (in a way) occupying the centre of the identity search. Displacement, as the act of removing something from its usual place, does not necessarily mean exclusion but rather an inclusion in a different place. For example, at one point Carri and Couceyro are rehearsing a scene in which Couceyro – playing Carri's role – repeats her lines after Carri makes suggestions about how to say them. This scene, presented to us through a refilmed rehearsal shot, emphasizes Carri's presence as the subject of gaze (and voice) given that she is telling the actress how to present it. In a way it displaces her, but only to replace her in a different position. In this scene Carri suggests suppressing certain pauses, giving these directions: "Podés decirlo más rápido.… Está bueno que hagas como una enumeración y también si te vas olvidando está bueno que pienses un instante y sigas" (You could say it quicker.... It's good to do it like a list, and if you forget along the way it's okay to think a bit and go on). Or, later, after the second shot of this scene: "No repetiría la palabra 'odio' porque es muy fuerte" (Don't repeat the word "hate" because it's very strong). This scene is repeated three times, with some variations in the words:

> I hate ladybugs, shooting stars, walking under bridges, train tracks, flocks of birds. I hate eyelashes falling out and having to make a wish when you blow out the candles on your birthday cake. Because I spent many years wishing for the same thing: that mom would come back, that dad would come back and that they would come back. Truthfully, it was always one wish, but I put it into three parts so that it would be stronger.[16]

In this scene Carri both questions herself (the duplication of Carri in Couceyro) and affirms herself as the director of the film, almost as if she was telling us that her gaze and voice should not go unnoticed. At the same time, she is representing her "fictional" identity with a fictional character, although she reminds us that both identity and documentary are fictional, but only up to a certain point. Carri includes testimonial and documentary voices and interviews in her film along with her very own participation to underline that this is not quite a fictional film. Nonetheless, *Los rubios* explores the fictionality of memory and the impossibility of accurately reconstructing memory. The director, who twenty years later remembers her life in 1977 when she was three years old, cannot reconstruct the history – neither hers nor her parents' – outside the form of a fragmented story. Those clouded and fragmented memories constitute her identity, as we can see when she refers to the memory of the very moment of her parents' detention – an event that she witnessed – and when one of the kidnappers put her in a car: "I think it was a red Ford even though I don't know if I imagined it or if it was like that, actually, I don't know if a lot of things then I remembered or if I went along creating them using things my sisters remembered" (2003).

A blurred memory is emphasized over the clarity of recollection. The voice weaves together disconnected memories and images and tries to give them sense. The gaze of the camera seeks new ways of representation for these new social subjects of memory examined by Carri's generation. The most controversial scene in the film has to do precisely with the representation of violence, in particular during a scene that uses Playmobil dolls to depict her parents' kidnapping. The reception of these images has provoked rather critical reactions. Kohan, for example, refers to the "depoliticization" of the kidnapping: "She suppressed a reality, that of political violence, not only in her game, but also in *Los rubios*, just as in her film are suppressed the past, the exercise of memory, or the possible bonds of a possible identity" (29).

Carri speaks of this scene stressing that it is about "kidnapping from the eyes of a child" (Kohan: 29). Childhood memories during a military dictatorship tend to be, as Elvira Martorell suggests, fragmentary, given that they concern what children hear and see. As such, any narration of these memory segments made twenty years later does not necessarily reconstruct the past but rather re-elaborates "that which has present-day power, *that part of the past that remains alive, unknowingly – in the present*" (141). Memories become "fictions that constitute a reality of the psyche always arising from a piece of historical truth" (143). In the same way, Carri, in exploring this tunnel of the fiction of memory, recreates not just the past but, as Martorell suggests, the images that are kept in the present; for example, those Playmobil images that not only allude to the disappearance of her parents, but also to the fact that the disappearance was interpreted by a child, with the imaginative and fantastic projection of a child (as with the spaceship that takes her parents away) having to face the absurd nonsense of official language. In that case it does not seem so strange that this representation de-normalizes the very concept of "disappearance" when it is interpreted from the perspective of a woman recovering her own childhood representation.

The scene of the kidnapping represents the disappearance of her parents and points to the erasures that disappearance produces in the symbolic sense. As Gilou García Reinoso (1997) suggests, disappearance "kills death"; that is, "it hints at making death disappear in support of life, making it humane" (382), and this scene, even with the problematic aspects that it might present, is attempting to provide a visual narrative of the concept of disappearance in the way that a child might have understood it. Violence is lost in Carri's representation partially because the vision proposed in *Los rubios* does not emphasize the accuracy of representation; rather, it depicts the fragmentation and opacity of representation.

VIOLENCE AND REVISION

Films made in Argentina soon after the collapse of the 1976–83 military regime represented violence as a way to expose human rights abuses without questioning representation itself. A good example of this moment can be found in one of the key films of this period, *The Official Story*, when students filled the blackboard with pictures of missing people and news about disappearances in an attempt to undo the totalitarian narrative of the so-called *Proceso de Reorganización Nacional*. Films produced during those years attempted to reconstruct the scenario of authoritarianism in which violence takes place. In this sense, films of the eighties responded to the gesture of revealing the truth as well as showing new ways of participating in the cultural redemocratization process, as Ruby Rich has suggested when discussing the New Latin American Cinema. I am thinking about films such as *The Official Story*, *La noche de los lápices*, and *Camila*. All of them explore images of state violence and undo the secrecy of state-based terrorism.

Films of the nineties are not so much about revealing the truth as they are about exploring representation itself. Not only do they account for the violence of the dictatorship, but also for the violence that the "wall of silence" (*indulto*, pardon, democracy as impunity) remade during the democratic transition. During this wave of democratization – marked by the impunity laws – the silence about the past that Stantic attempted to review was accompanied by the awareness of the limits of representation, violent loss, and the unrecoverable gap that the revision of the past necessarily implies.

In the late 1990s, the new generation of Argentine cinema undertook a somewhat different approach. The *campo* in Carri's film is a concept that refers both to the clandestine camp where Carri's parents disappeared and the *campo* (countryside) where Carri grew up. Using the same word for both implies an attempt to see a connection between the inside and the outside of the detention camp, and it signals a passage from the focus on the experience of her parents to her own experience as a daughter of two missing citizens.

During this newer wave of redemocratization, films propose narrative images that disrupt the meaning of previous years, as exemplified by the kidnapping scene in Carri's film. These images imply a revision of the past and they disrupt both the totalitarian narratives of the military regime and the narratives of democratization during previous years. Even with the emphasis on disappearance, *Los rubios* – as well as other films produced in the late nineties – explores captivity and survival as a prolonged event, not only for the militants, prisoners, and detainees, but also for the generation that experienced the last dictatorship during their childhood.

In her essay about the ethical dimension of the photographic images of war and violence, Susan Sontag (2003) argues that one of the problems of these visual representations "is not that people remember through photographs but that they remember only the photographs" (89). Sontag is cautioning us to consider that images "speak for themselves" in order to emphasize that photographs are always interconnected with the stories that explain them. The representation of violence in film also triggers a question about ethics and should be understood, as Barthes has suggested, as a "trace." In any case, the visual representation of violence is surrounded by language, text, and meaning, and without them, Sontag states, visual images "do not tell us everything that we need to know" (90). Through this interrelation between language and visual images, between representation and interpretation, between gaze and meaning, the depiction of kidnapping in *Los rubios* and *Un muro de silencio,* and the stories that go along with them, are pointing to real suffering and therefore, as Sontag suggests with photography, they bring to the discussion questions about the ethics of representation.

From *La noche de los lápices* to *Los rubios* the strategies of representation of violence have changed substantially and, in these two particular examples, it is clear that this passage underscores fragmentation and opacity rather than transparency and cohesion. This is not about an absence or an avoidance of depicting violence. In fact, violence is a central aspect of the so-called new independent cinema (of the late nineties and new millennium), but the strategies for representation are different. The emphasis is now more on repressed forms of violence that escape representation (*La ciénaga* and *El cielito* are two very good examples). Perhaps now the new generation of filmmakers who grew up during the last military dictatorship are exercising their vision of the past and addressing the traces of that violence, absurdly "normalized," not so much to explore the logic of authoritarianism as to expose the silent everyday atmosphere of tension and fear, the inexplicable nightmares surrounded by a climate of "normal life," the infantile explanations of a reality that refused any logical narrative, the terror and the games that children used to deal with it, and the suspicion (or the certainty) that catastrophe was taking place very close by. Violence here turns puerile as exemplified in Carri's controversial kidnapping scene in *Los rubios* because it attempts to represent violent events as a child understood them. Violence here turns opaque in a midst of unclear memories and refuses a transparent representation. Violence here triggers again questions about the ethics of representation in the construction of social memory and in the constitution of new subjects of recollection. In these different moments of the redemocratization process (the first one marked by the *Juicio a las juntas*, the second by the impunity laws, and the third by the attempts to derogate the impunity laws) we can see different problems posed by the representation of violence and human rights abuses and different strategies used to expose them, to silence them, or to question them. In all cases these films are about recollection and the project of reconstruction of memories. Perhaps one of the most powerful images of the last years in Argentine film takes place in *Crónica de una fuga*, by Adrián Caetano, a film about the escape of four detainees from the clandestine centre Mansión Seré, based on the testimonial account of one of the survivors, Claudio Tamburini. At one point, the character who interrogates the detainee Guillermo Fernández – in the fiction – is Guillermo Fernández himself, one of the survivors of that same detention camp. The borders between fiction and documentary collapse in these narrative images that account both for the history of Guillermo Fernández's escape from the camp almost thirty years ago and for the presence of Guillermo Fernández, now an actor in 2006, playing the role of a judge who interrogates his fictional double. Here is another duplication, as in Carri's and Stantic films (Carri/Couceyro, Silvia/Ana), which invites us to rethink the limits of representation and its violence in the construction of social memory.

WORKS CITED

Batlle, Diego. 2002. "De la virtual desaparición a la nueva ley: El resurgimiento." In *El nuevo cine argentino: Temas, autores y estilos de una renovación*, ed. Horacio Bernades, Diego Lerer, and Sergio Wolf, 17–28. Buenos Aires: Tatanka.

Baudry, Jean Louis. 1986. "Ideological Effects of the Basic Cinematographic Apparatus." In *Narrative, Apparatus, Ideology: A Film Theory Reader*, ed. Philip Rosen, 286–98. New York: Columbia University Press.

Calveiro, Pilar. 1998. *Poder y desaparición: Los campos de concentración en Argentina*. Buenos Aires: Colihue.

———. 2005. *Política y/o violencia: Una aproximación a la guerrilla de los años 70*. Buenos Aires: Grupo Norma.

Carri, Albertina. 2003. Los rubios. *El amante* 138. http://www.elamante.com/nota/2/2059.shtml (accessed 13 May 2007).

Castagna, Gustavo. 2002. "De una vanguardia a otra: ¿Hay una tradición?" In *El nuevo cine argentino: Temas, autores y estilos de una renovación*, ed. Horacio Bernades, Diego Lerer, and Sergio Wolf, 105–10. Buenos Aires: Tatanka.

Ciria, Alberto. 1995. *Más allá de la pantalla: Cine argentino, historia y política*. Buenos Aires: Ediciones de la Flor.

De Lauretis, Teresa. 1984. *Alice doesn't: Feminism, Semiotics, Cinema*. Bloomington: Indiana University Press.

———. 1990. "Eccentric subjects: Feminist Theory and Historical Consciousness." *Feminist Studies* 16: 115–47.

Escobar, Raú, and Fernando Martín Peña. 2001. "Apocalípticos pero integrados." *Film* 2001. http://www.filmonline.com.ar/nuevo/dossier/2001/movimientofalso/intro/apocalipticos.htm (accessed 12 Feb. 2007).

García Reinoso, Gilou. 1997. "Un agujero en las palabras." In *Ni el flaco perdón de Dios*, ed. Juan Gelman and Mara La Madrid, 381–88. Buenos Aires: Planeta.

Grant, Catherine. 1997. "Camera solidaria." *Screen* 38, no. 4: 311–28.

Jara, René. 1986. "Prólogo." In *Testimonio y literatura*, ed. René Jara and Hernán Vidal, 1-6. Minneapolis: Institute for the Study of Ideologies and Literatures.

Jelin, Elizabeth. 2003. *State Repression and the Labors of Memory*. Minneapolis: University of Minnesota Press.

Kohan, Martín. 2004. La apariencia celebrada. *Punto de Vista* 78: 24–30.

Mahieu, Agustín. 2002. "Nuevo cine argentino." *Cuadernos Hispanoamericanos* 627 (Sept.): 121–23.

Martorell, Elvira. 2001. "Recuerdos del presente: Memoria e identidad: Una reflexión en torno de HIJOS." In *Memorias en presente: identidad y transmisión en la Argentina posgenocidio*, ed. Sergio Guelerman, 133–70. Buenos Aires: Norma.

Peña, Fernando Martín, ed. 2003. *60/90: Generaciones de cine independiente*. Buenos Aires: Fundación Eduardo Constantini.

Nelly, Richard. 1993. *Masculino/femenino: Prácticas de la diferencia y cultura democrática*. Santiago de Chile: Francisco Zegers.

Sontag, Susan. 2003. *Regarding the Pain of Others*. New York: Farrar, Straus, Giroux.

Vezzetti, Hugo. 2002. *Pasado y presente: Guerra, dictadura y sociedad en la Argentina*. Buenos Aires: Siglo Veintiuno Editores.

FILMS

El cielito [*The Little Sky*]. Directed by María Victoria Menis. Todo Cine/Sophie Dulac Productions, 2004.

La ciénaga [*The Swamp*]. Directed by Lucrecia Martel. Cuatro Cabezas, 2001.

Crónica de una fuga [*Chronicle of an Escape*]. Directed by Adrián Caetano. K & S Films, 2006.

La historia oficial [*The Official Story*]. Directed by Luis Puenzo. Historias Cinematográficas Cinemanía, 1985.

Un muro de silencio [*A Wall of Silence*]. Directed by Lita Stantic. Aleph Producciones S.A., 1993.

Los rubios [*The Blonds*]. Directed by Albertina Carri. Cine Ojo, 2003.

NOTES

1. Lita Stantic and her partner, Pablo Szir, started making *Los Velazquez*, a film based on the novel *Isidro Velazquez* by Alberto Carri, Albertina's father. Both Pablo Szir and Alberto Carri disappeared during the military dictatorship.

2. Lita Stantic has played a fundamental role in Argentine cinema, especially as a producer – most likely the most well-known female producer in Argentina. She was, for example, president of the Cámara Argentina de la Industria Cinematográfica from 1986 to 1996 and founder of the Festival del Cine y la Mujer (http://www.litastantic.com.ar/unmuro/index.htm). Her work has been known above all in relation to Bemberg's films, of which Stantic was the producer of all except the final one (*Momentos*, *Señora de Nadie*, *Camila*, *Miss Mary*, *Yo la peor de todas*), and more recently she has produced some of the most important films that emerged in the mid-nineties; that is, the New Independent Cinema (such as, for example, Pablo Trapero's *Mundo Grúa*, Lucrecia Martel's *La ciénaga*, Adrián Caetano's *Bolivia* and *Un oso rojo*, and Diego Lerman's *Tan de repente*). In other words, Stantic's history in the film industry is connected as much to new cinema as to films produced at the beginning of the millennium, the "new" New Cinema.

3. Merely for means of reference, I wish to recall the Junta Trials that began in 1985 after the return to democracy, through which some of the main members of the military juntas were tried and sentenced to prison (Jorge Rafael Videla, Emilio Massera, Orlando Ramón Agosti). Nevertheless, the following years were marked by a series of impunity laws, starting with the Full Stop (*Punto Final*) of 1986 and the Due Obedience (*Obediencia Debida*) Law of 1987. Under these two laws, not only were the denunciations of human rights violations stopped, but also there was an absolution of responsibility granted to all those officers who acted under orders of their superiors. In 1989 and 1990, the Amnesty Laws (*Indulto*) pardoned those military officers charged in 1985. Most recently, this impunity process has begun to undo itself with the repeal of these two laws.

4. The discussion about gaze and film has a long history in film studies. The two names that are usually associated to the point of departure of these discussions are Christian Metz and Jean-Louis Baudry who in "The Imaginary Signifier" and "Ideological Effects of the Basic Cinematographic Apparatus" (respectively) introduced ideological representation in the process of identification of the spectator with the camera. The use of psychoanalytic theory, and in particular the mirror stage in visual studies, underlines the relationship between the gaze and the camera and the process of identification as a central aspect of the construction of the meaning of the film as well as in the constitution of the spectator

as subject. In the particular case of *Un muro de silencio*, the centrality of the gaze is linked to a dismantling of the authoritarian monopoly of vision, an exploration of new subjects of vision, the transformation of the images seen and the interpretations attached to them, and the process of unlearning the visions and perspectives learned under terror. The film can be thought of as Baudry claims through the image "mirror-screen" as a cultural and ideological interpellation to the spectator, as citizen, and as subject of memory.

5   A study by Ximena Triquell cited in Grant recognizes the number of Argentine productions in the first years of the redemocratization that deal with the *desaparecidos* compared to the production at the end of the eighties and start of the nineties. The percentages Triquell states speak for themselves about the decline of the representation of this theme: between 1984–86, 70 per cent of Argentine productions dealt with this topic. Between 1987 and 89, 3 out of 60 films dealt with the dictatorship, a number that drops further from 1990–92 when only 1 out of 45 films broach this topic (Grant 313, note 8).

6   I use here "eccentricity" thinking of Teresa de Lauretis (1990) when she refers to subjectivities that are both outside and inside of hegemonic forces. De Lauretis says: "They are excluded from the established discourse theory and yet imprisoned within it or else assigned a corner of their own but denied a specificity" (115).

7   I refer to testimonies that began with *Recuerdo de la muerte* by Miguel Bonasso (1984) and continued more recently with *Ese infierno* by Munu Actis, Cristina Aldini, Liliana Gardella, Miriam Lewin, and Elisa Tokar (2001), the testimony of Susana Jorgelina Ramus, *Sueños sobrevientes de una montonera* (2001), also concerning ESMA, the testimony of Claudio Tamburini and Norberto Urso on the Seré Mansión (*Pase libre* and *Mansión Seré*, both 2002), the testimony of Nora Strejelevich, *Una sola muerte numerosa* (1997), and the collection of testimony and narrative by Jorge Boccanera, *Redes de memoria* (2000), among others.

8   On many occasions Bruno speaks of "those boys" to refer to the militant generation of the sixties and seventies, brandishing an authority and distance that cannot be ignored.

9   For example, the association of ex-detainees / *desaparecidos* (http://www.exdesaparecidos.org.ar/aedd/example2.php) or the *Desaparecidos* Project (http://www.desaparecidos.org/).

10 This marginalization is represented within the inner story of Kate's film when we see, for example, a militant companion of Ana's raising suspicion over the survivor figure: "It's doesn't look good that they let you go" (this refers to her companions and their perspective towards the survivor, now a victim again, this time of the accusation of this other area of vigilance outside the detention centre).

11 The story of Julio's (Ana's husband) disappearance is narrated through

phone calls that are made to Ana over a six-month period from a clandestine centre, and even a secret encounter between Ana and Julio in a bar immediately after they are both kidnapped and Ana is freed.

12 "Creemos que el proyecto es valioso y pide en este sentido ser revisado con un mayor rigor documental, La historia tal como está formulada plantea el conflicto de ficcionalizar la propia experiencia, cuando el dolor puede nublar la interpretación de hechos lacerantes. El reclamo de la protagonista por la ausencia de sus padres, si bien es el eje, requiere una búsqueda más exigente de testimonios que se concretaría con la participación de compañeros de sus padres, con afinidades y discrepancias. Roberto Carri y Ana María Caruso fueron dos intelectuales comprometidos en los setenta cuyo destino trágico merece que este trabajo se realice."

13 The new independent cinema started around the late nineties when its directors (Pablo Trapero, Adrián Caetano, Martín Rejtman and Lucrecia Martel, among others) began to explore new creative spaces outside of commercial cinema and institutional financing. It can be said that Martin Rejtman's *Rapado* (1996) or Bruno Stagnaro and Israel Adrián Caetano's *Pizza, birra, faso* (1998), initiated this new cinema characterized by an independent cinema with a new generation of directors, generally non-professional actors, low production costs and, with some exceptions, a limited distribution and high participation in film festival circuits (Peña, 7–9; Battle, 17–28; Castagna, 105–17; Escobar and Peña, 1–6; and Mahieu, 121–23). The coincidences with the cinema of the sixties can be seen, argues Mahieu, not only in their independent production, but also in their search for a cinema that differs from the Argentine cinema that had come before, a search that speaks to a questioning of representativity and an interrogation of identity that, in some way, comes from the questioning of the earlier cinemas' systems of representation (Peña, 7).

14 "En 1999 comencé una investigación sobre la ficción de la memoria (hechos objetivos enfrentados a fantasías, relatos fragmentados a la imposibilidad de recordar ciertos elementos, y la imposibilidad de olvidar ciertos detalles librada al azar). En ese túnel me sumergí en aquel momento y esa búsqueda se convirtió en la primera media hora de *Los rubios*" (Carri 2003).

15 See Samanta Salvatori. "Las fotos del pasado en los films de la memoria." *Cine sin orillas*. http://www.cinesinorillas.com.ar/articulos/ivan-rubios.htm

16 "Odio las vaquitas de San Antonio, las estrellas fugaces, pasar por debajo de los puentes, las vías de los trenes, las bandadas de pájaros. Odio que se caigan las pestañas y tener que pedir un deseo cuando se soplan las velitas en los cumpleaños. Porque pasé muchos años deseando siempre lo mismo: que vuelva mamá, que vuelva papá y que vuelvan pronto. En realidad, el deseo siempre fue uno, pero yo lo estructuraba en tres partes para que tuviera más fuerza."

II.
PARADISE LOST

Barbaric Spectacles: Masculinities in Crisis in Popular Argentine Cinema of the 1990s[1]

CAROLINA ROCHA

SOUTHERN ILLINOIS UNIVERSITY, EDWARDSVILLE

When addressing representations of violence in films, one immediately thinks of the excessive and often outrageous mayhem that is customary fare in Hollywood cinematic productions. Graphic violence and ultra-violence have been the axis of numerous popular American movies since the 1960s – *Bonnie and Clyde* (1967), *A Clockwork Orange* (1971), *The Godfather* (1972), to name only a few – that have enjoyed global audiences and have thus influenced foreign filmmakers, both in subject matter as well as in the techniques deployed to depict violence. Some of the most popular Argentine films of the 1990s portray and dwell on the causes of violence. The depiction of violence, however, is carried out through minimal graphic scenes. The absence of takes showing gruesome mutilations, car chases, and spectacular explosions may indicate that what I will be addressing is a question of scale: scarce murders and less bloodshed probably do not disturb audiences as much as graphic scenes of violence do. While this may be true with regard to international audiences, for Argentine viewers many domestic films of the 1990s are shocking as well as revealing. Indeed, both commercial films and those created by directors grouped together under the umbrella of the New Argentine Cinema, capture aspects of contemporary Argentine society and the impact of post-1989 structural economic changes.

The *mise-en-scène* of many of these films grounded in a diegetic present exposes power struggles, but not as the result of diverging political views as was the case in the cinema of previous decades. Rather, these power struggles posit tensions that derive from the pursuit of economic profit at the expense of legality. Within this context, violence is largely perpetrated to eliminate those who stand for moral values and respect for the law. These victims are seen as obstacles by criminal characters who are unable and/or unwilling to restrain themselves in their search for financial gain. In depicting a society where profit-seeking prevails at the expense of the rule of law, many Argentine films showcase the implications of rule-breaking as a form of violence that, not only targets individuals, but also, and more importantly, affects the public sphere and the nation as a civilized space. Therefore, what many of these films present is the disintegration of the social fabric and the severance of ties among different members of the national community.

In this regard, the centrality of the representation of violence in Argentine society and cinema of the 1990s is particularly disturbing, for it problematizes the validity of the state, not only as a guarantor of certain basic rights for its members, but also as an entity that embodies and disseminates civilization.[2] While the civilization-versus-barbarism dichotomy has been present in the Argentine cultural and political imagination since the nineteenth century, I am not referring here to Domingo F. Sarmiento's concepts.[3] I am, however, interested in the tension of individual and society outlined by Sigmund Freud in *Beyond the Pleasure Principle* (1920) and *Civilization and Its Discontents* (1929), and the conceptualization of civilization by Norbert Elias in *The Civilizing*

Process (1939). These works are complementary in theorizing individual and social causes of violence in modern societies and are particularly relevant to my discussion of violence in Argentine cinema of the 1990s. In what follows, I briefly present Freud's and Elias's concepts.

In *Beyond the Pleasure Principle*, Freud explained the tension between individual and society, death and eros, as well as the motivation for human aggression and the ways in which societies have sought to curtail the eruption and production of violence. In this work, Freud first contended that men are propelled into action by drives. Among these, the "death instinct," present in all human beings, makes them prone to aggression and destruction. In certain individuals, the death instinct lures and prevails over the desire to live and let others live. This instinct also evinces the frail foundation on which human communities are built. If men carry the propensity to generate violence, how can the development and existence of societies be ensured? Freud answered this question in *Civilization and Its Discontents*. For him, civilization not only makes possible the enjoyment of fundamental rights but also helps curb human's tendency to resort to brute force. Nonetheless, for rights to be effective, the foundation of civilized societies needs to rest upon the penalization of criminality, or in Freud's words: "The first requisite of civilization, therefore, is that of justice" (Freud 1962: 41). Freud recognized that failure to impart justice both threatens individual and social life and also endangers the viability of civilized nations.

Drawing on Freud's ideas, sociologist Norbert Elias examined the emergence of civilization in the Western world. For Elias, the civilized ways of pre-World War II Europe could be best understood by examining the development of certain customs since the Middle Ages. For example, Elias posited that the constitution of a central authority came about to mediate among feuding parties and this led to the formation of a monopoly of physical power in which,

> ... not every strong man can afford the pleasure of physical attack. This is now reserved to those few legitimized by the

central authority (e.g., the police against the criminal), and to larger numbers only in exceptional times of war or revolution, in the socially legitimated struggle against internal or external enemies. (Elias 1978: 202)

Monopolies of physical power are, then, seen as a resource for groups to establish their own brand of leadership in a given society. What is particularly pertinent to my analysis is the fact that even within these monopolies of physical power that represent a civilized stage in the development of societies, those who resort to physical violence either have the support of authorities or have to be punished for their acts. In other words, in civilized societies, every violent action demands a response from authorities: either perpetrators act with the implicit support of the authorities or they are penalized for their criminal actions. Consequently, if central authorities exercising the monopoly of physical force cannot fully eradicate acts of violence, they have to maintain their legitimacy by rejecting those acts that defy the rule of law.

Interestingly, the inability to sanction those who employ violence presents a serious challenge to the development and continuity of a civilized nation. Law-breaking without sanctions proves to be particularly damaging for those who monopolize physical force in the sense that their very *raison d'être* as arbiters of civilization is interrogated. Indeed, the fictions that help bind the different groups or members of a given society around the recognition of authorities who monopolize the use of force lose their efficacy. This, in turn, leads citizens to question the efficiency of those who exercise the monopoly of physical force to use Elias's terms, or their capacity to lead the state. As the state's legitimacy is interrogated by its citizens, another implication of the failure to penalize undue violence surfaces.

Lack of justice and due process crucially disavows male hegemony in society. The breakdown of social order is inextricably linked to changes in gender roles. When "man is a wolf to man" to borrow Freud's expression (Freud 1961: 58), some men are more powerful than others. And, if some men are able to use force or violence without any moral or legal constraints, others feel weak and defenceless, and thus, need institutions to protect them and mediate in social life. But, what happens when institutions are unable to effectively impart rewards and punishments? In this case, lack of justice comes to stand as a kind of violence that civilized society deliberately inflicts upon its members – particularly men – , if we follow Freud literally. The unequal status of men, in turn, exposes a moment of crisis in which masculinity, as a social construct, is diminished, assailed, and challenged. Thus, the crisis of masculinity is engendered by the inability on the part of some men to abide by society's laws in order to resolve their conflicts. The disregard that some men show for society's laws also influences the masculine role of those who abide by them. In the absence of clear punishment for those who carry out criminal acts, law-abiding men also stand to lose, for their adherence to principles is ignored by authorities, giving way to the emergence of barbarism, or the law of the strongest.

In Argentina during the 1990s, important transformations took place as the state sought to occupy a less prominent role and let the forces of the market regulate public life. Argentine sociologists Alejandro Grimson and Gabriel Kessler offered an explanation of these changes when they stated that, "The former monopoly over violence within national boundaries has been replaced by a monopoly over tax revenue that characterizes any and all states" (2005: 54). Parallel to changes at the state level, citizens were also affected by the neoliberal *zeitgeist* and came to be viewed primarily as consumers and owners in detriment to their former role of citizens (García Canclini 2001). For Maristela Svampa, the process of decollectivization represented by a less crucial function of unions impinges on "the destruction of individual and social identities, affecting particularly the traditional shaping of the masculine world" (2005: 48). Political and socioeconomic factors had a lasting influence on the roles performed by men, particularly for middle- and lower-class men. In this article, I will explore the erosion of masculine middle-class roles or the crisis of masculinity as a result of the unleashing of violence by analyzing two of the most popular Argentine films of the 1990s.

These films depict violence against Argentine men by other Argentine men. The repetition of the adjective "Argentine" may seem superfluous, but I want to emphasize the competition and unresolved conflicts between groups within the same society. Unlike American war or science fiction movies, where the presence of foreign/nonhuman enemies legitimizes the use of violence, the movies that I have chosen, *La furia* (*The Fury*, 1997) and *Cenizas del paraíso* (*Ashes from Paradise*, 1997), show the unpunished victimization of innocent men perpetrated by their fellow citizens. Violence is possible as a result of a weakened state that appears ineffectual in sanctioning unlawful acts of violence, and hence unable to maintain the monopoly of physical force given its inability to reprimand criminal acts and ensure justice. As a consequence of the diminished power of the state, not only are citizens targets of violence, but also the representatives of the state succumb to violence. Because they stand in the way of groups seeking an unfettered road to wealth, they suffer physical aggression and mental abuse.[4] In these films, therefore, violence is employed to eliminate middle-class men imbued with moral values and ethic principles. As a result of the brutality depicted in these films, representatives of the judiciary who embody legality, order, and due process are also defeated by their violent adversaries. As fathers, their absence not only affects the dynamic of family life but also emphasizes the erosion of contemporary society as a civilized entity. Violence also affects their sons who experience it first-hand, and have to witness the destruction of their families. The death instinct prevails in those who inflict violence and who pose a challenge to civilized communal life.

LA FURIA AND *CENIZAS DEL PARAÍSO*

Both released in 1997, *La furia* and *Cenizas del* paraíso[5] quickly established themselves as the most popular films of the year in Argentina. In addition to their shared box office success, both films come from the same thriller/drama genre. Far from being documentaries, these movies present fictional plots that, nonetheless, deploy verisimilitude to represent contemporary Argentine society. They also bear striking similarities in their depiction of a society at the brink of implosion. In his review of *La furia*, Argentine critic Fernando López proposed a reading linking this film to current affairs in Argentina:

> It is a daily thing in this painful present of Argentines. Mafias have left their marks in events that no one can clarify; state officials and guardians of the law are involved in all types of crimes; judges are either separated from their cases, linked to numerous suspicions, or directly impeached; the shadow of corruption is everywhere as is the disturbing feeling that impunity reigns.[6]

Thus, in both films violence is deployed to highlight a crisis of the dominant order stemming from the failure of the state to provide justice and penalize criminal acts. For American film theorist Kaja Silverman, the dominant order is inextricably linked to the "the dominant fiction, which works to bring the subject into conformity with the symbolic order by fostering normative desires and identifications" (1992: 50). Consequently, the breakdown of the state affects the dominant fictions that sustain the orderly functioning of society. If impunity prevails, good citizens are indistinguishable from criminals. Therefore, what these films have in common is the representation of middle-class men who, though they adhere to the rule of law, are victimized by the success of criminals involved in corrupt dealings.

La furia begins with the investigation of a crime: a plane carrying a hefty drug shipment is seized by authorities in Buenos Aires. The following scenes are set in Misiones, somewhere close to the Paraguayan-Argentine border. The first part of the film focuses on Marcos Lombardi (Diego Torres), a young, idealistic middle-class man who wants to make a difference by working as a volunteer among the poor. One evening,

Marcos announces to his girlfriend, Paula (Laura Novoa), his intention to help one of his friends by driving him across the border. Paula opposes the idea, as if she knows that the trip will have dire consequences for Marcos and their future together. Indeed, when crossing the border, customs agents find drugs in Marcos's car, and without allowing any explanations, arrested Marcos in a way that recalls the disappearances of the most recent dictatorship (1976–83): his head is covered, he is led to a prison, and he is denied access to a public lawyer. Thus, the way Marcos is apprehended signals to the audience the prevalence of a certain disorder in society where men with more means – money, power, and weapons – arbitrarily decide the fate of other men who do not enjoy these same means.

Marcos's arrest at the border, a space that represents the jurisdictional limits of the national state, indicates a departure from civilized society and the realm of national laws. Indeed, the thriller will follow this character – whose innocence is cued to the audience – through his descent into hell and his encounter with police brutality and judiciary corruption. What appears more distressing is that the corruption that acts as a breeding ground for physical violence in this film, not only is confined to the margins of the nation, but also stretches to the centre of the national state. As news of Marcos's arrest reaches his father (Luis Brandoni), a stern judge in Buenos Aires, the thriller – will justice be carried out and how? – overlaps with a drama in which the strained father-son relationship is presented.

Also using the thriller/drama combination, *Cenizas del paraíso* explores the pervasiveness of violence as a result of some individuals' disregard of legality and self-restraint. The opening scenes show Judge Makantasis (Héctor Alterio) falling from the roof of a courthouse. In the following sequences, the audience witnesses a young man attempting to dispose of a bloody female corpse. The plot of *Cenizas del paraíso* is organized around the clarification of these two deaths. To complicate the plot line, all three Makantasis brothers confess to killing Ana, the young woman, whose bloody corpse is shown. Therefore, *Cenizas del paraíso* aims at restaging the events leading to the deaths of Judge Makantasis and Ana (Leticia Brédice) by reconstructing the past from a plurality of perspectives. As the title indicates, these deaths, whatever their explanation, reflect the impossibility of restoring the order, harmony, and happiness that has abruptly come to an end. The supportive and close-knit life of the Makantasis family is irreversibly changed, just as the lives of Judge Makantasis and Ana were cut short by violence. Therefore, the *whodunit* that informs the thriller is complemented by the drama lived, albeit in different ways, by the families of the two victims.

FALLEN MEN/BROKEN FAMILIES

Both *La furia* and *Cenizas del paraíso* stage the fall from grace of innocent middle-class men. This fall from grace is shown and provoked by the eruption of physical violence towards these defenceless men. If violence first affects men, the effects of uncontrolled violence are also felt within the family, disturbing the roles that men performed in it, both as father and sons. In *La furia*, Marcos's ordeal deprives him, not only of his freedom, but also of his job and his girlfriend for an indefinite period of time as the workings of justice, or better said, the workings of those who framed him are played out. Marcos's victimization at the hands of violent and corrupt men also extends to his father and makes evident the harsh and pervasive consequences of a society where men are wolves to men.

When Judge Lombardi finds out that his only son has been arrested for drug possession, he fails to perform his role as a father. Although he travels to visit Marcos in prison, he is so convinced that Marcos is guilty that he acts more as a judge than as a caring and concerned father. This fact does not go unnoticed by Marcos, who admonishes his father saying, "Do not interrogate me. Ask me questions as a father would do, not as a judge." Judge Lombardi, however, appears unmoved by his son's plea for support and compassion. Lombardi's failure to perform as a father is further illustrated when he visits his colleague, the judge who oversees his son's case and makes it clear that he does not expect any kind of privileges for Marcos. Quite the contrary, he states his confidence that justice will be carried out to the fullest. Judge Lombardi's actions not only reveal his naiveté regarding the way justice is enforced in remote areas but also signal a terrible blow to the father-son relationship and to the viability of the family unit.

The strained father-son relationship between the Lombardi's is presented from the beginning of the film. In the first part of *La furia*, the physical distance between father and son alludes to their ideological differences as well as to a familial tension between them. When Marcos reproaches his father for his professional demeanour and detachment in view of his plight, he also mentions something that belongs to the pre-history of the film. He blames his father for his mother's suicide and hints that it may have been caused by his father's inability to listen and empathize with others. This accusation allows us to consider two complementary insights. First, it shows that Lombardi's dedication to this profession was carried out at the expense of his family life and his roles of husband and father. Lombardi's failure to be a supportive partner triggered his wife's self-inflicted violence in the realm of his family when she committed suicide. Therefore, while working outside the familial space to ostensibly maintain law and order in his country, Lombardi could not maintain peace and harmony in his own household. The second insight is related to Lombardi's lack of empathy towards others. His stern demeanour indicates a failure to meaningfully connect with others and may also hint his detachment from current affairs. Lombardi's lacks suggest a type of masculinity in crisis that is stressed by his dysfunctional family life: he could not save his wife from suicide nor his only son from being charged with a crime he did not commit.

The failure to satisfactorily perform his role within the family is further highlighted by his overconfidence in the way that justice is enforced. By failing to connect the dots of Marcos's crime to his own role as a judge, Lombardi seems unaware that the violence that has reached his son is ultimately intended for him. In this regard, Lombardi's character appears as one who fails to grasp the changing coordinates of the society in which he lives, a fact that further undermines his roles both as a father and judge and stresses the problematic performance of his masculinity, both in the private and public realms.

Judge Lombardi's crisis of masculinity is emphasized by the fact that the younger Lombardi's arrest has been meticulously planned by a group that the judge is investigating. Indeed, the group's illegal political and economic interests have been jeopardized by the judge's strict probity and integrity. When Paula discloses the connections between a drug operation that has been assigned to Lombardi's office and Marcos's kidnapping, it is apparent that Marcos is an innocent victim of both his father's short-sightedness and the physical and mental abuse perpetrated by his father's enemies while in prison. This last development further emphasizes Lombardi's diminished influence within his family. Although he eventually attempts to save Marcos, his help comes almost too late, after Marcos has suffered from physical and sexual abuse in prison. If we consider Pierre Bourdieu's ideas about the relation between sexuality and power when he states that "the worst humiliation for a man is to be turned into a woman" (2001: 22), we can interpret Marcos's off-screen rape as an action intended to inscribe violence in his flesh as well as to mark his father's lack of power and authority. Thus, as a father, who cannot fully protect his son, Judge Lombardi bears the stigma of a diminished masculinity. I will return to the implications of this kind of masculinity within the nation after I analyze *Cenizas del paraíso*.

Similar to *La furia*, *Cenizas del paraíso* also centres around the ending of a period of plenitude perceived as such by those who later become victims of physical violence. In *Cenizas del paraíso*, it is Judge Makantasis, the patriarch of a family of three sons, who falls from a courthouse. Because of the way the camera depicts his falling, viewers first interpret it as a suicide. However, as the film progresses, it becomes evident that Judge Makantasis was pushed by a pair of hit-men hired by Francisco Muro (Jorge Marrale). Muro, a wealthy entrepreneur, is involved in illicit business deals that were being investigated by Judge Makantasis. Cornered by Makantasis's legal scrutiny of his businesses and unable to restrain himself from committing violence, Muro orchestrates the elimination of the judge in an act that clearly illustrates the "man is a wolf to man" dictum. Nonetheless, Muro's actions trigger an unforeseen event that challenges, not only his masculinity in the public arena, but also his authority within his family.

Judge Makantasis's murder is witnessed by Muro's daughter, Ana. Minutes before Makantasis's murder, Ana learns that her caring and doting father was involved in illegal transactions and was responsible for a series of murders among fellow businessmen. Unable to betray her father even when all evidence points to his culpability, Ana remains silent, only to be the witness of yet another act triggered by her father's greed and criminality. After this, Ana rebels against her father's use of violence by accusing him publicly and calling him a murderer. She herself contributes to the bloodshed caused by her father by committing suicide.

Ana's rebellion highlights Muro's inadequacy as a male, one who fails to perform his assigned role in his family. Instead of protecting his family and serving as a respectable role model, Muro repeatedly violates the laws of coexistence and civilized life, as he pursues financial gain and power – no matter the costs. Nonetheless, the fact that his crimes go unpunished by the legal system strengthens his hegemonic role in a society where rules are easily discarded. As the perpetrator of violence against an innocent man, Muro also poses a challenge to Makantasis's ability to perform his own roles as both husband and father. Muro first appears as an affectionate father until both his daughter and the viewers discover his controlling personality, his manipulation of information, and the possessive nature of his love for Ana. Thus, Muro's performance as a father is guided by his desire for power. The fact that Ana seeks to distance herself from her domineering father by moving out of his house points to a certain degree of disfunctionality in their relationship and emphasizes Muro's less-than-satisfactory role as a father. Muro's violence against Makatansis can be read both as a failure to curb his own possessive drive as well as his inability to establish a healthy relationship with his only daughter.

For his part, Makantasis is loved and respected by his three sons. Although he does not share the same house with them, he strives to stay involved in their familial and professional lives. Because of his common professional interest with Pablo (Leo Sbaraglia), Makantasis seems closer to this son and appears lenient and benevolent towards his other sons. When Ana arrives at their home, however, the normalcy of the Makantasis family life is disrupted. As Ana moves in, she slowly sets in motion the breaking of certain rules under the permissive stance of the Makantasis's father. Aware that Ana is the daughter of the man he is investigating, the judge prefers to believe in coincidences, allowing her to remain in his home instead of foreseeing a possible conflict of interests. As Muro's daughter Ana introduces disorder in the family, the judge is unable to control the situation.

The judge's mistaken assumption about Ana's innocence and her presence within his family points to Makatansis's failure as a father. He fails to realize that Ana slowly seduces all of his sons, pitting brother against brother and undermining the unity and well-being of his family. As Ana's seduction progresses and she feels more comfortable in the Makantasis home, she gains influence over the brothers while the father's authority recedes to a secondary position. This reversal of influence within the Makantasis family shows a strain in the performance of the judge's masculine role as a father and an authoritative family head and also reveals a weakening of family ties among the Makantasis as sons and brothers.

FAILING FATHERS AND LOST LAWS

So far I have been addressing the consequences of the crisis of masculinity that the fathers exhibit in *La furia* and *Cenizas del paraíso*. There is yet another dimension that merits consideration: both the fathers who are victimized by violence are judges and are outwardly committed to instilling the rule of law. Hence, I will be referring here to the implications that the crisis of masculinity has in the public sphere and how it poses a risk to the continuation of civilization.

In the final part of *La furia*, Judge Lombardi's masculinity experiences a series of blows. First, he is told that he is no longer in charge of the investigation of drug smuggling. Although he is not given concrete reasons for his separation from the case, it is clear that his probity and desire to enforce laws have made his superiors uncomfortable. This challenge to his professional judgment underscores a masculinity in crisis, now in the realm of his professional life. Curiously, it also makes him more receptive to reconsider his son's plight. It is in these circumstances that Lombardi, with the help of Marcos's girlfriend, confronts the true causes of his son's imprisonment and sets out to free him. He realizes that his investigation of drug routes prompted those in charge of illegal trafficking to retaliate against Marcos as a means to pressure him to collaborate. Lombardi's second trip to the border, then, is the reverse of his first: he travels with the mission of rescuing his son and making amends for the suffering he has indirectly inflicted on him – even if that means tampering with the law.

By finally assuming his role as a father, Lombardi attempts to restore his diminished masculinity only to face the fact that justice is not the panacea he thought it was; if he wants to be effective in freeing Marcos, he has to engage in the same illegal dealings as his opponents. Thus, while asserting his role as a concerned father, he uses his authority to violate the laws that he is supposed to defend and uphold. As he stages Marcos's rescue, he has to cross the divide between the legal and the illegal, symbolically shown when he orders the prison guard to escape by breaking the prison's gate. The momentary success that he attains while managing to take Marcos to meet his girlfriend is jeopardized by the fiery persecution of police, who are both corrupt and unaware of the plot that had put Marcos in jail. This chase forces Lombardi to realize that in order to ensure Marcos's survival there has to be a scapegoat to take his place. It is at this moment that he decides to surrender himself to save his son.

The final images of *La furia* stress Lombardi's diminished masculinity as a result of violence and the ensuing rule of barbarism in the nation. Marcos and his girlfriend flee to a neighbouring country and are able to elude the chase. The bird's-eye shot of Lombardi standing alone on the Argentine side of the border is a powerful scene as it encapsulates his helplessness next to the criminal thugs. This scene allows viewers to infer the terrible fate that the powerless judge will find at his enemy's hands. Lombardi's defeat is not only personal; rather, it stands as a setback to the civilization that was supposed to prevail in the nation as a result of the rule of law. When the legal side that Lombardi represents is overwhelmed by those who are violent, civilization recedes in the nation while barbarism takes over. The failure of the legal system unleashes basic instincts of aggression between men. This impacts society as family bonds are severed, and justice, the bedrock upon which civilization is built, disappears.

The ending of *Cenizas del paraíso* also provides a pessimistic reading in relation to the father's murder and the failure of the legal system to identify and bring his killers to justice. Indeed, Judge Makantasis did not heed his son's advice to take care of himself. He felt that, as a representative of the state, he would somehow be spared a violent death, the common *modus operandi* of Muro's hit men. Makantasis not only underestimated his opponent's capacity for violence and corruption but also failed to take adequate measures to guarantee his sons' well-being. Hence, his lack of power that reflects a masculinity in crisis touches that of his sons. The three Makantasis brothers, although alive, not only are deeply traumatized by their father's violent murder, but also are the only suspects apprehended to solve both Ana's and the judge's deaths. In this context, their father's death comes to signify the overthrow of legality and justice and the subsequent triumph of violence triggered by those where the death instinct prevails over compliance to laws. The haunting last scene that shows them descending in an elevator symbolizes the moral defeat that they suffered as a result of impunity and corruption. This sense of defeat also impinges on Makantasis's perception of their masculine roles. Although they all claim a false culpability in Ana's death that is later clarified, their inability to have their father's murderers prosecuted makes them victims of violence in the absence of justice.[7]

The death of Judge Makantasis leaves his sons fatherless and constitutes a terrible loss for the family: his disappearance stands in stark contrast to his nemesis's freedom. Moreover, Makantasis's death makes possible the spread of barbarism at the expense of civilized justice. As Judge Teller (Cecilia Roth), the person in charge of the investigation into Ana's death, gets closer to reaching the truth, threats and warnings curtail her freedom of action and remind her that she, too, could face a violent end. Consequently, Muro's untouchable status signals that impunity reigns and justice cannot touch powerful men. Even though Muro suffers a severe loss when Ana commits suicide, his kind of masculinity based on power and control remains unchallenged by the institutions and officials that represent the state. With a limited scope of action to take those suspected to trial, civilization recedes. Hence, brute force prevails over the laws that guarantee and regulate peaceful coexistence in Argentine society.

CONCLUDING REMARKS

The depiction of violence presented in *La furia* and *Cenizas del paraíso* reflects the implications of the state's inability to sanction acts of violence. The absence of justice contributes to a shrinking of civilized coexistence and the subsequent supremacy of barbarism both in the private sphere and in the public space. The representation of violence in these two Argentine films avoids gruesome and graphic scenes to emphasize, instead, the subtle consequences of the triumph of barbarism and its impact on masculine roles, both in the family and in the nation. *La furia* and *Cenizas del paraíso* present the negative effects derived from a society that fails to punish physical aggression and criminality by exposing the ways in which male victims experience violence as a process of emasculation. In the realm of the family, fathers are eliminated; their absence deeply marks the surviving sons by weakening the family unit. The victimization of fathers also decreases society's order and weakens the institutions that represent legality and the state.

WORKS CITED

Bourdieu, Pierre. 2001. *The Masculine Domination*. Stanford, CA: Stanford University Press.
Butler, Judith. 2004. *Precarious Life: The Powers of Mourning and Violence*. London: Verso.
Elias, Norbert. 1978. *The Civilizing Process. The History of Manners*. Trans. Edmund Jephcott. New York: Urizen Books.
Freud, Sigmund. 1961. *Civilization and Its Discontents*. New York: Norton.
———. 1975. *Beyond the Pleasure Principle*. Trans. and ed. James Strachey; introd. Gregory Zilboorg. New York: Norton.
García Canclini, Néstor. 2001. *Consumer and Citizens: Globalization and Multicultural Conflicts*. Minneapolis: University of Minnesota Press.
Grimson, Alejandro, and Gabriel Kessler. 2005. *On Argentina and the Southern Cone: Neoliberalism and National Imaginations*. New York: Routledge.
López, Fernando. 2005. "Un justiciero en la piel de un juez." *La Nación*. http://www.lanación.com.ar/97/06/05/s05.htm (accessed 9 May 2007).
Martins, Laura. 2007. "Bodies at Risk: On the State of Exception. (Lucrecia Martel's *La Ciénaga* [*The Swamp*])." In *Argentinian Cultural Production during the Neoliberal Years (1989–2001)*, ed. Hugo Hortiguera and Carolina Rocha, 205-216. Lewinston, NY: Edwin Mellen.
Rocha, Carolina. 2007a. "Crímen/es irresuelto/s en *Cenizas del paraíso* de Marcelo Piñeyro." *Revista de Estudios Hispánicos* 41: 117–34.
———. 2007b. "Riding against the Wave? Caballos salvajes and its critique of neoliberal cultural" *Studies in Latin American Popular Culture* 26: 167–77.
Silverman, Kaja. 1992. *Male Subjectivity at the Margins*. New York: Routledge.
Svampa, Maristella. 2005. *La sociedad excluyente: La Argentina bajo el signo del neoliberalismo*. Buenos Aires: Alfaguara.

FILMS

Cenizas del paraíso. Directed by Marcelo Piñeyro. Artear, 1997.
La furia. Directed by Juan Bautista Stagnaro. Argentina Sono Film SACI, 1997.

NOTES

1. A preliminary version of this article was published in *Ciberletras*. Rocha, Carolina. "Barbaric Spectacles: Masculinities in Crisis in Popular Argentine Cinema of the 1990s," *Ciberletras*, July, 2009, http://www.lehman.cuny.edu/ciberletras/

2. Laura Martins presents an example of the withdrawal of the state from public life in "Bodies at Risk: On the State of Exception. (Lucrecia Martel's *La Ciénaga* [The Swamp])" in Hugo Hortiguera and Carolina Rocha, eds., *Argentinian Cultural Production during the Neoliberal Years* (1989–2001) (2007), 205–215.

3. I refer to Sarmiento's dichotomy when analyzing Marcelo Piñeyro's *Caballos Salvajes* (Wild Horses 1995) in *Riding against the Wave? Caballos salvajes and its Critique of Neoliberal Culture* (Rocha 2007).

4. Grimson and Kessler have described these tensions as follows: "One is the tension between the state (Argentina) and society (Argentines) resulting from people's increasing hostility toward the former's ineptitude and degradation. Another is the tension existing between individuals (Argentines) and community (Argentina); in this view individual interests seeking egotistically to maximize benefits hurt the nation" (Grimson and Kessler 2005: 66).

5. For an analysis of *Cenizas del paraíso* as a detective story, see my article, "Crímen/es irresuelto/s en *Cenizas del paraíso* de Marcelo Piñeyro" (Rocha 2007: 117–34).

6. "Es cosa de todos los días en esta penosa actualidad de los argentinos. Mafias que han dejado su huella en episodios que nadie termina de esclarecer; funcionarios públicos y guardianes de la ley involucrados en toda clase de delitos; jueces separados de sus causas, envueltos en una maraña de sospechas o directamente sometidos a juicio político; la sombra de la corrupción por todas partes y la inquitante sensación de que reina la impunidad."

7. In *Precarious Life: The Powers of Mourning and Violence*, Judith Butler reflects on the consequences of September 11, 2001. Butler states that, "Lives are supported and maintained differently, and there are radically different ways in which human physical vulnerability is distributed across the globe. Certain lives will be highly protected, and the abrogation of their claims to sanctity will be sufficient to mobilize the forces of war. Other lives will not find such fast and furious support and will not even qualify as 'grievable'" (Butler 2004: 33). In *Cenizas del paraíso*, the different status of lives and deaths reinforces the fact that some lives are more important than others. The difference of human lives and deaths both challenges the notion of equality in democratic societies and alludes to the different position of individuals regarding their closeness/distance from those who oversee the monopoly of physical force.

Far from Heaven: On *El cielito*, by María Victoria Menis[1]

GABRIELA COPERTARI

CASE WESTERN RESERVE UNIVERSITY

Heaven on earth in the life of Félix, protagonist of *El cielito* ["*Little Sky*," "*Little Heaven*"] – an Argentine film directed by María Victoria Menis[2] and released in Argentina in 2004 – is going to be, as the title of the film announces, very brief. Above all, it will consist of a space of protection and love for a man and a baby, whose very relationship constitutes the heaven that both are going to inhabit for a little while. If this relationship can be thought of as a heaven, it is because it seems to exist apart from the all-pervading violence that surrounds it; it is precisely conceived as a shelter against that violence. But, as I have anticipated, this *cielito* is not going to last.

Violence has undoubtedly occupied an important place in contemporary Argentine cinema (in films preceding and following the 2001 crisis) and, more broadly, in contemporary Latin American cinema. It has moreover been argued that "within a new cinematographic world ... violence is the new trademark of Latin America" (Sánchez-Prado 2006:

48).³ Ignacio M. Sánchez-Prado is specifically criticizing a representation of violence as "natural" and "aesthetic," as it is represented in *Amores perros* (2006: 50). He argues that "[a]ll references to violence should be a critique of violence, a comprehension of its profound economic, social and political roots" (2006: 51). What makes *El cielito* a particularly interesting film in which to analyze the representation of violence in the aftermath of the Argentine crisis of 2001 are the relations that it explores between social exclusion and violence. *El cielito* focuses on the consequences of the violence of social exclusion, on the one hand, in the relations between traditional gender roles that are, at the same time, racially and socially marked within the model of a patriarchal family, and, on the other, on marginalized youth. Moreover, the film contrasts the diverse ways in which the consequences of social exclusion manifest themselves in the city and the countryside, that is, in rural violence and urban violence.

This is not to say that *El cielito* is the only Argentine film that tackles violence as an economic, political, and social phenomenon. In fact, it has a rather prestigious antecedent in the representation of social violence in the city: *Pizza, birra, faso* (Adrián Caetano and Bruno Stagnaro, 1997),⁴ the film that has consistently been celebrated by critics as inaugurating, in 1997, a New Argentine Cinema.⁵ Both films deal with the violence of social exclusion produced by the neoliberal reforms implemented during the 1990s (whose consequences seem not to have abated in the six years that separate the filming of both films, at least not for the most vulnerable and unprotected residents of Argentina) and with the consequences that such violence – social exclusion, marginalization – has on its victims whom it leaves without employment, opportunity, or, essentially, a future. While *El cielito* explores these consequences both in the countryside and in the city of Buenos Aires, *Pizza, birra, faso*'s plot develops in Buenos Aires.

In analyzing the impact of neoliberal economic and social reforms on Argentine society in the 1990s, Alejandro Grimsom and Gabriel Kessler write that by the mid-nineties, with "[t]he reconversion of the productive apparatus and the growing protagonism of the financial and service sectors of the economy" (2005: 104), there started to emerge "two phenomena that came to characterize the decade as a whole: contingent jobs and unemployment," which "have affected the working class in particular and Argentine society as a whole" (2005: 105). They also describe the emergence "[w]ithin the framework of an unstable job market" of "a segment of the population, made up primarily of young people, that subsists by combining legal and illegal activities" (2005: 107), such as "different kinds of work with robbery," or, for example, by alternating "contingent jobs with petty crime when unemployed" (2005: 110). In this context, work "no longer occupies the key position as basis for the construction of individual identity and peer relationships" (Grimson and Kessler 2005: 113) and "becomes strictly instrumental and, as such, more closely resembles a source of supply" (Grimson and Kessler 2005: 114).

This is exactly the situation we will find in *El cielito*: a laid-off factory worker vegetating in the countryside; one of those young men "that subsists by combining legal and illegal activities" (Grimson and Kessler 2005: 107) – Félix, who seems to be progressively escaping, more than migrating, in search of opportunities, being these of working or stealing or both, from the country to the city; and a representative of that vast urban youth with no chance of finding a job, caught up in the world of crime. The film seems unequivocally to be staging an inverted image of a national identity narrative anchored on an image of Argentina as a land of opportunities and social mobility, related to the image of immigration/migration as a path of work and progress – a narrative of national identity that has come into crisis with the crisis of Argentina. When the possibility of employment disappears, not only as a means of sustenance, but also as a foundation for social identity and for a sense of belonging – as an organizational principle for family relations and for social relations in general – social and personal identity narratives also disintegrate, as occurs in *El cielito*.

In what follows, I will focus on the analysis of the different ways in which the countryside and the city are represented, paying particular attention to the consequences of social exclusion on family and gender relations in the countryside and the city, to conclude with the analysis of the religious images in the film's *mise-en-scène*, and of the meaning of Félix's flashbacks of his childhood and of his relationship with the baby he will make his own. These last three elements will contribute, as I will show, to the imaginary creation of the "cielito" to which the film's title refers.

The film tells the story of a young occasional thief, Félix, who wanders seemingly in search of work downriver, "río abajo," as highlighted by the song in the soundtrack that accompanies various segments of the plot. The first part of the film takes place in Río Tala, the tiny coastal village where Félix initially arrives. Inquiring about possible jobs, Félix meets a man named Roberto, who reveals that he had been left without work when he was fired from a factory and who offers Félix room and board in exchange for help with the family's source of sustenance: the preparation of homemade preserves with the fruit they harvest and the sale of them by the roadside. While Félix helps Roberto's wife, Mercedes, who is in charge of this task, and witnesses Roberto's increasingly frequent drunkenness and violence, usually directed toward Mercedes, Félix grows ever more fond of the family's baby, "Chango" (a colloquialism that could be roughly translated as "kid"). When Mercedes, faced with the impossibility of enduring her abusive situation, disappears (presumably commits suicide) and Roberto completely falls apart, Félix escapes to Buenos Aires with the money he finds in the house, Roberto's revolver, and the baby, who from then on he will claim as his own.

Once in Buenos Aires, Félix rents a room in a tenement house for himself and Chango, until both are mugged and must sleep in the street. Once more, while inquiring about work, Félix meets someone in Buenos Aires: a young man whom they call Cadillac and who does dirty jobs, most likely robberies and assassinations, seemingly for the police. Cadillac proposes that Félix help him with those jobs and takes him to his house, where he lives with his teenage sister; once again Félix is temporarily integrated within a family. In his first – and last – job with

Cadillac (the assassination of a man), Félix leaves Chango with Cadillac's sister, and while he observes in shock the murder Cadillac has committed, he is, in turn, killed by a neighbour who has witnessed the act.

The film juxtaposes two spaces in Félix's journey: the countryside and the capital city, clearly differentiated through the film's aesthetic choices in representing them, although they are practically homogeneous with respect to the desolation and lack of opportunity that define them. As Horacio Bernades summarizes, the countryside is filmed "in establishing shots that reflect all its quietness and lack of geographical accidents, and in medium shots that register the doses of tension, repressed violence, and unresolved conflicts that may lie behind closed doors" (2004). The supposed tranquillity of the countryside seems to have carried over into its modes of representation. Nonetheless, such stability and quietness contrast with the hidden violence of the plot that unfolds in this landscape. In the city, on the other hand, we witness an inversion: if the quietness of the countryside's landscape contrasted with the violence in the interior of the house, in the city the "interiors that serve as places of refuge" contrast with "the harsh, hostile, and ever-dangerous streets" (Bernades 2004). The use of a handheld camera that usually follows Félix when he walks in the streets adds roughness to the representation of urban spaces.

From the opposition of the developments occurring in each of these two spaces, and from the way in which these spaces are represented, it might be supposed that the journey downriver to Buenos Aires implies a greater decadence, a downfall; in fact, it ends in Félix's death. The harshness of urban life (Félix is mugged, evicted from the tenement house because he cannot pay, and ends up sleeping on a bench in a park along with other homeless individuals), its violence made evident through the depiction of criminal activity by delinquents and the police (or crimes carried out for the police) and in the vigilante justice taken by residents facing urban violence and insecurity, might suggest that the bucolic portraits of the rural landscape constitute a silent and peaceful contrast to the merciless city. However, in spite of Félix's deteriorating situation, there is no such idealization of Argentina's countryside,⁶ at least in the present time, as can be clearly seen in the design of family and gender relationships in the countryside and the city.

We can infer from what Mercedes tells Félix that she was the housemaid – of indigenous or *mestizo* origin – whom Roberto – of European descent – married and with whom he continues to maintain a hierarchical, master-servant relationship: Mercedes must pick the fruit, cook and sell the preserves, do the housework, care for her son, and fulfill her wifely "duties" when Roberto exacts them from her by force. Roberto, in contrast, since losing his job at the factory, does nothing except drink and violently act out his frustration on Mercedes. In what used to be a patriarchal family structure, reproducing itself over the centuries, there has been a significant change. This change also affects the model of social relationships and has to do precisely with Roberto's loss of employment and his inability to re-insert himself socially and through work.

It is significant that Mercedes speaks lovingly of Roberto's father, who gave her all of the preserves recipes, and whom she holds up as a model and defends from Roberto's attacks. Her depiction of Roberto's father makes apparent the contrast between a productive and protective father – even toward his employees, whom he might have exploited but also took care of – and a non-paternal and unproductive father (Roberto), who does not work, does not look out for his own, and exploits his wife. Here there is not protection along with exploitation, as there was in the case of Roberto's father.

It is also particularly interesting that all the characters come from somewhere else, that they have migrated to their present location. Félix says that he comes from the countryside near Paraná, Mercedes tells Félix that she is not "from here" (so she is either a domestic migrant like Félix, or an immigrant from a bordering Latin American country), and Roberto's grandparents also arrived from another place, "from another country" – Mercedes says – and things presumably went well for them in Argentina. Roberto clarifies that harvesting fruit and selling preserves and sauces was the work of the entire family: "My family always did it, and lived well. But things have changed. I never liked this."

These stories of migration and immigration condense an entire century of Argentine history. Félix and Mercedes represent what Natalio Botana would call, in contrast to "the society born of immigration, relatively white, which flaunts its European origins," the "Creole [*criolla*] society, which not only includes Argentine Creoles [the indigenous people, the *mestizos*], but also includes today the immigrants hailing from bordering countries" (2002: 84). They are/were im/migrants in search of employment. Roberto's grandparents, judging from Roberto's appearance and the fact that they came from another country, might have been European immigrants, who progressed in the past within the countryside economy. Roberto's status as a laid-off worker is indicative of the situation of many industrial workers who found themselves excluded with the de-industrialization of the country. In Roberto's case, he cannot re-establish himself (he says that he does not like rural labour), and it is Mercedes who ensures the production of homemade goods that, more than to an agricultural model, seems to respond to an economy of survival.

The family is disintegrating with the disappearance of employment as a means of sustenance and of industrial labour as Roberto's social identity, leaving its offspring abandoned. Félix joins a family in which, although both a father and a mother are present – a traditional family model – one fails to carry out his paternal duty and the other commits suicide, whereupon Félix comes to occupy a maternal role in relation to both Chango and Roberto.

In Buenos Aires, in contrast, Félix briefly becomes part of a family with no authority figures, a family of orphans, although the siblings fulfill traditional gender roles. Cadillac's sister prepares meals and stays at home to care for the baby, and Cadillac and Félix head off "to work," that is, to commit crimes. In the city, there are neither mothers nor fathers, and the characters do not even find themselves in a survival economy; there do not seem to be employment opportunities for these poor young people, who live in a shantytown, and the only alternative for them seems to be a descent into the world of crime. The very fact that Cadillac refers to his criminal activities as "laburitos" (little jobs) is intended to show that the world of labour has been replaced by the world of crime.

In the case of the countryside, the film seems to argue that the survival economy (to which the image of the countryside is reduced) has totally collapsed. The images of the countryside, before Félix flees it, show the progressive decomposition of that world following Mercedes' disappearance: the dog Roberto kills, decomposing in the mud; the crates of abandoned fruit; fruit spilled across the floor or rotting in baskets in the sun; the buzzing of flies around the putrefaction; the interior of the humble house also destroyed during one of Roberto's drunken rages, in which he knocks everything off the shelves in a metaphorical instantiation of his disappearing world: the sweets, preserves, glasses, and jars. Yet Félix's "migration" to Buenos Aires (which is really more like an escape) does not imply a viable alternative.

During his bus trip to the city, Félix sees through the window a demonstration on the road, a protest of *piqueteros* that induces him, significantly, to concentrate on the baby in his arms. The *piqueteros* are themselves emblematic of the lack of employment and constitute a form of political protest against this lack, and they appear represented as such in the film. Félix's absolute apathy toward political activism, visible in his withdrawal into his own private world, in his function as a "saviour" father to Chango, refers to his impossibility of finding himself represented by this collective political project. Moreover, Félix is represented as a passive character, totally devoid of agency, who remains inactive even when he finds no other option but crime: he is a bewildered spectator while Cadillac murders the targeted man.

In both cases, then, in the countryside and in the capital city, we find completely disintegrated worlds where, if a few ties of solidarity still remain – most obviously in the way Félix fathers Chango, but also when Roberto and Cadillac offer Félix help and take him to their homes – it is unclear in the latter case to what extent the ties are of solidarity or of interest: Roberto and Cadillac help Félix on the condition that he "work" for them.

We find generalized orphanhood. Not only do the siblings in Buenos Aires lack parents, but both Mercedes and Félix have lost their families. Félix never knew his parents, although his case (he was raised by his grandmother) is different, as I will later discuss. The characters' orphanhood, that is, the lack of a protective mother and father or a mother and father in general, seems clearly to refer in the film to a generalized social orphanhood resulting from the absence of a protector or benefactor state, which has completely abandoned its most vulnerable citizens.

For this reason it is interesting that in the film's *mise-en-scène* religious images of the Virgin with baby Jesus or of a saint with a baby have such an important presence. When Félix arrives at the bar where he meets Roberto and inquires about work, we repeatedly see an image of the Virgin with baby Jesus on the wall of the bar. Later in the film we will see images of a saint with a baby: both on the wall of the tenement house where Félix and Chango stay, and in Cadillac's house. The saint in these images is Saint Cayetano, the highly venerated patron saint of bread and work, on whose feast day the unemployed make offerings in order to find work. When Félix arrives at the house of Cadillac and his sister, where we learn that the "little jobs" that support them are criminal acts, variously sized images of the saint abound and seem to highlight ironically the loss of all hope in Cadillac's chances of finding work. But what is most significant in this *mise-en-scène*, however, is not only the saint's role in the religious or social imaginary, that of providing or ensuring the employment of those who pray to him, but what we actually see in the saint's image. Analogous to that of the Virgin, it presents a man holding a baby in his arms, the protective father or mother; precisely what is lacking here. It is fitting then that, in this sequence, on two occasions, we see Félix holding Chango, and, behind and next to him, on the wall, the image of Saint Cayetano holding the baby. The juxtaposition of both men with babies in these shots makes clear the role that Félix wants to fulfill for Chango: the protective parent, when neither the state nor religion, and not even parents, provide the protection expected of them.

Now, in opposition to that homogenous present without horizons, both in the city and in the countryside, there exists for Félix a paradise, or rather two paradises, which function as a refuge. Nonetheless, the first one is a lost paradise, which resides in the past, the rural past. And the second one is a very brief paradise, just "a little heaven," which fails to build a future.

The first paradise (the lost one) is recovered by the film through the flashbacks in which Félix remembers his childhood, when he was being raised and cared for by his grandmother. In these flashbacks, a saturation of light floods the contrast between brilliant shades of red and green, and the image of the river, the countryside, and the sky. These landscape images frame the figure, sometimes fragmented, sometimes complete, of a woman – Félix's grandmother – performing household chores or rural labour, from the point of view of a child, of whom we see only occasionally the small hands, or face reflected indistinctly in the water, while he plays and watches the woman. It is Félix as a child, following with his gaze the protective figure of his grandmother, in a rural environment, deprived in a material sense yet rich in affective terms. Two songs: one a lullaby and the other a folk song – "Río abajo" – announce and accompany the appearance of some of these flashbacks, which constitute Félix's daydreams, his fantasy of a protective refuge against the hostile present in which he is immersed. This is the paradise that Félix tries to recover upon making Chango his reason for living, upon identifying himself with Chango as an orphan, and assuming the protective maternal and paternal role that his grandmother embodied for him, as can be seen when the second flashback occurs. Félix is singing Chango to sleep with a lullaby, and his singing voice is superimposed upon that of his grandmother singing the same song, while he remembers his own childhood. In his destitute present, Félix recovers the protective figure of his grandmother by assuming it himself in relation to Chango.

Félix's flashbacks represent everything that he currently lacks: protection and love as a refuge, as a paradise against the hell of the present. It is highly significant, in this sense, that many of the film's point-of-view shots from Félix's perspective are shots of the sky. In Félix's first journey, the train ride that will end in Río Tala, shots of Félix in the train alternate with point-of-view shots of the landscape and *the sky* (what Félix sees out the train window). It is the "sky" that he figuratively searches for on his journey. During his bus trip to Buenos Aires, at one point the image of the sky merges with the memory of Félix's grandmother. And finally, when Félix arrives at the tenement house where he is renting a room, his gaze happily registers, through a small window, a tiny piece of the sky: a visual, figurative equivalent of the heaven that Félix believes he has just found by recreating, in his relationship with Chango, the kind of relationship he had with his grandmother. He and Chango together represent the recovery of a private, tender paradise, which, nonetheless, like the piece of the sky seen through the house window, will be small and brief: a *cielito*, a little heaven.

Protecting another in whom he sees himself is Félix's way of once again feeling protected as he was by his grandmother. Félix is, in fact, his grandmother, but he is also Chango or, better yet, simply one "chango," who needs protection. In fact, the film's final image, which finds Félix dying in the street, has all the aesthetic characteristics of his flashbacks, yet is different: it is a fantasy in which we now see the grandmother and child together, he in her arms, as in the images of Saint Cayetano and the Virgin, only now the child is no longer Félix but Chango.

The film therefore ends with an image of Félix's heaven, in which past, present, and future merge in an image of fullness in which the lost paradise of the past is recovered in a fantasy (almost a daydream) from which the grandmother and Chango (a child as Félix was in the past) smile at Félix, who was able in the little heaven of his imagination to be his grandmother and his child simultaneously, to protect himself by becoming the protector of another orphan like him. It is in this imaginary dimension that Félix can erase the violence of the present and the context that produces it by saving Chango and, at the same time, saving himself through his own gaze upon a space of well-being, protection, and shelter, which he associates with his grandmother. This space inhabited by the three of them thus constitutes a fantasy of protection and shelter, of continuity of the past in the future; a continuity that has no place in the disintegrated world the film represents.

Despite the years that have passed since the crisis of the neoliberal model in Argentina in 2001, and despite the policies implemented in the last years to lessen its social consequences, the structure of distribution of wealth seems not to have been essentially modified for the most vulnerable sectors of the population. It is not surprising, therefore, that *Pizza, birra, faso* and *El cielito* six years later (both centred, as we said, on the representation of the violence of social exclusion and its consequences) have significantly similar endings. "Córdoba's" project in *Pizza, birra, faso* of emigrating to Uruguay with his pregnant girlfriend in order to begin a new life away from delinquency and build a family is cut short precisely by his death: in what would be his last robbery before emigrating, he is killed by the police. Likewise, Félix's project in *El cielito* of starting a new life and a new family with Chango in Buenos Aires is ultimately destroyed when he meets death at the hands of vigilante justice. In both cases, the possibility of change has vanished in the face of total exclusion that destroys at the same time the illusion of family as a place of refuge and shelter and the expectation of a future.

Translated by Steven Wenz

WORKS CITED

Aguilar, Gonzalo. 2006. *Otros mundos: Un ensayo sobre el nuevo cine argentino*. Buenos Aires: Santiago Arcos.

Bernades, Horacio. 2004. "Crónica de un marginal y un niño." *Página/12*, October 22. http://www.pagina12web.com.ar/diario/espectaculos/6-42634-2004-10-22.html (accessed 29 May 2007).

Botana, Natalio R. (conversaciones con Analía Roffo). 2002. *La república vacilante: Entre la furia y la razón*. Buenos Aires: Taurus.

Eseverri, Máximo, and Ezequiel Luka. 2003. "Introducción." In *60/90 generaciones: Cine argentino independiente*, ed. Fernando Martín Peña, 11–27. Buenos Aires: MALBA Colección Constantini.

Grimson, Alejandro, and Gabriel Kessler. 2005. *On Argentina and the Southern Cone: Neoliberalism and National Imaginations*. New York: Routledge.

Page, Joanna. 2009. *Crisis and Capitalism in Contemporary Argentine Cinema*. Durham, NC: Duke University Press.

Sánchez-Prado, Ignacio M. 2006. "*Amores perros*: Exotic Violence and Neoliberal Fear." *Journal of Latin American Cultural Studies* 15, no. 1: 39–57.

FILMS

El cielito. Directed by María Victoria Menis. Todo Cine S.A, 2003.

Pizza, birra, faso. Directed by Adrián Caetano y Bruno Stagnaro. Palo y a la bolsa cine, 1997.

NOTES

1. The research for this article was funded, in part, through the auspices of the Foreign Travel Grant program of the Baker-Nord Center for the Humanities, Case Western Reserve University. I would also like to thank Jennifer Driscoll Colosimo and Jorge Marturano for their reading of this article and their insightful suggestions. Finally, I am grateful to Steven Wenz for his translation.

2. *El cielito* is María Victoria Menis's third feature film. She has also directed *Los espíritus patrióticos* (1989), *Arregui, la noticia del día* (2001), and *La cámara oscura* (2007).

3. Ignacio M. Sánchez-Prado is referring here to the big success in international markets and among critics of films like *Amores perros* (Alejandro González Iñárritu, 2000), *Cidade de Deus* (Fernando Meirelles and Kátia Lund, 2002), and *La virgen de los sicarios* (Barbet Schroeder, 2000), which, "along with other cultural manifestations such as the Colombian literature of the *sicarios*, or the increasingly popular Latin American 'crime fiction,' has changed the form in which the metropolitan discourse conceives Latin America. To use Sylvia Molloy's term, the 'magic-realist imperative' is now accompanied by a 'violent imperative'" (2006: 50).

4. It is therefore interesting that Horacio Bernades, in his review of *El cielito*, should compare it with *Pizza, birra, faso* in its way of filming the city (2004).

5. See, for example, Aguilar (2006: 14), and Eseverri and Luka (2003: 14).

6. As Joanna Page states in her reading of *El cielito*, "the narrative structure of *El cielito* … moves from the barbaric countryside to the equally barbaric city, refusing to permit the establishment of space external to, or in any way separate from, violence and degeneration" (112).

An Argentine Context: Civilization and Barbarism in *El aura* and *El custodio*

BEATRIZ URRACA

WIDENER UNIVERSITY

Recent Argentine cinema, lamented veteran Argentine director Fernando Solanas, is devoid of authenticity, self-knowledge, and historical memory; it lacks "an Argentine context."³ His nostalgia for the politically engaged films of his own generation, or even for the specific socioeconomic contextualization that characterized many films of the late 1990s, may be well-founded, but as Francine Masiello has observed, Argentina is a "nation in which even accounts of minor detail serve to allegorize the national dilemma" (Masiello 2001: 3). Two recent examples – *El aura* (*The Aura*, Fabián Bielinsky, 2005) and *El custodio* (*The Minder*; Rodrigo Moreno, 2006) – show that the uniquely Argentine foundational myth of civilization and barbarism still informs the nation's cinematic consciousness. As we explore the representations of violence in contemporary Argentine cultural production, we find Sarmiento's dichotomy inextricably linked to "the elaboration of the monstrous, of that 'other' that irrupts in the universe of civilization with the intention of questioning it and undermining it" (Lusnich 2005: 16).[4] That "other," I will argue, is deployed in the criminal act, committed by an improbable subject who contains within himself an element that is imperfect but also uncontrollable, and who achieves his full potential as a result of his interaction with a specific environment.

Violence, as many critics have argued, is intrinsic to the cinematic medium, "part of its deep formal structure" (Prince 2003: 3).[5] This essay follows the trajectories of two shots (a word used here in its full filmic and violent double meaning): the accidental killing of Carlos Dietrich, a *baqueano* mistaken for a deer in *El aura*, and the well-placed, silenced bullet that kills Artemio, the Minister of Planning, in *El custodio*. Neither is a particularly violent film in the traditional Hollywood manner: both victims die of a single, painless, unexpected shot; the representations of their deaths lack both gore and confrontation; and the films focus on the depth of the killers' psychological development. Although *El aura* offers more in the way of fast-paced action scenes than *El custodio*, Dietrich's death is less graphic than Artemio's. The *baqueano* is glimpsed through the trees by the viewer and by the shooter, who averts his eyes as he pulls the trigger thinking that he has a deer in the crosshairs. The minister, however, has his forehead neatly pierced point-blank by a very intentional bullet, and the scene's absolute silence contributes to the viewer's ability to focus solely on the slowly spreading deep-red bloodstain on a white pillow and the tranquil sound of waves that displaces the blast of gunfire. In both cases, the violence and its perpetrator are portrayed as products of the spaces in which the action takes place: the untamed forests of Argentina's wilderness in *El aura*, the urban corridors and parking lots of Buenos Aires in *El custodio*. In examining the motives, circumstances, and consequences of the killings and the techniques employed to portray the two protagonists and their environments, this article seeks to interpret the films as representative of a key concept in the nation's cultural production: that the civilization-barbarism dichotomy survives in the oppositions, contradictions, contested spaces, and unresolved conflicts that define both the characters and the places where they live. As representative examples of a trend that has rarely been interrupted since Sarmiento described the dichotomy, these films point towards a society where interpretive strategies of social and individual issues continue to utilize established parameters of national identity formation.

FILM SYNOPSES

Fabián Bielinski completed *El aura* months before he died in 2006. Internationally renowned for his 2000 blockbuster, *Nine Queens*, Bielinski delivers here a psycho-noir drama distinguished with prestigious awards at the Cartagena and Havana film festivals as well as in his native Argentina. With the exception of a few scenes that frame the movie's beginning and end, *El aura* is filmed almost entirely in Bariloche, in southwestern Argentina. It is within its impenetrable forests that an unnamed taxidermist (Ricardo Darín) accidentally kills a man while on a hunting trip, unleashing a series of events that involve him, as a stand-in for the victim, in executing the plans to rob a casino's weekend profits. The taxidermist, who suffers from epilepsy, periodically experiences a series of warnings, or "auras," during which he is incapable of action and must give himself over to the oncoming seizure. Due to a miscalculated detail, the heist ends in bloodshed, but Darín's character survives and returns to his Buenos Aires studio taking his victim's dog with him.

El custodio is Rodrigo Moreno's first full-length film. It received a series of prestigious awards in 2006, including the Alfred Bauer at the Berlin Film Festival, and won for Best Director and Best Actor at the Bogotá Film Festival. The story features the daily routine of a bodyguard, usually a secondary character, a faceless extra, but one that in this case fills the screen in nearly every scene while the rest of the film's action occurs in relative obscurity. Everyday, Rubén (Julio Chávez) follows the minister (Osmar Núñez) to meetings, media interviews, and private events, ostensibly to protect him from threats that never materialize. While the attractive and successful politician dashes from wife to lover to closed-door gatherings, Rubén's own private life consists only of sporadic visits to his sister Beatriz in a mental hospital or to a prostitute in a sordid apartment. As Moreno acknowledged, any interpretation of *El custodio* is necessarily a backward reading of the film based on its unexpected ending (Robbins 2007): after shooting his boss in the head as he sleeps, Rubén drives off for a liberating, cleansing swim at Mar del Plata, while the viewer has only a few minutes left to interpret Rubén's every action as foreshadowing the murder.

These two narratives hinge on some of the same principles: a lone, male anti-hero and a path to violence that appears devoid of freedom of choice; a highly controlled, "civilized" environment that contains a dormant element of barbarism which makes violence possible; a non-diegetic past which hints at the cause of the protagonist's initial loss of individuality and autonomy and of the ensuing violence but does little to complete the psychological puzzle. In addition to the plot of the foiled heist in *El aura*, the choice of "Rubén" in naming Chávez's character and other minor details evoke an obvious and recent precursor, Adrián Caetano's *A Red Bear* (2002), cementing Bielinski's and Moreno's position as expositors of the next stage of the New Argentine Cinema.[6]

There are also similarities in the ways in which the two directors depict the protagonist. The taxidermist lies his way into being someone else, taking his victim's place in a series of complicated plans that he must piece together from the partial notes and photographs he left behind; Rubén spends his life as another's shadow, screen, protector, whose access to the lives of others is brief and partial as doors close and curtains are drawn in his – and the viewer's – face. Abandoned by his friend and jilted by his wife, the taxidermist attracts the interest of a band of criminals intrigued by his access to Dietrich's heist plans, photographs, and keys. Rubén is almost always alone, surrounded either by people who fail to acknowledge his presence or by his chaotic family members, all of whom depend upon his constant, reassuring presence to continue with their carefree lives. Both are damaged personalities, one paralyzed by his seizures and his inability to become the criminal mastermind he always dreamed he would be; the other running from his past and bottling up the pressure inside him. Both are misunderstood artists: the taxidermist is a meticulous man who excels at making dead animals look real but who resents his friend Sontag's lack of respect for the products of their profession; Rubén likes to draw portraits, especially nude women, but his artistic talent is mocked by one of Artemio's friends, adding to the long list of the bodyguard's humiliations.

THE TAXIDERMIST

El aura is a film about a loner whose insignificant daily existence as a maker of realistic fakes is thrust into protagonism when he joins his friend Sontag on a hunting trip in the south, the "most uncontaminated place in the Argentine imagination" (Rocha 2006: 211). Through Sontag's eyes we begin to piece together the personality of the taxidermist as someone who thinks of himself as a criminal mastermind capable of carrying out perfect, precisely timed heists, but who is also damaged by a paralyzing illness that takes hold of his body and mind and prevents him from any kind of action. The "auras" are filmed with a camera that spins around and above the subject, while a series of sounds alert us to the imminent seizure and let us inside the taxidermist's mind: a whistle blowing, a heavy door slamming. Indeed, the longest speech Darín delivers in this film is to describe the sensations to Diana, Dietrich's wife:

> Suddenly things change. It is as if … the world stopped and a door opened inside your head that lets things in.… Noises, music, voices …, images, smells.… It tells me that the seizure is imminent, that I can do nothing to avoid it, nothing.… It is horrible and perfect because during those seconds you are free, there is no option, no alternative, nothing to decide. Everything adjusts itself, tightens. And you give yourself up.

The taxidermist, whose every movement in his workshop is precisely calculated to produce a perfect, lifelike result, suffers from a paralyzing frustration when it comes to acting out his fantasies. He rejects Sontag's concept of "macho" violence, which hinges on "having the balls" to kill a defenceless animal and beating up his wife, but struggles to define himself as anything more than a listener, a watcher, and a daydreamer. As they stand in line at the museum's office, waiting to be paid, he and Sontag find themselves in the midst of one of the taxidermist's fantasies. His mind – and with it, the camera – flashes forward to reconstruct a crime that has not taken place, as if his eyes and imagination were those of a film director describing and sketching a scene. His eyes are, indeed, a camera – he has a photographic memory – , but with that comes paralysis, the stillness of a photograph: he is "waiting … for someone to do something." While the viewer debates whether he and Sontag have a criminal past together or whether one of them is daydreaming, Sontag breaks the suspension of disbelief with a mocking, "Who do you think you are, Billy the Kid?"

The taxidermist does, eventually, find himself capable of violence – but only to overcome his aversion to shooting animals and to kill in self-defence. Otherwise, he remains vulnerable, repressed, in need of the weak protection afforded by the Tegretol in his pocket and the medic-alert medallion he wears around his neck and which repeatedly falls out of his shirt like a semi-religious talisman, a reminder of the illness engraved upon it.

As Sergio Wolf proposes, many examples of the New Argentine Cinema seem to be "preceded by a former film we did not see" (Wolf 1993: 176). In the absence of a flashback, this "former life" is a non-diegetic element that makes us wonder but does not fully explain the present nor provide a more complete picture of the character's reality or motivations (179). *El aura* includes such an element in the protagonist's life. At the museum, the conversation between the taxidermist and Sontag alludes to past situations of shared crime, a reputation for being "the best player" at this game, and a veiled reference to failure:

Sontag: Do you remember that time when ...?
Taxidermist: I remember every time.

While we remain in the dark as to the nature of these remembrances, the taxidermist always remembers because he has no choice, but also because he cannot be separated from his weakness, from the enemy within, the "other" that forces him into situations in which he has no control. He is damaged, flawed, unlike the "perfect" stuffed animals he builds for the museum, whose skin he stretches over the bones like a mask. But, like them, in the end he learns to wear the mask that will bring to life his fantasy of being a cinematic superhero, a gun-wielding robber with extraordinary mental abilities.

When the hunting trip takes the two men deep into Argentina's frontier country, and after Sontag departs abruptly, the taxidermist is left alone to become protagonist, director, and audience of his own film. In preparation, he watches Dietrich's first planned heist take place, as if he wanted to be part of it, like a spectator might want to be part of a movie. While cops and robbers shoot at and pursue each other, Darín's figure wanders among them, unnoticed but noticing the smallest details. At this time he becomes, like an actor, an impostor who blunders into performing the role of Dietrich's "friend from the capital" and implementing the dead man's plans. Like the foxes we observe him stuffing in the film's opening scenes, he is metaphorically wearing someone else's skin: he puts on one of Dietrich's ties to enter the casino where only the "civilized" and properly attired crowd gather at the weekend. This allows him to infiltrate a band of thieves, take charge of the details, direct their every move based on the fragmentary script he finds in Dietrich's cabin, play along with the other actors, and fill in the gaps in his knowledge like a reader or a viewer might do. At every turn, he lies, creates a fictional situation, fleshes it out as he goes along, as if he were filling a wolfskin with putty. Thus the taxidermist finds himself embodying, if not Billy the Kid, then its Argentine equivalent.[7] Dietrich had been a *baqueano*, and in reading Sarmiento's description of that character we find that it describes the taxidermist's new role, with his near-perfect photographic and spatial memory:

> The *baqueano* is a reserved, serious gaucho, who knows twenty thousand square leagues of plains, forests, and mountains like the palm of his hand. He is the most complete topographer, the only map a general takes along to direct the movements of his campaign.... As modest and reserved as a mud wall, he is in on all the secrets of the campaign; the fate of the army, the success of a battle, the conquest of a province, all depend on him.... (Sarmiento 1845: 66)

He does not flaunt his abilities, but he is confident of them in the face of taunts and threats from everyone around him: "a *baqueano*," Sontag calls him derisively when the taxidermist assures him that he does not need his help to return to the cabin through the forest, "You had to have some kind of ability, to compensate." The other robbers also realize in the end that with the taxidermist's useful photographic memory and unusual attention to detail comes the unforeseen, the dark, monstrous animal inside the mask: "You are badly made," says Sosa, one of his accomplices, when he comprehends the problems the seizures cause at the crucial moment.

RUBÉN

Although there is hardly a scene in *El custodio* without Rubén, his role is essentially that of someone's shadow, a non-entity, a role which could be played by anyone. Whether he finds himself following or waiting for the minister, or listening to his sister's meaningless drivel, Rubén is nothing but a passive actor in someone else's life, a foil, a screen that protects others from the perils of a world we can only glimpse through the closed windows of cars and nondescript public buildings. No one really knows him, not even his sister, who believes he is "a straight man, incapable of fraud." On the job, Rubén is what he does: a purely cinematic creature, an *actor* interpreting, but not really *being* the same as a full-fledged character, at least not until he takes a step "out of character" and shoots Artemio. To emphasize the "monstrous other" that coexists within him, the two sides of Rubén's performance, Moreno often shows his image at the same time as his reflection in a mirror.

Rubén's private life is limited and chaotic: a visit to his sister's hospital, for example, begins with a shot of a dirty coffee cup and a full ashtray, things his obsessive-compulsive personality would never tolerate at home. Beatriz's long hair is dishevelled, while his is short and slicked back. In his professional life, everything has a place, clothes fit perfectly, and schedules are predictable. Despite the relentless taunts on the part of Artemio's family and staff, Rubén often behaves like a caged animal, calmly pacing with his hands behind his back, as if they were tied by an invisible rope. He loses his cool in only three scenes, where among the deliberate greyness of the film a red object alerts us to the bodyguard's state of mind. In the first one, he grumbles at Beatriz, whose hair is a muted shade of red, because she has been telling others what he does for a living. In the second, he chides his niece, Valeria, when he discovers that she has taken his drawings out of their hiding place (Valeria is holding a red snack bag during this scene). These two sparks of muted anger have to do with keeping his identity secret, which is consistent with the director's intention of giving us as little information as possible about this character. The third time, Rubén's barely contained anger is given a somewhat freer rein, as if it had accumulated within him to the point of near overflow. Thus Rubén's birthday celebration at a Chinese restaurant ends, before the meal even begins, with the entire family being thrown out. The bland atmosphere of the place is, in this case, punctuated by red trim, a waitress's red dress, and red gift-wrap. On the way out, Rubén screams at a small, young Chinese woman, torn between his desire to attack the waiters and the expectation that he help keep the disturbance to a minimum.

By contrast with these "preparation" scenes, the final shooting is an act of unprovoked, extremely cold-blooded calculation, and it takes place in a nondescript grey room with a red bucket in the background. It may well be Rubén's only act of individual volition, and the ensuing killing, as Joel Black argues, is "the bloodiest, the most gruesome, and the most violent." Rubén blasts "apart the brain, the seat of the will, where all executive decisions originate" (Black 1991: 2), and in the process frees himself to follow his own path, which leads to the cleansing, purifying sea, representing a "more primitive or 'natural' state."[8]

Two circumstances appear to bring about this ending: ostensibly, Rubén wants to swim at Mar del Plata because he has never been in the sea. But that sea, which he can only glimpse through the glass of a large picture window, is inaccessible because, at the moment when he is considering a colleague's offer of a bathing suit, Rubén is urgently recalled to the minister's side. When Artemio arrives in Mar del Plata, the first thing he does is ask Rubén to open the car window, then loosens his tie and breathes in the sea air, gestures of freedom that are unavailable to Rubén. As he smokes, a tiny silhouette dwarfed by the huge picture windows, a second camera begins to record the scene from the outside, and we see the sea reflected on his face behind the glass that cages him. It is only in the last scene, as he sits in the car facing the waves, that his carefully combed hair appears, finally, slightly unruffled.

Rubén's character is vulnerable and repressed, more interested in protecting himself than his employer. With few exceptions, he appears onscreen enclosed within a shell – the bullet-proof vest – and spends a lot of his time inside the minister's car. During car rides our point of view is dominated by the rosary dangling from the rear-view mirror like a conspicuous talisman, similar in effect to the medal that falls out of Darín's shirt in *El aura*. This rosary, a clear reference to the red heart that graced the same space in Caetano's *A Red Bear*, is the last thing we see, hanging between us and the sea, in the final scene. The Rubén who shoots Artemio is an enemy within the minister's team but also within

Rubén himself. As a victim, Artemio makes no sense: he is simply there at the point when Rubén's beast, too long held in check, finally stirs.[ ]

There is one more piece missing from this psychological puzzle: the fragments of a past attributed to Rubén when another bodyguard, waiting in the hallway with him, recognizes him:

> *Carrillo:* Weren't you a machine gunner? At the border, no?
> *Rubén:* How do you know?
> *Carrillo:* My brother used to work with you. Don't you remember Carrillo?
> *Rubén:* … It could be …
> *Carrillo:* You should be higher up, shouldn't you?
> *Rubén:* Why?
> *Carrillo:* You were famous once.

This unspoken past may well refer to the unspeakable parts of Argentina's history, where everything still has a bearing in the present, but Moreno's generation has opted for filming a reality they know for sure, rather than offer the "false didacticism" of filmmakers of the 1980s (Wolf 1993: 180). Just as the minister represents the political present, Rubén's non-diegetic history as a *milico* is clearly meant to evoke a certain political past – Argentine "figures of authority, meant to protect, are seen as persecutors" (Rotker 2002: 5). As we start watching the film for the first time, when the frame fills only one third of the screen, and throughout all the scenes where we are made aware that what we have is a partial, veiled view, we are reminded that we can never know the full story.

SPACES

Sarmiento identified the wilderness as the space of barbarism, while for him the elements of civilization were located in the cities, particularly the capital. But as Maristella Svampa has argued, the dichotomy can also be understood in temporal terms: barbarism was Sarmiento's present and civilization was a future, a project to be realized (Svampa 1994: 165). It seems fitting, then, that Rodrigo Moreno chose a "Minister of Planning" to be protected by Julio Chávez's character, someone who nonchalantly dismisses the provinces – he tells a governor that "your province is the least complicated." It is also significant that whatever plans and projects he carries out behind closed doors and in meaningless, mumbled speeches are ended by Rubén's weapon. What all this "civilized" planning has produced, according to Rodrigo Moreno's view of the capital, is a series of "transitional spaces" where Rubén's life passes: urban corridors, hallways, elevators, waiting rooms, and stairways of buildings that are as purposefully unidentifiable as they are impersonal, constraining, and suffocating. They are grey, modern buildings constructed out of straight lines and lots of windows through which the also grey skies of what we assume to be Buenos Aires – but is really a city carefully stripped of landmarks – can be glimpsed. These spaces, inhabited by "pacers" like Rubén as well as by cleaning staff, waiters, and chauffeurs, recall the half-built structures and nondescript sky-scapes of Trapero's *Crane World* (1999) and are a faithful representation of what Marc Augé has termed the "non-places of supermodernity," in which the "user" is also stripped of his identity (Augé 1995: 103) and of Deleuze's "any-space-whatever," in which "the source of control, the center of power, is difficult to apprehend" (Shiel 2001: 12). In these spaces, characters are bound to others by "modes of social interaction defined by the precarious and the temporary, the transactional, and the contractual" (Urraca 2007: 130); as a constant of the New Argentine Cinema, these modes of social interaction provide a picture of modern relationships in urban Argentina.

One recurring shot, in particular, underscores the symbiosis between Rubén's self-containment and his working environment. It is an aerial view of the parking lot from an upstairs window, sometimes glimpsed by Rubén, other times by the viewer while Rubén is downstairs waiting for the minister to get inside the car. The parking lot is effectively an urban well surrounded by tall buildings. Within it, the minister's staff and his convoy, which looks like a set of toy cars from above, perform a careful choreography each time he enters or exits a vehicle. Rubén and his colleagues "dance" around the accurately positioned cars, adopting a military stance, hands behind their backs, looking up at the sky to avoid their employer's gaze. This space makes us privy to the techniques of Rubén's work, and duplicates the containment that defines his character. Everything in his professional life moves, like the cars, with precisely calculated timing and gracefulness. But it also encloses, like a prison or a too-small bullet-proof vest, any human yearning to colour outside the lines.

Coincidentally, *El aura*'s opening scene takes us inside the ultimate transactional non-place: the ATM lobby where the body of the taxidermist is slowly regaining consciousness after a seizure, and where a beeping sound is slowly revealed as coming, not from hospital equipment, but from the machine where his card is still inserted. The fact that the character played by Ricardo Darín in *El aura* is, by profession, a taxidermist points to the conjunction of two worlds within his life: the "civilized," represented by the way he turns lifeless wild animals into realistic museum dioramas, and the barbaric, represented by his adventure in the forest, where he encounters those animals in real life and must confront the very real ways in which they kill and die. In his workshop, with classical music playing, the taxidermist is very much in control, an artist who knows exactly where each piece goes, and who chooses, from a perfectly organized drawer, the pair of eyes that will give his fox a realistic semblance of life. The museum, as Francine Masiello has pointed out,

> ... brings nature and artifice into contact, showing the transformation of popular culture under the lens of formally constituted disciplines.... [t]he museum draws into collision the famed oppositions of civilization and barbarism, translating the languages of the latter for the advantages of the former.... (Masiello 2001: 235)

We go to a museum to see the dioramas that, upon contact, reveal themselves as fake; indeed, the ones in the movie are in various states of disrepair. As the taxidermist accidentally leans upon a deer, its horn falls off, and he carefully returns it to its place on top of the animal's head. When he finds himself in the midst of "real" nature, however, things are not as easy to fix. The hunt then emerges as one of the film's primary motifs: man against animal, man against man, man against woman, animal against animal. Sontag and the taxidermist came to kill deer, and what they find is a "wounded animal," a "hunted" human being, in Diana, Dietrich's battered wife. She cannot escape because, as she confesses to the taxidermist, "I already did it once. And Dietrich looked for me and found me. He is going to find me. Always." They also find Dietrich's dog, a wolf-like creature with knowing eyes and a bloody snout which has been killing the neighbour's sheep and which evokes Plautus's saying "*homo homini lupus*" [man is wolf to man]. The camera transforms the unwilling hunter into the hunted subject through wide-angle shots that dwarf his presence in the midst of the immensity of Argentina's wilderness. Whether he stalks the deer in the forest or a wounded criminal through the town's unfamiliar streets, we always find ourselves stalking Darín's character in the crosshairs of the camera's lens.

The wilderness contains the certainty of violence but also refuges, museum-like spaces like Dietrich's forest cabin, full of notebooks, photographs, tools, weapons, and hunting trophies – a guide to a dead *baqueano*'s past. And a part of the wild is brought back to the city at the end of the film, when we see Dietrich's dog quietly watching, half in light, half in shadow, as the taxidermist resumes his work. For him, the civilized and the barbarous have become intricately woven as he has accepted his own dualism reflected in the figure of the dog. The wilderness, as Richard Slotkin has argued in a different context, is "a realm of mystery in which there is an interchange of identities between the soul of the hunter and that of its prey" (Slotkin 1973: 479). What the wilderness brings out in him is the ability to let go, as he does during his "auras," and liberate himself from the constraints of family, job, and illness to delve into self-knowledge and self-realization, to stand above himself and look down, as the camera allows us to do, at this insignificant man among the trees and understand his true purpose.

CONCLUSION

As these two films demonstrate, the Argentine context Solanas declared missing is actually vibrant, present in cinematic representations of violence and violent types that continue to refer to older Argentine foundational myths and relate them to present-day social and individual situations. Whether these twenty-first-century reinterpretations of Sarmiento's dichotomy mirror contemporary Argentine socio-political realities is less important than the fact that the artist's lens is still shaped by this tradition. Along with many other works of the New Argentine Cinema, Bielinski's and Moreno's works privilege stories that focus on the individual's attempts to navigate a highly controlled "civilized" environment where barbarism has never ceased to provide periodical disruptions, be they in the form of state-sponsored violence and corruption, the empty promises of neoliberalism and globalization, or the relentless growth of the metropolis and its hold on the country's wilder nature. Both films propose a perception that ordinary individuals are powerless and devoid of freedom of choice, as much in the natural wilderness as in the midst of the urban corridors of political power, and hint that there is an "other," an impostor, a monster within them that will gain his moment of protagonism through unpredictable, barbaric violence. Ricardo Darín and Julio Chávez give life to complex characters whose binary composition reflects that of their environments and of their country at large. The violence comes from inside them and yet appears to be also outside, taking over their volition at the moment of pulling the trigger, as one averts his eyes and the other looks, for the first time, at the camera that records the shot.

WORKS CITED

Alberdi, Maite. n.d. "Entrevista a Rodrigo Moreno." *La fuga* http://www.lafuga.cl/articulos/entrevista_a_rodrigo_moreno/ (accessed 14 June 2007).

Augé, Marc. 1995. *Non-Places: Introduction to an Anthropology of Supermodernity*. London and New York: Verso.

Black, Joel. 1991. *The Aesthetics of Murder: A Study in Romantic Literature and Contemporary Culture*. Baltimore: Johns Hopkins University Press.

French, Karl, ed. 1996. *Screen Violence*. London: Bloomsbury.

Girard, René. 1977. *Violence and the Sacred*. Baltimore: Johns Hopkins University Press.

Ludmer, Josefina. 2004. *The Corpus Delicti: A Manual of Argentine Fictions*. Pittsburgh: University of Pittsburgh Press.

Lusnich, Ana Laura, ed. 2005. *Civilización y barbarie en el cine argentino y latinoamericano*. Buenos Aires: Biblos.

Masiello, Francine. 2001. *The Art of Transition: Latin American Culture and Neo-liberal Crisis*. Durham, NC: Duke University Press.

Molteno, María. n.d. *El custodio*. http://www.cineismo.com/criticas/custodio-el.htm (accessed 14 June 2007).

Poblete, Joel. 2006. Rodrigo Moreno, director de *El custodio*. Mabuse. http://www.mabuse.cl/1448/article-74875.html. November 7 (accessed 14 June 2007).

Prince, Stephen. 2000. "Graphic Violence in the Cinema: Origins, Aesthetic Design, and Social Effects." In *Screening Violence*, ed. Stephen Prince, 1–44. New Brunswick, NJ: Rutgers University Press.

Robbins, Jon. 2007. Interview with Rodrigo Moreno. http://www.newdirectors.blogspot.com/April (accessed 14 June 2007).

Rocha, Carolina. 2006. "¿Idealismo en tiempos de mercado? La cinematografía de Piñeyro de los 90." *Nuestra América* 2: 211–26.

Rotker, Susana. 2002. *Citizens of Fear: Urban Violence in Latin America*. New Brunswick, NJ: Rutgers University Press.

Sarmiento, Domingo Faustino. 1845 [2003]. *Facundo. Civilization and Barbarism*. Trans. Kathleen Ross. Berkeley: University of California Press.

Shiel, Mark, and Tony Fitzmaurice, eds. 2001. *Cinema and the City: Film and Urban Societies in a Global Context*. Oxford: Blackwell.

Slocum, David. 2001. *Violence and American Cinema*. New York and London: Routledge.

Svampa, Maristella. 1994. *El dilema argentino. Civilización o barbarie*. Buenos Aires: Taurus.

Urraca, Beatriz. 1993. The Literary Construction of National Identities in the Western Hemisphere: Argentina and the United States, 1845–1898. PhD diss. University of Michigan.

———. 2007. "A New Cinema for a New Argentina." *Cuaderno Internacional de Estudios Humanísticos y Literatura*. 7: 128–51.

Wolf, Sergio, ed. 1993. *Cine argentino: La otra historia*. Buenos Aires: Letra Buena.

FILMS

El aura [*The Aura*]. Directed by Fabián Bielinski. Buenos Aires: Patagonik Film Group, 2005.

El custodio [*The Minder*]. Directed by Rodrigo Moreno. Buenos Aires: Rizoma Films, 2006.

Un oso rojo [*A Red Bear*]. Directed by Israel Adrián Caetano. Buenos Aires: Lita Stantic Producciones, 2002.

Mundo grúa [*Crane World*]. Directed by Pablo Trapero. Buenos Aires: Producción Cinematográfica Argentina, 1999.

NOTES

1 Fernando Solanas and Sissako Abderrahmane, "Diálogo Cine-Política" (A conversation at the 9th Buenos Aires International Festival of Independent Cinema, Buenos Aires, April 3–15, 2007).

2 All translations are mine.

3 See also Black (1991): 16; French (1996): 5; Prince (2000): 2; Slocum (2001): 4.

4 Moreno places a smoking Rubén behind a lamppost in a scene where we only see the cigarette smoke blowing out the side – a clear quotation of *A Red Bear* where another Rubén, also played by Julio Chávez, does a similar thing to confuse his attackers in a tavern shoot-out. Bielinski's film borrows the robbery of salaries and the references to "el Turco," a distant Buenos Aires figure who gives the orders in *A Red Bear* as well as in his own *El aura*.

5 Josefina Ludmer also equates the mythical figure of Billy the Kid with Argentine models, such as Juan Moreira (Ludmer 2004: 87).

6 Slotkin, cited in Slocum (2001: 12).

7 In his study of sacrifice, René Girard explores both the concept of the overflow of accumulated violence and of choosing a victim simply because he is "vulnerable and close at hand" (Girard 1977: 2, 10).

ID.
THE RE-SIGNIFICATION OF SOCIAL AND GEOGRAPHICAL SPACES

Postnational Boundaries in *Bolivia*

IGNACIO LÓPEZ-VICUÑA

UNIVERSITY OF VERMONT

The films of Israel Adrián Caetano are characterized by their way of looking at Buenos Aires, seeing the underside of modernization, the violence in everyday interactions, and the uncertainty of individual and collective destinies in Argentina. Caetano has developed a way of talking about the contradictions of neoliberal modernity in Argentina, exploring the lives of characters that are trapped in impossible situations, which appear to have no resolution other than personal sacrifice or death. At the same time, in Caetano's films the familiar spaces of Buenos Aires become defamiliarized, appearing strange and even hostile. The downtown boulevards and monuments in *Pizza, birra, faso* (*Pizza, Beer and Smokes*, 1997), the neighbourhood bar in *Bolivia* (2001), the suburban neighbourhood in *Un oso rojo* (*A Red Bear*, 2002), in a movement away from the city centre and further out towards the periphery, emerge as immediately recognizable spaces that nevertheless reveal a different face of Buenos Aires, spaces from which the characters are estranged as if the city itself had suddenly turned against them. In his most recent film, *Crónica de una fuga* (*Chronicle of a Flight*, 2006), Caetano delves into an episode from the period of military dictatorship, departing from the portrayal of contemporary urban settings in Buenos Aires. This paper will concentrate on *Bolivia*, with some reference to *Pizza, birra, faso* and *Un oso rojo*. In this essay, I attempt to situate *Bolivia* as a reflection on the instability of national boundaries brought about by neoliberalism, on the intolerance and violence that accompanies it, and on the limits and possibilities of the post-national space that emerges among the fragments of the nation. As the characters are confronted with forces that exceed their ability to control or even fully understand, racism and xenophobia emerge in a vain attempt to stabilize national identities and social positions. Caetano's filming style emphasizes the disempowerment of the characters and their inability to control their own destinies in the age of neoliberal globalization. At the same time, it positions the viewers as witnesses to the fragmentation of the nation, opening up the question of how the fragments of the national project fit together in an (uncertain) postnational space.

One could argue that in Caetano's films the protagonists are forced to cross certain boundaries in order to survive. In *Pizza, birra, faso* and *Un oso rojo*, the main characters are forced to turn to crime as the only viable way to protect their families from misery. Perhaps the violent path they choose reflects the extent to which they are being pushed out of the working class and left exposed to the brutality of economic adversity. In both cases, the protagonists are forced to choose personal sacrifice: Cordobés in *Pizza, birra, faso* dies trying to ensure a future for his pregnant wife, and Oso in *Un oso rojo* faces prison or becoming a fugitive after robbing a bank in an attempt to provide for his wife and daughter, whom he will not be able to see again. These films are structured around both narrative inevitability and an overarching sense of being trapped in a situation with no solution. By showing the ways in which the characters are cornered, the films expose the injustice of the neoliberal model's consequences for Argentina, displaying at the same time an ethics of defiance against the current order and irreverence towards national discourse, which has lost credibility as more people are pushed to the margins. In *Pizza, birra, faso* such irreverence is directed towards the monuments and symbols of modernity in Buenos Aires (the Obelisco and downtown boulevards) while in *Un oso rojo* the most striking moment occurs when Oso's shoot-out with the police is cross-cut with images and sounds of children (including his daughter) singing the Argentine national anthem in school. Both films make significant use of *cumbia villera* at key moments associated with crime, taking full advantage of the music's association with lower-class resistance to bourgeois norms and embrace of delinquency and violence. These elements in Caetano's films support Remedi's claim that *Un oso rojo* espouses a "neogauchesca" aesthetic. For Remedi, the film embraces – and invites the viewer to embrace – a position outside of law and order, "because it is a bad law and because it is an immoral and unjust order" (2006: 156). Similar to the *gauchos* in nineteenth-century Argentina, characters like Oso live on the frontier between law and illegality, between civilization and barbarism. But, according to Remedi, the frontier no longer lies between the city and the country, and instead it now exists within cities, and even defines life in contemporary urban spaces (2006: 148).

Bolivia is unique, however, in that the plot does not so much embrace defiance of the established order as it explores a sense of tragic failure that taints everyone's life. It is the most stark and bleak of the films (it is shot in black and white) and carries furthest the elements of neorealism present in Caetano's work. Even more significantly, in *Bolivia* the crossing of boundaries shows characters at their most vulnerable and passive. The film stages the unravelling of the national community in the microcosm of the café-bar, but the fact that the narrative has a Bolivian immigrant at its centre suggests that this unravelling cannot be understood merely in terms of the nation itself but must include a critique of de-nationalization in the Southern Cone as a result of neoliberal policies. The fact that Freddy has crossed national boundaries is significant because *Bolivia* explores how borders of exclusion (race and class) are constructed in everyday interactions and in language. In what follows, I will concentrate on how *Bolivia* uses neorealist film language to communicate a sense of helplessness and perplexity in the face of ruthless economic conditions and will then go on to discuss how this perplexity reflects a larger uncertainty about the future of the national community in a time of breakdown of national borders.

BOLIVIA AND NEOREALISM

Bolivia is shot in black and white, using 16 mm, which gives it a grainy, quasi-documentary look. It is organized around long takes, often at table-level. The camera moves in a wandering gaze that is not particularly attentive to narrative (since narrative appears rather repetitive or even banal) focusing instead on objects and details: beer glasses, cigarettes, smoke, hands, cash. These objects, as well as music, sounds, and even the camera's gaze become detached from the narrative, giving rise to what Christian Gundermann describes as "loose objects" (2005: 241) that interrupt the hermeneutic process, making a reading of the action or plot more opaque and dense, defying any easy interpretation of the film's story. In his reading of Italian neorealism, Gilles Deleuze argues that neorealism can be more accurately defined, not by its socially engaged content, but by its way of looking at things. For Deleuze, the neorealist image breaks with the conventions of narrative cinema by establishing a new kind of image, the *time-image* (as opposed to the *movement-image*). This new way of presenting images creates "optical and sound situations": protagonists become primarily observers of reality as they are increasingly more helpless with regard to narrative action. But reality is viewed as a series of elements or objects whose connection to each other is unclear, opaque (Deleuze 1989: 2–4). As Laleen Jayamanne remarks in regard to Deleuze's text, the neorealist way of viewing gives us a space that is emptied of traditional spatio-temporal coordinates and rules of perspective, lacking connection between parts: "Because of these qualities action becomes difficult, if not impossible, in such spaces and mutates into a kind of aberrant movement. What emerges in this impasse is a cinema of the seer and not of the agent. This is because 'I see' does not mean 'I understand' in this economy" (Jayamanne 2001: 138).

Hence in the film, characters 'see' the superficial effects of neoliberalism: they see each other losing jobs, falling into debt, being unable to make ends meet. They also see immigrants taking "Argentine" jobs and they see themselves being demoted to the same category as immigrant workers. What they fail to see/understand is that the idea of the national community as a unitary space is no longer possible in the current global moment as the new economic policies have irrevocably shattered the possibility of resistance to capital organized around a national-popular discourse. Thus characters like Oso, Don Enrique, and their bar buddies criticize immigrants (and display hostility against Freddy) because their way of viewing things is limited by their own subject position as "white" Argentines. Oso's claim that "any Bolivian, any Paraguayan" can come to Argentina and "make it," while people like him and Don Enrique have to struggle to get by, reveals not only the way they look at immigrants but also the way they see (or fail to see) their own position in Argentine society. The film pushes the viewer, on the other hand, to see/understand the similarity between the displacement Freddy experiences and that of Argentine workers and to make the connection between the realities of poverty and unemployment in Argentina and the larger process of unsettling of borders in South America. The film thus forces the viewer to see Freddy (the outsider or stranger) as another victim of economic displacement; in turn, it also forces us to see a likeness between Argentines marginalized by economic hardship and the immigrants they distrust and resent.

In *Bolivia* Freddy as well as the patrons of the café appear helpless and perplexed in face of social exclusion. Characters are viewed almost as objects (or as disempowered subjects) of a process of economic marginalization they cannot fully understand, which gives rise to a situation where tensions, distrust, and fear quickly erode the men's civility towards each other and their own sense of social standing/position. The action takes place almost entirely in a café bar (identical to so many others in Buenos Aires), and, as the film progresses, the space becomes increasingly claustrophobic and tense.

The film renders this space strange and hostile, suggesting that "[t]here is something sinister about this bar like thousands of other bars" (Gundermann: 244). When the film opens, Freddy, an undocumented immigrant from Bolivia, has arrived a week ago in Buenos Aires and is being instructed in the details of his job. The dialogue is heard before the people speaking are seen. The camera moves around the empty café focusing on objects and, eventually, on the sign taped on the window, "*Se necesita cocinero/parrillero*" (Cook/parrillero wanted). The boss, Don Enrique, asks Freddy if he "has papers," to which the latter replies that they are "being processed." The fact that Don Enrique says nothing further suggests their mutual understanding of Freddy's illegal status.

The regulars in the café are a group of taxi drivers, an occupation that in Buenos Aires often absorbs downwardly mobile, educated professionals and that therefore hints at the hard times these men are experiencing. Among them, Oso (Bear) is in financial trouble and in danger of having his car taken away, which would seriously compromise his livelihood. As Oso's desperation increases, he drinks more, and as Don Enrique attempts to confront him about the money he owes him (around 100 pesos) not directly, but by using Freddy, the feelings of hostility and resentment among the men play out in more sharp and violent ways. In the end, Don Enrique instructs Freddy to throw Oso out, and after the fighting that ensues, Oso shoots Freddy in the street, killing him. During the very short time that Freddy works at the café (two days), he bonds with Rosa, an attractive young waitress whose father is from Paraguay and whose mother is Argentine, which makes her of ambiguous ethnicity, although she identifies as Paraguayan. Since Don Enrique and one of the cab drivers both express sexual interest in Rosa at different times, Freddy's friendship with Rosa is viewed with suspicion and contributes to making the other men jealous.

As Oso becomes more frustrated with the people to whom he owes money, and who are threatening to have his car taken away, he vents his xenophobic feelings by talking about how "these immigrants" have it so easy, such as the Uruguayans who are "screwing him" by not extending his car loan. While Don Enrique, the boss, tolerates this behaviour to a certain point, eventually he decides to stop allowing Oso to eat or drink on credit, demanding that he pay up or leave. The tension between Don Enrique and Oso triggers the latter's resentment against Freddy, who is instructed to stop serving him food or drink, and ultimately also instructed to throw him out of the bar. Oso confronts Don Enrique, for not speaking to him directly, but this does not prevent him from continuing to harass Freddy by calling him "Boliviano de mierda" and by making references to "negros" and "Paraguayos." Although Oso represents the most extreme form of xenophobia Freddy has to face, however, the film shows him also being harassed by the police for no reason, being treated as expendable (after his death, in the final scene, Don Enrique simply replaces the "Cook wanted" sign on his window), being constantly asked about Perú, and called (insultingly) "*boliviano*," "*paraguayo*," and "*negro*" by drunk patrons. On the surface it would appear that the main concern of the film is racism. However, a closer look reveals that *Bolivia* constitutes a larger reflection on the unravelling of the nation and that it expresses a sense of helplessness in view of the breakdown of social hierarchies and positions.

Bolivia was made at a time when xenophobic feelings were running high, when local authorities and the media were calling for sanctions against, and expulsion of, illegal immigrants. The film consistently makes the viewer aware, however, of the artificiality of the term *boliviano* and points to the semiotic ambiguity in the use of the word, as will be discussed below. Caetano problematizes the idea that the expression *boliviano* merely indicates a national origin. Instead, the film explores how the label functions as a category that denotes precariousness and vulnerability in the present economic order.

As used by the xenophobic patrons of the café, the words *boliviano*, *paraguayo*, and *negro* express, by means of racial language, a condition of dispossession and insecurity, analogous to Agamben's notion of "bare life" (Agamben 1998), which threatens to encompass Argentine workers, not only immigrants. According to Caetano, the main theme of *Bolivia* is not racism but "the collision among people of the same social class, they are workers about to be left out of any class at all, and thus they are intolerant towards one another. Basically, they are trapped in a situation they cannot escape."[1] This idea of being "trapped in a situation they cannot escape" can be applied to the protagonists of *Pizza, birra, faso* and *Un oso rojo* as well. In *Bolivia*, however, boundaries are even more unsettled because they question the very limits of the nation, unlike in Caetano's other films where the nation remains the ultimate point of reference and intelligibility. In other words even the harsh critique, defiance, and despair directed against the nation in Caetano's films ultimately presuppose a coherent sense of the nation, with the exception of *Bolivia*, where it is the very definition and limits of the national community that is at stake.

From the very beginning, *Bolivia* exposes the artificiality of national boundaries and identifications. The opening credits show a football match between the national teams of Bolivia and Argentina on television, while neo-Andean music plays in the background. In the opening dialogue between Freddy and the boss, Don Enrique asks if Freddy learned to cook meat in Perú, prompting him to respond that he is from Bolivia, not Perú. This is the first in a series of similar exchanges that illustrate the uncertainty of national borders, even when those identities are claimed proudly or defensively. Immediately after this opening scene, there follows a conversation among the taxi drivers who patronize the café-bar. One of them is trying to locate a street on the map, and Don Enrique responds that it should be in that area with the streets that have names of Central American countries, such as Perú. These exchanges emphasize the artificiality of national identities in the Southern Cone, identities that must be constantly reaffirmed by means of external symbols like football teams, national anthems, or flags, but that clearly are in danger of being confused with one another as easily as street names. By citing this everyday situation, the film opens up a larger theme, which is the confusion and uncertainty of social hierarchies and positions.

Prejudice and violence against others, the film makes clear, stems from a sense of insecurity in one's own position. It is significant that the instances of xenophobia come from the cab drivers, who are in a position of downward social mobility. As a result of the neoliberal process, working class men are now forced to compete for jobs that were not attractive previously, which causes competitiveness with and intolerance toward immigrant workers. This situation renders hypervisible any workers from a class formerly considered inferior, with whom one is now forced to share the same space. The fear of losing status and of being left out of any class exacerbates this. For a while, Don Enrique and Oso bond over their suspicion of foreigners: "It's those damn Turks, gypsies, foreigners," Oso complains, who come here and "make money," while people "like us" work and never prosper. Don Enrique agrees and, in reference to Freddy, comments: "they play dumb and then before you know it they're your boss." But as soon as Don Enrique tries to get Oso to stop drinking and to pay his tab, the two men's resentment against each other becomes evident. Oso criticizes Don Enrique for hiring illegal workers, while people in Buenos Aires can't find jobs. "There's misery here," he complains. "But you give a job to any damn Paraguayan."

Clearly the insecurity felt by those who are being pushed out of their traditional positions clashes with the mobility of those crossing borders of class or nation. Because the characters feel threatened by a process they don't fully understand, xenophobic prejudice and racist labels emerge as a way of discursively stabilizing and reinforcing boundaries that are in flux. The hostility against Freddy and other immigrants is stronger because there is an increasing inability to mark clearly who belongs where, not only geographically but also in terms of status.

A significant scene illustrates this instability. In the morning, some customers have fallen asleep at their tables and Don Enrique asks Freddy to make them leave since they are not consuming anything. Freddy wakes them up, asks them to leave, and they react by complaining and almost immediately begin to call Freddy "negro" and "Paraguayo." On the evening of the same day, Freddy walks out (he has not yet found a place to stay) and is stopped, questioned, and harassed by the police. After this unpleasant scene, Freddy walks into a nearby café, orders some coffee, and falls asleep at the table. The man who serves him (whose face we don't see) appears to be a 'white' Argentine with the same build as Freddy's boss, Don Enrique. The symmetry between the morning scene at the café and the evening scene at an almost identical café, along with Freddy's rapid shift in roles and positions, underscores the instability of social boundaries. In this light, the use of racist and xenophobic language can be seen as an effort to summon national/ethnic categories in a last-ditch attempt to stabilize social roles and hierarchies, a strategy that, in the end, can only result in violence against those who are most defenceless.

Even though Freddy is clearly the victim of xenophobic violence, one could argue that those who attack him are also victims, rather than villains in any traditional sense. *Bolivia* resists locating a unitary source of social injustice, exclusion, or violence. Social injustice not only affects nearly everyone but it also comes from nearly everywhere. Oso's verbal (and ultimately physical) violence against Freddy can be seen as an attempt at retaliation against an unjust order whose agents remain invisible and intangible. The very fact that Freddy is in Buenos Aires is the result of forces whose violent effects exceed the national sphere. In his conversation with Rosa at the cantina, Freddy tells her that in Bolivia he used to work in the coca and fruit fields, until the "Yankees" came and burned everything. Thus *Bolivia* points to transnational forces that are displacing workers in the region, showing the underside of transnationalization, the globalization from below that is redefining boundaries in the Southern Cone.

THE NATION IN FRAGMENTS

During the 1990s Buenos Aires became an increasingly transnational city, with growing numbers of fancy shopping malls and boutiques, as the economy became more open to transnational capital. At the same time, however, the realities of poverty in the streets and slums of the city belied the triumphant official narrative of progress and integration into the first world. The contradiction between the public discourse of modernity and the everyday realities of insecurity and marginalization set the stage for a situation in which the poor came to be perceived as a threat to the neoliberal narrative. In this context, it is important to understand how the presence of undocumented immigrant workers (nothing new in Buenos Aires) fits within the struggle to define Argentina's identity at the beginning of the twenty-first century. Towards the end of the 1990s, the Menem government announced that the presence in Buenos Aires of immigrants from border countries showed that Argentina had entered into the first world, having become an attractive destination for foreigners. But, the government stated, immigrants from border countries like Bolivia, Paraguay, and Uruguay were also to blame for the high percentage of unemployment and for the increasing insecurity associated with crime (Grimson and Kessler: 117). As Grimson and Kessler have shown, however, this was hardly the case. Since the mid-1800s, immigration from border countries remained constant, fluctuating between 2.3 and 2.8 per cent (Grimson and Kessler: 124). What changed in the 1990s, according to the authors, was that ethnic diversity became "hypervisualized" in response to increasing economic and job insecurity. It was not only that local authorities and the government found it convenient to blame immigrants for Argentina's economic troubles. It was also that the reality of neoliberal globalization clashed with the perceived modernity Argentina was supposed to be experiencing. Traditionally, Argentina was seen by its elite and middle classes as a country without blacks or Indians (even though this contradicts history and fact). Because of the large amount of immigration from Europe, especially in Buenos Aires, it was possible to sustain the myth that Argentina was essentially a white country, and that Argentines had "descended from ships."

During the time of Perón, Buenos Aires was "invaded" by a multitude of working-class masses from the interior, brought in to work in the industries. These *mestizo* masses were referred to by the frightened middle classes as *cabecitas negras* (little black heads). Even though the term is racist, this does not mean that ethnic or racial identities were articulated politically. Rather, the expressions *negro* and *cabecita negra* became categories to express subalternity within a class-inflected system. Therefore the ethnic connotations of these terms were subsumed under class domination and exclusion rather than functioning as specific ethnic identities. According to this logic, immigrants from border countries (and migrants from provinces of the interior) were rendered invisible from the point of view of ethnicity: they were simply subsumed among the poor masses considered as "black heads," and their specific country or region of origin was irrelevant. According to Grimson and Kessler, in the 1990s this situation became to some extent reversed, giving rise to a "tendency to ethnicize formerly invisible differences." Thus, where previously the urban poor were referred to as *negros*, now they began to be referred to as *bolivianos* or *paraguayos*, shifting the emphasis from perceived colour and ethnicity to perceived *foreignness*.

In this new regime of visibility, Argentines whose ethnic traits are indigenous or *mestizo*, as well as those who are the children of immigrants, are suddenly rendered foreign. This essentially means turning the urban poor into "foreign" elements in the city. In Grimson and Kessler's words: "Although affirming that Argentina has entered the first world, neoliberal national imagery denationalizes its social effects" (2005: 127). That is to say, while neoliberalism pushes working class people out of the class system and into a situation of uncertainty and vulnerability, it also reterritorializes an exclusionary discourse of the nation in order to mark poverty as external and foreign to the nation. This helps to explain the sense among Argentines that immigration from border countries has increased and that *bolivianos* and *paraguayos* are taking their jobs. Since the perceived increase in immigration cannot be explained by actual figures, it must be explained as a change in the regime of visibility. Traditionally seen as part of the urban poor, immigrants, in the age of globalization, began to be seen as "foreign." What is more, poor Argentines, whether from the interior, or whether children of immigrants, also began to be seen as "foreign" and out of place in what should have been a modern, prosperous, first world city. Although immigration from border countries remained below 3 per cent, rising unemployment and the increasing job insecurity were linked, in the social imaginary, to the greater visibility of the urban poor, the "blacks" now perceived as "Bolivians."

    Understanding this discursive shift can help us better appreciate the simultaneous critique of racism and deconstruction of ethnic/national categories in *Bolivia*. By situating all of his characters in a position of vulnerability and dispossession, Caetano emphasizes the similarities, rather than the differences, between undocumented workers and national workers displaced by neoliberalism. In a sense, then, we can see Freddy as a figure for Argentines' sense of abandonment by the economic system. We could even go so far as to see the term *boliviano* as illustrating what everyone is becoming: foreigners, dispossessed in their own country. As the neoliberal system creates a situation of exploitation across national borders, it also weakens those national discourses that had sustained common Argentines by providing a sense of integration and belonging.

    Let us recall at this point that the neorealist way of seeing, in Deleuze's analysis, positions characters as puzzled, and to some extent helpless, observers of a reality in which the connection between things is unclear. In Caetano's films, the protagonists' choices are presented as a puzzle that defies solution. The tagline to *Pizza, birra, faso*, for example, is: "Four friends. One town. One way out." The 'way out' is, of course, Cordobés' sacrifice by turning to crime (and dying as a result) in order to provide for his wife and the baby she is expecting. In *Un oso rojo*, Oso 'solves' his dilemma by concluding that he must turn to crime again, provide for his wife and daughter (as well as his wife's boyfriend), and choose to separate himself from them indefinitely. In *Bolivia*, however, no such solution, not even as ironic defiance or tragic sacrifice, presents itself; it remains the starkest of the films, making the viewer as helpless as the characters in face of their circumstances.

Critics often comment on the use of music in Caetano's films. In particular, the use of *cumbia villera* to signal delinquency (or defiance against the established order) is significant in *Pizza, birra, faso* and *Un oso rojo*, as mentioned above. In *Un oso rojo*, the nostalgic music of tango (played on a *bandoneón*) punctuates a scene in which Oso spends time with his daughter, a moment that points to the past and signals an impossible future, as Oso concludes that the best thing for his wife and daughter is for him to stay away from them. The tango music becomes detached from the plot, however, making its meaning ambiguous. Is it meant to be nostalgic or are we meant to understand it as a trashed object from Argentine cultural history? In the scene where the national anthem is superposed over the shoot-out scene with the police, what would be the correct 'reading' (or the correct way of putting together the parts) of this scene? Is it meant to be ironic? Is it meant to affirm a *neogauchesca* defiance against the narrative of national identity, as Remedi might suggest? Is it meant to put to shame the institutions that claim to integrate everyone into the nation while excluding people like Oso? Or is it meant to allegorize the nation *as* violent and criminal (as Oso remarks, "*toda la guita es afanada*")? The openness of the music's function within the narrative suggests that music and sound indeed become detached, loose objects in these films.

Music that is immediately recognizable as Argentine (*cumbia villera*, tango, the national anthem) punctuates significant moments in the films, but its significance remains open, hovering between ironic critique, sadness, or even in its very ironic detachment, suggesting the ruin of certain signifiers of national identity. Keeping this in mind, I want to suggest that the use of *cumbia villera* works somewhat differently in *Bolivia*. In one scene, Freddy and Rosa go dancing to a local *bailanta* (popular dance club) where many immigrants go. In fact, one of the cab drivers asks

Rosa if she went to "that cantina where all the Bolivians gather" (which she denies). The music (intra-diegetic in this case) does not designate 'delinquency,' but rather is associated with a gathering space for those outsiders, who (somewhat ironically) listen to and dance to the same music as lower-class *porteños*. Although *cumbia villera* is associated with the Argentine lower classes, it is also to some extent a hybrid product, originating in Colombia, reinvented in Argentina's *villas miseria*, and circulated throughout the Southern Cone. In *Bolivia*, it becomes a music for immigrants. Significantly, it is in the scene at the cantina that Freddy and Rosa's bonding (although almost accidental, and certainly short-lived) occurs. The film uses neo-Andean music at key moments (opening credits, Freddy's long dream-like sequence following his phone conversation, and final credits), but it is significant that it is *cumbia villera*, and not neo-Andean music, that provides the sound-image that accompanies the coming together of the displaced in Buenos Aires. Perhaps this is not surprising, as neo-Andean music joins tango as discarded objects of national cultural histories, left without a stable narrative of the nation to anchor their meaning.

Freddy and Rosa's bonding, surrounded by other immigrants, provides a glimpse of a post-national community, a space that can be considered post-national to the extent that it depends upon displacement (significantly, it is in this scene that Freddy tells Rosa about his reasons for migrating from Bolivia). Rosa and Freddy's bonding thus carries the potential for a non-national community that emerges in the context of the ruin of the nation, once the nation is in fragments. *Bolivia* opens the question whether these fragments can be put together in other ways, creating a community, not based on a hegemonic discourse of the national popular, but on its reverse, on the displacement and heterogeneity Gareth Williams calls "the other side of the popular" (Williams 2002). *Bolivia* shows us a precarious, transient form of community that does not (and perhaps cannot) realize itself in the space of the film. Unfortunately, the film's tragic ending appears to foreclose this possibility, suggesting that, at the present moment, the breakdown of the nation is overwhelmingly dystopian. Ultimately, the displacement and slippage of identity categories occasions a neo-racist discourse that summons up national and ethnic categories (*argentino*, *paraguayo/boliviano*, *negro*), even though their reference to national histories has been suspended as a result of globalization. National/ethnic categories remain as empty signifiers, serving, not to construct a national-popular project, but rather to reaffirm and justify exclusion. It is one of the paradoxes of neoliberal globalization that, while it opens up borders to the flow of information and money, it must at the same time increase control and repression over the flow of bodies displaced by neoliberalism's social effects.

Unlike *Un oso rojo*, for example, where resolution is provided in the form of a defiant embrace of crime and banishment from 'good society,' *Bolivia* confronts the viewer with a radical impasse, with meaningless sacrifice, with an absence of any satisfying resolution. It remains the most bleak of the films, exploring how boundaries of exclusion are experienced and constructed in everyday language and in quotidian interactions. As nations come undone and their borders become increasingly uncertain, subjects of these nations are left more exposed and marginalized, and hence become more intolerant of one another. On the one hand, the film suggests the artificiality of national identities, as immigrants are referred to as *peruano*, *boliviano*, *turco*, *indio*, and *negro*. In this regard, the film offers a glimpse of Buenos Aires as post-national space. On the other, however, it also shows the violence and intolerance that result from the unraveling of the national project, leaving us with a puzzled, helpless look upon the new configurations that are emerging in the wake of the nation.

WORKS CITED

Agamben Giorgio. 1998. *Homo Sacer: Sovereign Power and Bare Life*. Trans. Daniel Heller-Roazen. Stanford, CA: Stanford University Press.

Deleuze, Gilles. 1989. *Cinema 2: The Time Image*. Trans. Hugh Tomlinson and Robert Galeta. Minneapolis: University of Minnesota Press.

Grimson, Alejandro, and Gabriel Kessler. 2005. *On Argentina and the Southern Cone*. New York: Routledge.

Gundermann, Christian. 2005. "The Stark Gaze of the New Argentine Cinema: Restoring Strangeness to the Object in the Perverse Age of Commodity Fetishism." *Journal of Latin American Cultural Studies* 14, no. 3: 241–61.

Jayamanne, Laleen. 2001. "Deleuzian Redemption of Bazin: Notes on the Neorealist Moment." *Toward Cinema and Its Double*. Bloomington and Indianapolis: Indiana University Press. 135–48.

Remedi, Gustavo. 2006. "De *Juan Moreira* a *Un oso rojo*: crisis del modelo neoliberal y estética neogauchesca." *Ideologías y literatura*, eds. Mabel Moraña and Javier Campos, 147–65. Pittsburgh: IILI.

Williams, Gareth. 2002. *The Other Side of the Popular: Neoliberalism and Subalternity in Latin America*. Durham, NC: Duke University Press.

FILMS

Bolivia. Directed by Israel Adrián Caetano. Prod. La Expresión del deseo, 2001.

Un oso rojo [A Red Bear]. Directed by Israel Adrián Caetano. Lita Stantic Producciones, 2002.

Pizza, birra, faso [Pizza, Beer and Smokes]. Directed by Israel Adrián Caetano and Bruno Stagnaro. Palo y a la Bolsa Cine, 1998.

NOTES

1   Cited in background notes contained in *Bolivia* DVD (New Yorker Video, 2005).

Contesting Spaces, Contesting Discourses in *Bolivia*, by Adrián Caetano

NATALIA JACOVKIS

XAVIER UNIVERSITY

Since 1995, Argentine cinema has been going through a period of steady growth in importance and quality, a process reflected in the popularity of its films in the national market and in international film festivals. This situation has consolidated the reputation of Argentine productions among specialized cinematographic circles around the world, and this group of films has been labeled the "New Argentine Cinema."[1] Among the directors that emerged, we can name Adrián Caetano, Lucrecia Martel, Lisandro Alonso, and Pablo Trapero, among others. It is difficult to describe common traits of something that is far from being a homogeneous movement, but it could be said that most of these films explore and rearticulate the crisis of disintegration that form their historical backdrop: that of the end-of-the-century Argentina, with the collapse of the *menemista* dream.[2] These films foreground, in many different ways, the devastating effects that the application of neoliberal policies had in Argentina.

In this article, I will study one of these films, *Bolivia* (2002), by Adrián Caetano. I will focus on how the film recuperates a very recognizable social space of Argentine modernity, the bar, to represent the violence that neoliberalism brought about in the country's social network. I would like to remark, thus, that even the title of the film is not neutral and points to this process of deterioration and the high levels of violence that it entailed in the affected population. I will argue that *Bolivia* foregrounds the problematic nature of both the discourse of neoliberalism and of its predecessor, the discourse of modernity, as the bar becomes an unstable space that at the same time contests and reproduces hegemonic discourses. *Bolivia* asserts the necessity to conceptualize the crisis not in terms of a monolithic idea of nation but rather taking into account the transnational flows that are a part of the insertion of Argentina in the logic of late capitalism. At the same time, *Bolivia* shows how many of the discourses that became hegemonic in the nineties are not a rupture but a continuation, under a slightly different rubric, of popular tropes of modernity – in particular, the dichotomy civilization vs. barbarism that permeated Argentina's cultural productions since the late nineteenth century.

The erosion of the state started in Argentina with the dictatorship that came to power in 1976. The process, however, accelerated and became painfully obvious during the nineties. Of course, the process had a great impact in Argentina's cultural production. In the specific case of cinema, Ana Amado points out that many of the films of the "New Argentine Cinema" deal with "topics most current to cinema in all world cinematographies: the disillusioned middle-class young people, youth as a marginalized segment by the severity of market and consumer society and the city as backdrop of their directionless journeys." This remark points to the universal effects that globalization has had around the world. However, although some topics may coincide in different national cinemas, the aesthetic choices are always different from one another. At the level of the image, as Christian Gundermann has studied, many of the new Argentine films "engage in a formal, abstract reconfiguration of what 'reality' means both for and in the cinema.... The neorealist and avant-garde experiments of the 1960s ... are the most apparent aesthetic antecedents of this cinema" (2005: 241). These aesthetic choices serve both to stage the crisis of national disintegration that is one of its underlying and recurring themes and to formally foreground and subvert the dominant neoliberal discourse, which affirms a society harmonically united under free-market laws.

The film *Bolivia*, released in 2002 but shot during the two previous years, is an example of the trend discussed above. Narrating the story of a Bolivian immigrant in Buenos Aires, it focuses on the impact of Argentine society's fragmentation on the individual. The film portrays a country in state of social emergency. The plot is simple, almost non-existent. Freddy, a Bolivian immigrant who lives in Buenos Aires, finds a job as a short-order cook in a bar frequented by taxi drivers. He has the hope of being able to send money to help his family, who stayed in Bolivia, and eventually of reuniting with them in Buenos Aires. In the bar he meets and interacts with a diverse range of characters: Don Enrique, the owner; Rosa, a waitress from Paraguay, who is as exploited as he is; Cordobés, a gay street-vendor; and Oso and Marcelo, two other usual patrons. The unstable balance in which they coexist, among strong tensions, is a reflection, at another level, of Argentine society; and the final outbreak of violence that kills Freddy is painfully close to the Argentine spectator taking into consideration the December 2001 crisis.

Bolivia recuperates a very recognizable social space of Argentine modernity, the bar, but also renders it problematic because it locates it at the centre of conflicting discourses about social reality. In Argentina, throughout the twentieth century the bar has been essential to understand the everyday life of the city and how the inhabitants relate to their social network. It became an important space of socialization, where people would meet and talk for hours, and where the main focus was human interaction and spending leisure time. Anne-Marie Fortier has analyzed the extent to which cultural identity is embodied and memories are incorporated "as a result of iterated actions" (1999: 48). In this sense, spending time in a bar became an example of a ritual that, in Fortier's words, "cultivated a sense of belonging" (1999: 48). But the spaces in which these rituals take place are not neutral, mere recipients of the actions of its occupants. The bar in *Bolivia*, I argue, can be conceived in terms of a Foucauldian heterotopia, which "presuppose a system of opening and closing that simultaneously makes them both isolated and penetrable" ("Of Other Spaces" 1999: 26). Héctor D. Fernández L'Hoeste has noted how useful this concept is to better understand inequality in Latin American cities because they are "singular areas of the social space characterized by the coexistence of antagonic functions," where what is interesting is "the interconection among these spaces and not the primacy of one over the other one" (1998: 14). Foucault recognizes the heterotopic quality of modern urban spaces against modernity's ideal of representing it as an utopia. Edward Soja, elaborating on the concept, explains:

> Through such forms of spatial regulation the heterotopia takes on the qualities of human territoriality, with its conscious and subconscious surveillance of presence and absence, entry and exit; its demarcation of behaviors and boundaries; its protective yet selectively enabling definition of what is the inside and the outside and who may partake of the inherent pleasures. (1996: 161)

Accordingly, in *Bolivia*, although the bar is supposedly a space where its customers can unwind and relax, the patrons' ways of conducting themselves are highly regimented. Don Enrique, the owner, becomes the arbiter of acceptable behaviour in the bar, stating what can and can't be done in that space, who is included and who is excluded. According to him, the bar is a site where "one comes to relax and to have a beer." Any situation that could potentially lead to conflict should be avoided.

For example, when el Cordobés, the gay street vendor, seems to become a little too friendly with Freddy, Don Enrique advices him to stop directing his attention towards the cook, although he wasn't being disruptive. Oso and Marcelo, two of the patrons, are also very attentive to who comes and goes. Marcelo tries to control Rosa, while Oso seems to be up to date on everybody's affairs. It is important to remark, as Peter Johnson has, that "heterotopias are fundamentally disturbing places" (2006: 87). Following Gilles Deleuze's elaborations, he considers Foucault's concept of heterotopia an attempt:

> ... to overcome the dilemma of every form of resistance becoming entangled with or sustaining power. Heterotopias in this way light up an imaginary spatial field, a set of relations that are not separate from dominant structures and ideology, but go against the grain and offer lines of flights or ... 'a passage which is an enclosure.' (2006: 87)

In this sense, as I will explain in more detail, the bar is an unstable space that simultaneously contests and reproduces hegemonic discourses and cannot escape the power relations that are deeply rooted in the social nexus. The bar in the film, on one side, goes against the grain of hegemonic contemporary discourses, in the sense that it offers a respite to its patrons from the alienation that the emphasis on the individual and the breakdown of old forms of socializations provoke in them. It is the space where they perform the everyday ritual of just hanging out there, interacting and unwinding. However, as Johnson points out, it can't be separated from dominant structures and ideologies, and it is this contradiction that creates the tensions that will erupt at the end of the film.

The dynamics and interactions observed in the bar among its customers, Don Enrique, Freddy, and Rosa foreground the changes that took place in contemporary Argentina by the insertion of the country in the global logic of late capitalism. Regarding people's responses to changes in public discourses brought about by globalization, Gareth Williams notes:

> [This process] transforms Latin American modernity's models of fictive ethnicity production into an indefinable hybrid mix of discipline/control-based apparatuses. Meanwhile, undisciplined migrant populations attempt to eke out a meager existence in ... the street corners of the intentionally disorganized, deregulated, and denationalized labor markets of the neoliberal order's informal economy. (2002: 108–9)

A response to this is, according to Williams, that "abandoned and isolated people hang on (sometimes fanatically) to historically sedimented truth – local, regional, or even neighbourhood identities – as if they were natural" (2002: 109). As a result, there is a generalized "climate of fear and disengagement that nevertheless lends structure to the international division of labour, and upholds the reign of the marketplace, the illusory withdrawal of the state, and the consumption, as the dominant ideological realities and institutional practices of our times" (2002: 109). In *Bolivia*, on one side, its patrons try to rebel against the rhetoric of neoliberalism that affirms the hegemony of the marketplace and the primacy of consumption. At the same time, they embrace a social imaginary that posits them as the white, modern, and civilized inhabitants of Buenos Aires against the threat of invasion by dark-skinned immigrants. This social imaginary is based on the basic paradigm of Argentina's national identity and the collective representations that sustain it. Many scholars have pointed to a process that they refer to as the "latinoamericanización" of Argentina during the nineties. During the greater part of the twentieth century, most Argentines felt that they belonged to the middle class (Minujin and Kessler 1995). However, alongside this perception is the inescapable fact of Argentina's economic decline in the second half of that century. One of the consequences, Ariel and Victor Armony remark, was that "along with Argentina's decadence during the second half of the twentieth century, a myth of past and future national grandeur definitely shaped public discourse" (2005: 44). This discourse separated Argentina from the rest of the Latin American countries and posited it as a "European" nation only geographically located in Latin America. However, this long-standing illusion was shattered during "*menemismo*," which saw large parts of the Argentine population fall below poverty lines. Therefore, the country began to resemble more and more its poorer neighbours.

In the neoliberal paradigm, a person's worth is measured by his or her ability to consume. Strong individualism is emphasized as acceptable and necessary behaviour in contemporary society. Pierre Bourdieu has characterized neoliberalism as a new global discourse that forms a political program for the methodological destruction of all the collectives (1998). Against this rhetoric, the patrons of the bar still struggle to maintain old forms of solidarity. They reject the primacy of the economy and constantly complain about money (or the lack thereof). Oso constantly reminds Don Enrique, when the latter insists that he pay his tab, that he helped him some time ago, so he should now wait until things get better for him. Marcelo is trying to help Oso as much as he can. By spending so much time in the bar, they try to cultivate a "sense of belonging" that will provide them with roots amid the chaos of contemporary life. It is a way for them to resist the hegemonic discourses that makes them invisible for a neoliberal society since they are not able to consume and participate in the supposed benefits of a free-market economy.

However, this "sense of belonging" is attached to another paradigm, one that was essential in shaping Argentina's biggest national myth. I'm referring to the one that posits the country as white, modern, and European. In the late nineteenth and early twentieth century, millions of European immigrants settled in the country, then seen as young, rich, and having an unlimited potential. This was encouraged by the elite, who wanted to populate the country with white immigrants while at the same time exterminating the native indigenous population, viewed as "barbaric" and a source of backwardness. These immigrants and their descendants "would form the core of the middle classes, but they would also join the ranks of a nascent working class that soon adhered – through Peronist redistribution policies – to middle class values, lifestyle and aspirations" (Armony 2005: 44). The increasing economic problems of the country and its failure to achieve its supposed potential "engendered a narrative of victimization, which became the staple of almost every political point of view: there is someone who is liable for robbing Argentina's wealth, and worse, for steering the country away from its glorious destiny" (Armony 2005: 44). This narrative of victimization appears very clear when the consequences of *menemismo* began to be felt in the country's general population. Emanuela Guano has studied the discourses and practices of the impoverished middle class in Buenos Aires in the nineties, who "strove to generate a consensus on Buenos Aires as a quintessentially white and middle class city whose 'modernity' was being eroded by the presence of a large mestizo lower class" (2004: 71). When, in the late nineties, this middle strata found itself confronted with their failure to adapt to the neoliberal policies and a consequent descent into poverty, they developed "a common strategy of reproducing social difference through a discourse that posited a white, middle class, and modern 'normalcy' as the only legitimate modality for spatial and cultural citizenship in Buenos Aires" (2004: 70). This gave rise to discourses that "marked poor, dark-skinned individuals as 'not belonging' in white Buenos Aires" (2004: 70). During the 1990s, another "form of symbolic violence was the widespread habit of blaming these 'others' for Argentine's predicaments" (2004: 75). This strategy recalls the trope of civilization and barbarism, as originally formulated by Domingo Faustino Sarmiento, which was essential to the process of nation-building in the country. Argentines' discourse of modernity posited a civilized and white population that should constitute the modern Argentine state against a backward, violent, and primitive indigenous and *mestizo* population that lacked the proficiency to be incorporated into the public sphere. Henri Lefebvre has argued that discrimination is spatially reproduced through a discursive economy of representations that valorize "certain relationships between people in particular places" and in this way building up "consensus" on these places as well as an identification of who belongs to them (1991: 56). In *Bolivia*, the interaction among characters in the bar, not only reproduces, at a smaller level, xenophobic attitudes towards illegal aliens in Argentine society that is part of the above-mentioned narrative of victimization, but also puts in evidence the sense of loss that the new parameters of acceptable behaviour imposed by neoliberalism brought about. Both Freddy and Rosa are conceived by the patrons as disruptive figures who do not belong there. Oso criticizes Don Enrique for employing a non-Argentinian. Marcelo tells Freddy to be careful with Rosa, as she is supposedly a tricky person. She poses a double treat: as a woman, she is a stranger in the all-male environment; as a foreigner, she can arise the same xenophobic sentiments Freddy does if she steps outside the submissive behaviour that is expected from her.

The bar is an unstable space where different temporal forms of social relationships coexist within its limits. At the bar, this is symbolized by the clock that never works correctly and that Don Enrique constantly asks Freddy to fix. This repeated action provokes the sensation of a suspended time. Against the primacy of anything but an economic logic, old forms of solidarity still subsist, but they are constantly in tension with the uncertainty and confusion brought about by globalization. The patrons spend their time being idle, not engaging in any productive (from an economic point of view) activity. Moreover, the bar could be considered as a site of resistance to the homogenizing aesthetics that globalization brought about in the nineties to the Latin American metropolis where, as Jean Franco points out, "everything looks familiar because it looks like everywhere else" (2002: 191). The bar in *Bolivia* is old, modest, and has survived the changes brought about by the nineties to these particular spaces, when most of them were recycled and redecorated with the same homogeneous bright lights and colours of furniture. It is the place where the patrons go to look for old forms of community bonds that the impact of neoliberal discourse and its emphasis on individualism put an end to. Therefore, on the surface, old forms of socialization that mostly disappeared still subsist within this space, especially in the relationship between Oso and Marcelo. The latter is always there to listen to all of Oso's complaints about his economic situation; he tries to iron out the differences between Oso and Don Enrique and to help him economically. Oso is a typical lower middle-class individual excluded from the system by the economic transformations of the nineties.

However, the personal exchanges between patrons in the bar also illustrate what Bauman has called "the changing pragmatics of interpersonal relations" within the logic of globalization, which "are now permeated by the ruling spirit of consumerism and thus cast the other as the potential source of pleasurable experience, and partly to blame: whatever else it is good at, it cannot generate lasting bonds" (2000: 206). In *Bolivia*, Oso doesn't know how to react and adapt to the new reality. Although he is deep in debt, unable to pay his bills, he keeps ordering food and coffee in the bar. He constantly reminds Don Enrique, when the owner tries to recover what he owes him, that he had helped him when Don Enrique was broke. Therefore, according to him, Don Enrique should wait until he solves his economic problems. He also asks Mercado, another taxi driver that frequents the bar, to go with him to visit a car dealer to ask him to defer the payments of his loan, in order to be able to save his car. This becomes another disappointment for Oso. Mercado not only doesn't help him but stops frequenting the bar. Oso's reaction in view of his problems is to blame the immigrant: "Here comes any son of a bitch and makes money. Does this happen to you? Not to me, and I bust my ass off working." This quote illustrates not only the increasing xenophobia of great parts of the Argentine population, but also the lasting effects of the illusions of certain discourses of modernity that formed the national myth that we referred to above: that of Argentina as a land of opportunities, of an unlimited potential, where social mobility is possible if one works hard enough. As we pointed out, the failure to make this dream come true resulted in a narrative of victimization and in always blaming an "other" for this letdown. In this sense, Oso attributes the impossibility of making that dream come true not to the deep structural changes from last decade but to the immigrants that come from border countries to take away the opportunities of the Argentinians.

Though concerned with the effects of neoliberalism in Argentine society, the film also foregrounds the illusory nature of the many discourses that were part of the process of nation-building in the country. The film subverts in different ways monolithic fictions of nationality. When Freddy asks Rosa about her national origin, she answers that her father is from Argentina, her mother from Paraguay, where she was born, she has been living in Buenos Aires for four years and can't wait to leave the city. Freddy doesn't seem very surprised by her answer. At the same time, as Carlos Scavo points out, the exclusion and other effects of neoliberal policies in the social fabric need participating fictions to compensate. The initial opening credit sequence shows one. The credits flash by alongside a televised soccer match between Argentina and Bolivia, with the TV announcers praising the home team and deriding Bolivia's performance. In Argentina, there is nothing better than the national soccer team to create a myth of social unity that transcends social classes and particular situations,[3] or, in the case of local soccer teams, to create a sense of belonging to a certain group. For a country like Argentina, triumphing over its poorer neighbours still offers some small comfort. The derogatory comments of the TV commentator towards the Bolivian team anticipate the xenophobia and racism Freddy will go through throughout the movie, just for being a poor immigrant.

The instability and antagonism that permeate the interactions among the characters in *Bolivia* points to the collapse of the idea of the modern nation. The bar is a site that, in terms of Fernández L'Hoeste, is characterized "by the coexistence of antagonic functions" (14). While its former function, that of a place of idleness, remains, it also becomes witness to the discursive strategies of differentiation and exclusion that Argentina's middle class developed to cope with the failure of the neoliberal dream. *Bolivia* is part of the group of films that, according to Joanna Page, use the nation as the *mise-en-scène* (2005: 305).[4] However, she remarks, it is not the unified nation of modernity but the nation as "a porous entity: specifically, the nation as unfinished project, hybrid, transculturated, marginalized and positioned as dependent within the asymmetrical structures of globalization" (2005: 311). In this film, attention is drawn to the necessity to analyze contemporary Argentina in all its complexity, abandoning any attempt to homogenize it. It doesn't, however, leave aside the notion of nation in favour of a more diffuse one of transnational territory. Octavio Ianni points out that one of the discourses that accompanies the imposition of neoliberalism is that of the "end of geography" (1998: 38), where the attributes of traditional nation-states are diminished and we talk about a world designed based on transnational interests. What actually happens, according to Ianni, is that the most typical and sedimented institutions of dominant capitalist societies expand even further their sphere of influence (1998: 63). *Bolivia* points in this direction. While taking into account the transnational flows of people and merchandises that affect contemporary Latin American societies, it also emphasizes the asymmetries that this process entails.

Although Don Enrique pretends that the bar is a neutral space where people come to spend their idle time, it becomes witness to questions of inequalities and relationships of power. As Rossana Reguillo affirms, "the ... social body that perceives the threat of corruption, the loss of sense, the transformation of values, and an uncontainable and amorphous violence responds with the expansion of mechanisms of vigilance" (2002: 188). As noted above, Don Enrique acts as the arbiter of tolerable behaviour in the bar. Nothing escapes his gaze, which is represented in the movie through multiple close-ups of him, quietly observing what goes on in his bar. Marcelo is very attentive to Rosa's increasing friendship with Freddy, probably out of jealousy. Similarly, all the customers meddle in everybody else's life.

Freddy is the object of derogatory and racial slurs by the bar patrons. Rosa is sexually harassed by some of them and also by Don Enrique. It is also implied that "el Cordobés," a gay street vendor that frequents the bar, wasn't given the job as a meat cook because of his sexual orientation.

However, none of the characters is a defenceless victim. Freddy and Rosa, in particular, display small strategies of resistance to cope with the daily exploitation they are subjected to (Noriega). When he is stopped and harassed by the police, Freddy dodges the questions until they let him go. Later, he walks up to an open bar where, in a situation that parallels the one where he had to throw out a customer in Don Enrique's bar for being asleep, he orders a coffee and prepares to spend the night there, since he doesn't have any other place to sleep. Rosa, meanwhile, rejects being considered a mere sexual object by the bar patrons and by Don Enrique. At the beginning of the film, it is implied that she has a relationship with Marcelo, when she arrives late for work in his cab. Later, however, she rejects Don Enrique's overtly sexual invitation to give her a ride home. The night she goes out with Freddy, she also refuses Marcelo's repeated requests to "go for a drive" with him.

Freddy's and Rosa's small acts of resistance have their correlation in the bar through small details that define the relationship between both of them. As Gustavo Noriega has remarked, they share tips, "a mode of communal exchange that contrasts with the infinite complaints about money of the rest of the characters in the film." The bond between Freddy and Rosa doesn't go unnoticed by either Don Enrique or the patrons, and questions of power come into play again. Marcelo and Don Enrique try to break their link, talking ill of her to him. Finally, Freddy is not passive in front of the insults he receives. Although at first Don Enrique manages to protect him and calm him down, it is precisely Freddy's reaction, hitting and breaking Oso's nose, due to his racist and xenophobic slurs, that triggers the final tragedy of the character. Drunk and beaten up by Freddy, Oso leaves the bar with Marcelo, who tries to take him home. In the car, Oso takes a gun from the glove compartment and shoots Freddy, who was standing at the bar entrance watching him leave.

Bolivia continuously transmits to the spectator a feeling of latent violence that seems inevitable and uncontainable. At the level of the image, this is achieved through an increased feeling of claustrophobia. *Bolivia* is one of the most recognizable examples of the neo-realistic tendencies of some films of the New Argentine Cinema. It was shot mostly with non-professional actors (only Enrique Liporace, who plays Don Enrique, is a recognizable figure). It was shot in "real" locations, and this, combined with the restriction of the camera movement, produces a documentary effect. In this aspect, it recalls the political films of the late sixties; whose most famous representative is probably Pino Solanas and Octavio Getino's *The Hour of the Furnaces* (1968). This documentary was part of a broader continental project that came to be known as "New Latin American Cinema," whose characteristics include:

> … the emphasis on national popular cinema, the attempt to adopt and transform neo-realism in the context of Latin America, and the effort to break with the distribution and exhibition circuits of commercial cinema, incorporating new working-class and peasant audiences into more democratic cultural practices. (King 1990: 85)

These films proposed a gaze towards the referential world based on the totality of collective experience. Contrary to them, however, one of *Bolivia*'s main characteristics is its fragmentation, the isolation and the anonymity of the characters. The film starts and finishes with the same advertisement asking for a cook, which points to the fact that Freddy's tragedy is all too common in contemporary Argentina. Very little do we know about the characters. We never see them with their families, and, if it is mentioned, they are all separated or distanced from them. As Noriega points out, "its creatures are basically enclosed, isolated in the bar, but also on the shot.… The director chose to isolate each character in the shot and link them through the edition process." The camera is there to register every corner of the bar, the gazes and exchanges among the characters, to describe situations and characters, an operation that serves to build up the subterranean tensions that pervade the film and will boil over at the end.

The bigger setting for the film, besides the bar, is that of the city of Buenos Aires. The city appears to be as disturbing as the bar itself. After Freddy's first day of work, he is stopped in the streets by two policemen that threaten him with deportation if he is working illegally. He is also ripped off by the owners of an illegal telephone booth when he tries to call his family in Bolivia. It seems to be an example of the way Franco, among others, describes the big Latin American metropolis at the turn of the century:

> The ideal order that made the city such a powerful symbol for the national community and for civic conduct, even if it never really coincides with the real city, is now impossible to reclaim. Indeed, one could argue that the vibrancy, the ephemeral encounters, the vertiginous changes, the infinite ruses of survival has made the city the trope of disorder.... And though cities are still administrative centers, real power is concentrated in the anonymous modern buildings that house high-tech communities, insurance firms, and banks or in the shopping malls. (2002: 191)

The anonymity of the characters therefore coincides with the decentralized mode of exercising power that characterizes contemporary societies. Contrary to the bar's claustrophobic atmosphere, the film conveys a sense of a city as a vast urban sprawl in which its central core is diminished. As Adrián Gorelik has studied, neoliberal discourse has also affected the sphere of urban planning. Its consequent policies have transformed public space and infrastructure in a hunting ground for business and real estate developers (2004: 193). According to Gorelik, the logic of this city is the logic of the "shopping center," which doesn't presuppose any longer expansion and homogenization but contrast and fragmentation (2004: 200). Parallel to the process of impoverishment and decay, gated neighbourhoods and country clubs proliferated in the mid-nineties in Buenos Aires' suburbs, preying both on a discourse of fear and of exclusivity. These enclaves catered to the small section of the population that was benefiting from the neoliberal economic policies. Significantly, the most recognizable spots in Buenos Aires (9 de Julio, Plaza de Mayo) are not present in the film. We are shown an urban cartography that, on one side, would be recognized by anybody familiar with Buenos Aires. But, on the other side, what we see are undistinguished neighbourhoods, local cafés, or a dancing club with mainly working class or immigrant customers. This movement of defamiliarization is paralleled at the formal level. Analyzing the initial sequence, composed of still frames of objects natural to the bar: bottles, a knife, ashes, a rag, Gundermann points out that "it is as if we saw a bar for the first time, one of those places that we have frequented thousands of times.... There is nothing familiar in this familiarity" (2005: 244). Therefore, we encounter a series of marginal sites rendered unfamiliar at the level of the image. Don Enrique's bar only becomes a temporary centre because it is a site of communication, but it reflects the dislocations that the imposition of neoliberal economic policies brought about in Argentine society.

To sum up, in *Bolivia* the multiple and often contradictory discourses interact within the same physical space, the bar, and foreground the tensions and violence that undergo contemporary Latin American societies. While contesting hegemonic neoliberal discourses, the film also positions itself against the intended logos of modernity as a comprehensive discourse. Instead, it points out that the xenophobia that is depicted has its roots in the divisive Argentine nation-building discourse. *Bolivia* seeks an alternative in a more flexible discourse that would take into consideration the global flows that affect Latin America in the late twentieth century. As Lopez-Vicuña argues, the film "force[s] a rethinking of community and collectivity by imagining the nation's fragments entering into new, unforeseen assemblages" (2005, 2000). As it is illustrated by the relationship between Freddy and Rosa, while these flows accentuate the unequal division of wealth and power, the film affirms that they may also contain the potential for new forms of solidarity that transcend rigidly fixed national boundaries.

WORKS CITED

Amado, Ana. 2002. "Argentine Cinema: When Everything is Fringe." *The Thinking Eye: Latinoamerican and Spanish Cinema Online Magazine* http://www.elojoquepiensa.udg.mx/ingles/revis_01/secciones/veranali/artic_04.html (accessed Dec. 2004).

Armony, Ariel, and Victor Armony. 2005. "Indictments, Myths, and Citizen Mobilization in Argentina: A Discourse Analysis." *Latin American Politics and Society* 47, no. 4: 27–54.

Bauman, Zygmunt. 2000. "Making and Unmaking of Strangers." In *The Bauman Reader*, ed. Peter Beilharz, 200–218. Oxford: Blackwell.

Bordieu, Pierre. 1998. "The Essence of Neoliberalism." *Le Monde Diplomatique*; http://mondediplo.com/1998/12/08bourdieu (accessed July 2004).

Fortier, Anne-Marie. 1999. "Re-Membering Places and the Performance of Belonging(s)." *Theory, Culture and Society* 16, no. 41: 41–64.

Gorelik, Adrián. 2004. *Miradas sobre Buenos Aires: Historia cultural y crítica urbana*. Buenos Aires: Siglo Veintiuno Editores.

Guano, Emanuela. 2004. "The Denial of Citizenship: 'Barbaric' Buenos Aires and the Middle-Class Imaginary." *City and Society* 16, no. 1: 69–97.

Gundermann, Christian. 2005. "The Stark Gaze of the New Argentine Cinema: Restoring Strangeness to the Object in the Perverse Age of Commodity Fetishism." *Journal of Latin American Cultural Studies* 14, no. 3: 241–61.

Fernández L'Hoeste, Héctor D. 1998. *Narrativas de representación urbana: un estudio de expresiones culturales de la modernidad latinoamericana*. New York: Peter Lang.

Foucault, Michel. 1986. "Of Other Spaces." *Diacritics* 16: 22–27.

Franco, Jean. 2002. *The Decline and the Fall of the Lettered City: Latin America in the Cold War*. Cambridge, MA: Harvard University Press.

Ianni, Octavio. 1998. *Teorías de la globalización*. México: Siglo Veintiuno.

Johnson, Peter. 2006. "Unravelling Foucault's 'different spaces.'" *History of the Human Sciences* 19, no. 4: 75–90.

King, John. 1990. *Magical Reels: A History of Cinema in Latin America*. New York, London: Verso.

Lefebvre, Henri. 1991. *The Production of Space*. Oxford: Blackwell.

López-Vicuña, Ignacio. 2005. *New Urban Cartographies: Space and Subjectivity in Contemporary Latin American Culture*. PhD diss., University of Pittsburgh. http://etd.library.pitt.edu/ETD/available/etd-05202005-125316/unrestricted/lopezvicuna_etd2005.pdf (accessed 25 Mar. 2007).

Minujín, Alberto, and Gabriel Kessler. 1995. *La nueva pobreza en la Argentina*. Buenos Aires: Verlap S.A.

Noriega, Gustavo. 2002. "Freddy toma soda." *Fipresci Argentina* http://www.fipresciargentina.com.ar/archivo/bolivia.htm (accessed 12 July 2004).

Page, Joanna. 2005. "The Nation as the Mise-en-Scène of Filmmaking in Argentina." *Journal of Latin American Cultural Studies* 14, no. 3: 295–304.

Reguillo, Rossana. 2002. "The Social Construction of Fear: Urban Narratives and Practices." In *Citizens of Fear: Urban Violence in Latin America*, ed. Susana Rotker, 187–206. New Brunswick, NJ: Rutgers University Press.

Scavo, Carlos. 1995. "Marginalidad en las ciudades." In *Argentina hoy: crisis del modelo*, eds. Naum Minsburg and Héctor W. Valle, 233–82. Buenos Aires: Ediciones Letra Buena.

Soja, Edward W. 1996. *Thirdspace. Journeys to Los Angeles and Other Real-and-Imagined Places*. Oxford: Blackwell.

Williams, Gareth. 2002. *The Other Side of the Popular: Neoliberalism and Subalternity in Latin America*. Durham, NC: Duke University Press.

FILMS

Bolivia. Directed by Israel Adrián Caetano. Prod. La Expresión del deseo, 2001.

NOTES

1. In a recent article, Tamara Falicov has analyzed a parallel and related process: the "boom" in commercial blockbuster movies in Argentina's film industry, which were in part produced by large television channels that were utilizing state subsidies for these projects. This contradicted the essence of the film legislation passed in 1994, aimed at providing less commercial filmmakers the resources necessary to make their films. See Tamara Falicov, "Argentine's Blockbuster Movies and the Politics of Culture Under Neoliberalism, 1989-98" *Media, Culture and Society* 22 (2000): 327–42.

2. For several different analyses of what has been called "The New Argentine Cinema," see Ana Amado, "Cine Argentino" *Confines* 11 (2002): 87–94; or Horacio Bernades, Diego Lerer, and Sergio Wolf, *Nuevo Cine Argentino. Temas, Autores y Estilos de una Renovación* (Buenos Aires: Ediciones Tatanka, 2002).

3. The best example of this is the 1978 Soccer World Cup, played in Argentina and won by the national team. In the middle of a brutal and repressive period of military rule, the success united the nation in a joyous outpouring of nationalism where the genocide practices of the regime were suddenly forgotten.

4. In her article "The nation as the *mise-en-scène* of filmmaking in Argentina," Joanna Page conclusively argues against a current trend in Latin American film studies in the American academia, that of the dismissal of the study of national cinematographies in favour of a transnational approach. According to her, this critical approach not only is not supported by empirical facts but also "masks the asymmetries of exchange that still limit production and distribution for all but a very few of the continent's films" and reproduce the language of the global market, therefore "reinforcing its structures" (305).

The Violence of the Site[1]

ZULEMA MORET

GRAND VALLEY STATE UNIVERSITY

"The city, programmed to be functional, with a checkerboard design, gets swamped by and multiplies in individual and collective fictions."
("La urbe programada para funcionar, diseñada en cuadrícula se desborda y se multiplica en ficciones individuales y colectivas.")
– Néstor García Canclini
Imaginarios urbanos, 107

"This city is like an octopus."
("La ciudad es como un pulpo.")
–Reny, in Vagón Fumador.

Nomadic, orphaned, stray, inhabitants of the night, jobless, and lawless – these are some of the characteristics of the protagonists in the three films selected to guide my discussion on violence in Argentine culture during the nineties and the beginning of the new century. *Un día de suerte*[2] (*A Lucky Day*, 2002) by Sandra Gugliotta, *Vagón Fumador*[3] (*Smokers Only*, 2001) by Verónica Chen, and *Hoy y Mañana*[4] (*Today and Tomorrow*, 2003) by Alejandro Chomski were all filmed at the beginning of the year 2000, all are set in Buenos Aires, and all follow the wanderings of their young protagonists. The themes and approaches of these films are representative of the New Latin American Cinema, a trend that became noticeable during the nineties and continued during the first years of the present century. They also reflect the influence of the expansion of a globalized urban culture, such as the disarticulation of political power and the lost sense of community.[5] This discourse has been called "dirty realism" [*realismo sucio*], and it speaks of a new cinema that addresses the questions that come with life in the big city: corruption of values, identity crises, marginality, and extreme poverty (Christian León 2005: 23).[6]

Although the New Argentine Cinema is not exempt from such introspection when dealing later with the economic crisis of the nineties, it also consists of a new discourse that addresses urban violence, social marginality, and identity uprooting that could be considered "dirty realism." One of the most significant characteristics of the New Argentine Cinema is the visual treatment of space, in cities as well as in country landscapes, or the treatment of the new, mobile borders in a centre/periphery relationship. As Sergio Wolff makes clear in his essay "The Aesthetics of the New Argentine Cinema: The Map is the Territory," the movie directors who officiate as the pioneers of this new trend attempt a new reading of Buenos Aires' lesser-known spaces or a return to peripheral places (2002: 29).

Throughout this essay, I will address the concept of space as complementary to the construction of the main characters and as a frame through which the violence of site can be perceived even when these characters wander in cities and downtown areas, often in the "centre" of the urban space. As Edward Casey reflects in his phenomenological analysis of the construction of place, "Bodies and places are connatural terms. They interanimate each other.... Places also gather experiences and histories, even languages and thoughts" (1996: 25). Taking these concepts under consideration, I will explore the extent to which space defines the interactions of the protagonists and the city of Buenos Aires in the three selected movies.

The main characters in *Un día de suerte*, *Vagón Fumador*, and *Hoy y Mañana* are all urban dwellers of Buenos Aires who move to peripheral areas, drawing mobile frontiers between centre and periphery and erasing territorial limits in their individual search for survival. Elsa and her friends, in *Un día de suerte*, travel to shady neighbourhoods to deal illegal drugs and prescription medicines. *Vagón Fumador* is a more complex story that focuses on two night strollers: Reny is a female singer in a band and lives alone; Andrés is a taxi boy who lives by street prostitution around the Plaza San Martín and the cash machines on Lavalle Street and its surroundings. We recognize evidence of violence during their sexual encounters in public spaces. The case of Paula, the protagonist in *Hoy y Mañana*, brings out the complexity of the relationship between identity and market goods, for she chooses to prostitute herself just for one night in order to pay the rent of her small studio apartment located in a non-marginal area. Her action shows us the level of helplessness in which she lives. These characters, as city wanderers, are exposed to all kinds of violent, daily life situations, in their jobs and in their personal and social relations.

The city of Buenos Aires is the main setting of these three movies that all establish a close association between violence, gender, and social class interactions. As observed by Christian León,

> Confronting the fact that learned society, which sustains national identity, has lost its legitimacy in the present, [this new cinema] elaborates miscegenated codes that include elements from globalized western culture and from the local imaginary. It shows the street culture as a hybrid space composed of the deterritorializing effect of the media imaginary and the

re-mapping of territory by the marginal world according to its own subaltern codes. (2005: 31)[7]

The city is an active force in the setting-up of social bodies and ties. Elizabeth Grosz, in her essay "Bodies-Cities," describes a series of general effects on those who live in such cities. She concludes that the city always leaves its traces on the subject's corporeality, corresponding to the transformation of the city as a result of the information revolution:

> The subject's body will no longer be disjointedly connected to random others and objects through the city's spatiotemporal layout; it will interface with the computer, forming part of an information machine in which the body's limbs and organs will become interchangeable parts. (1999: 387)

Because of the traces that the city leaves on its subjects, we know that every city is a polysemic construct. Cities are neither innocent nor guilty for the actions that they provoke. Their set-up, development, and inner movements influence all kinds of changes in their inhabitants' lives. The city is the same and, at the same time, always different, because – as Grosz further emphasizes –

> The city's form and structure provides the context in which social rules and expectations are internalized or habituated in order to ensure social conformity or, failing this, position social marginality at a safe distance (ghettoization), and this fact means that the city must be seen as the most immediate locus for the production and circulation of power. (1999: 386)

For example, in one scene in *Vagón Fumador*, the two protagonists, Reny and Andrés, are sitting outside on the roof of a tall building (*rascacielo*) and looking down on Buenos Aires. There, Reny tells Andrés, "The city is a monster, it forces you to buy things, to consume … they don't see the monster, the brutality, in pieces, bit by bit."[8] This lyrical scene with the couple regarding the city from the terrace of a tall building at night is not the same image or representation of the city that appears in *Un día de suerte*, where spaces are filled with the shouts of *piqueteros* (picketers) at public protests, the noise of helicopters flying over, the loud discussions of neighbours during the protests, and the distant sound of gunshots. The city in *Un día de suerte* is a city under siege due to events such as the electricity shortage that took place in the southern neighbourhoods of Buenos Aires the year the movie was shot.

The city and its daily practices – work, entertainment, drug use – simultaneously welcome and expel passers-by. The night shops, hotels, and open sport courts are places where young people go to make out or exchange products. Those places delineate or map the night city, the city of transgressions, where creatures wander without making any substantial or lasting connections with each other. The dialogue between Reny and Andrés in a pizza parlour that could be on Lavalle Street or anywhere downtown is a good example. They talk about where they are from and say, "*Estamos viajando a la velocidad de la luz*" (We are travelling at the speed of light). Later, while eating a piece of pizza, they add, "*La pizzería es una nave espacial*" (The pizza place is our space-ship), and "*Lavalle es la galaxia de al lado*" (Lavalle is the galaxy next to ours). *Vagón Fumador* constructs a city with fragments that reflect individuals, streets, lights, mirrors, and creatures that are duplicated in other shop windows. There is no centre, no core, no map; the city is built fragmentarily, producing a constant imaginary exchange with its inhabitants. The games played at night establish an ironic relationship with the ones that the young people on roller skates play around the monument of *El Libertador*, a memorial built in honour of the national hero, José de San Martín. Another ironic reference to the value of monuments that are meant to represent the nation is found in a scene with Elsa and her friends. They are playing around monuments and one of them starts imitating the voice of the pope (or an Italian priest more generally) reading a text about Italy. In some way, these jocular spatial movements demystify the importance of such authoritative figures as San Martín, the "Father of the Land," and the pope.

Urban games and fragmentary realities applicable to First World countries and their alienating relationship with the computer universe are also suggested in other scenes in *Vagón Fumador*. Cash machines and cell phones are signs of the city at night and seem to complement, as if they were a communication prosthesis, the silence imposed by the lack of direct communication among the people who circulate through it. The borders between centre and periphery dissolve. In *Un día de suerte*, a group of young people go to smoke marihuana in a peripheral field where they imagine cows that later become imaginary bridges to downtown, since the cows reappear walking through the streets of a peripheral neighbourhood in Buenos Aires.

Drug dealers, both with their bodies and through their illegal exchanges, also alter the borders of the diverse peripheral villages (*barrios*), stretching the frontier of legal activities into illegal practices and transforming accepted actions into forbidden ones. Elsa and her friends work in the city in "funky" positions such as pamphleteers, pollsters, or promoters of valueless products for social consumption; in their free time, they sell merchandise consisting of goods smuggled by a network of young people. These youth have discovered smuggling as a way of surviving, but this is the case in the margins of all big cities such as Buenos Aires, creating a hidden and illegal trend that must be recognized. Regarding this issue, Marc Hatzfeld, in his analysis of the French neighbourhoods and peripheries, explains,

> The neighbourhoods – or the neighbourhood clans – each offer different services so that in that universe – a parallel one, to a certain degree, but tolerated by most – the informed clientele knows where to go and from whom to buy a product or service. Garages, apartments or parking lots serve as workshops, the tontine system often works as pirate banks

and hidden hierarchies at the network level come up to the surface. (2007: 59)[9]

Buenos Aires is the space where all the protagonists' vital transactions take place. The interiors – of houses, bars, coffee shops – show a progressive decline in living conditions. None of the action in these films, however, is set in an interior. For most of the time, the characters cruise the city looking for something that seems lost or that cannot be found. In this way, we recognize both the streets of downtown and others that lie further from downtown and reach the peripheral neighbourhoods. Another category of the urban landscape to be considered is the category of "no-places" (*no-lugares*), emphasized in *Vagón Fumador* as alternative spaces where characters spend idle time or earn money through illicit sexual exchanges. In his anthropological reading of the city, Marc Augé defines these no-places as the contemporary spaces of circulation, distribution, and communication. Airports, gas stations, and big shopping malls are no-places, but cash machines and transportation ticket machines, which are mute in their dialogue with us and, in general, all networks, are also no-places that bring images or information to a particular group of individuals with the eventual help of satellites (Augé 1993: 28).

Much of the *diegesis* in *Vagón Fumador* occurs around cash machines, bars, candy stands, the corners of movie theatres, the roofs of skyscrapers, parks, and other areas passed through during the night. The camera is used in an attempt to capture the fragmentary quality of reality and emphasizes such mobility by cutting out heads, eyes, faces, and gestures. A poetic treatment of the night expresses the disorientation of characters in their search for clients or a group of friends. As Luciano Monteagudo writes in a review of this film,

> There is a very particular appropriation of the city in *Vagón Fumador*.... It is very unlikely that the elegant Plaza San Martín would be one of the sex-for-sale sites of Buenos Aires,

> but the film transforms it into the meeting place of Andrés and his friends and clients, a coven of taxi boys howling in front of the Círculo Militar building and around the monument of El Libertador San Martín. Such vampirization of the city – there is something deeply nocturnal in Chen's film – gives it a sense of strangeness. Accompanied by an excellent soundtrack by Edgardo Rudnitsky, the camera, as if it were mounted on Andrés' roller skates, goes through the streets in slow motion and stops to focus on the texture of a face or on the dynamics of a gesture, both able to enrich the neon landscape. (2002: 1)[10]

There are several places in the film that are void of life, such as the abandoned swimming pool where the characters swim and play in the water or the empty train car at the end of the film, which express the extreme loneliness in the characters' lives, the devastations they have suffered, and the futility of words. Andrés and Reny send cell messages and go to cash machines, and Reny's gaze is the complicit voyeuristic gaze of the audience during Andres' sex scenes. The no-place, therefore, is the space of others, but without their presence, the space is transformed into a spectacle, a spectacle in its own right trapped in words (Augé 1993: 2). That "other" (*otro*) of Augé is no longer the other of postcards or tourist advertisements, but that of the unemployed, the uprooted, the immigrant, the homeless, the orphan, all of them searching for a space in which to live and fulfill their desires.

We could easily extend this definition of no-place to the shop-window street where Paula, the protagonist in *Hoy y Mañana*, circulates. She is an actress, but she also plays another role – that of a prostitute – to earn money and pay her debts. Paula's performance is also set in some kind of shop-window that lies on the border with a no-place, since she stops being a subject to become an object of consumption, like Andrés, for a certain price in a strictly commercial transaction. This perennial interaction between the young protagonists and the city, however, presents a conflictive relation framed by the violence that crosses the city and its history. The violence of the site as it appears in these films is a sudden spot in the visual narrative that leaves a fading trace that is more difficult to define, for it forms layers of meaning within the opacity of the discourse. We can agree with Christian Leon's analysis of films by the Colombian director Víctor Gaviria in that the unsettling effect of some movies is linked to the traumatic encounter with the "real" (*lo real*). Understood in Lacanian terms,

> The real can be represented by the accidental, the little noise, that small piece of reality that confirms that we are not dreaming ... that reality is not insignificant since it makes us aware of another hidden reality behind the void that is in fact the representation. (Lacan 1999: 68)[11]

What wecall a spot is more precisely a hole, or a void. The selected movies are testimonies of such a spot or hole or void, pointing out both the lack and the presence of reality and constituting a form of violence in each of the addressed representations.

As I have suggested before, the type of violence found in the Argentine films analyzed in this essay is related to the historical events that occurred in the city during the economic crash of 2001 and which, though never part of the *diegesis* of these movies, certainly influence the ways the characters behave. The violence in these movies is found and expressed through the situations of the characters in the places where they move, and, in some cases, it does not have "words"; it is a silent state of violence crossing the protagonists' lives, as when Reny cuts her arm and finds herself alone in the bath without any kind of emotional support, or when Elsa's girlfriend attends a party on the terrace of the small studio where she lives and her boyfriend makes love to her without considering her desires, using her as an object to satisfy his own sexual needs.

The main characters in these films feel the consequences that social violence has upon their lives, and they cannot escape from them. For example, because Paula (the young protagonist of *Hoy y Mañana*) cannot find a job, pay the rent of her small studio, or borrow money from her father, she decides to go out and work as a streetwalker. She feels free to choose this action, but her choice is made in a state of desolation without any other means of support. She is telling the truth when she shouts, "I am not a whore!" (*¡No soy una puta!*), but she has to sell her body in order to pay the rent; she has to act, to play a "character." She engages in the only work she can find to provide a solution during a critical moment in her life.

Violence is reflected in the city because events leave their imprint on the social body. For example, the lack of employment in Argentine society is in truth a "political event," and it imposes its effects on the young protagonists' lives. When Elsa, the main character in *Un día de suerte*, is looking for a job to be able to save money to travel to Italy, *piqueteros* demonstrating in town form the background of her cruising through the streets of the city. This is due to the fact that:

> The newly impoverished sector's relationship to politics and collective action has also been transformed.... Then, following the events of December 2001, the impoverished middle class, no longer ashamed, took to the streets forming neighbourhood assemblies and pressure groups made up of people whose savings had been frozen and then devalued in the banks. (Grimson and Kessler 2005: 99)[12]

Watching these new films, the spectator is forced to analyze the relationship between the political context surrounding the main plots and the fates of the leading characters. These films show the devastation of society and its subsequent effects on individuals who appear unable to construct a future for themselves. The violence that the city produces in the lives of its citizens extends into other territories. In *Hoy y Mañana*'s final scene, Paula decides to end her service to a client who has already paid her. While they meet in the hotel room, the screen shows scenes of a wildlife documentary where a tiger is eating a small prey. The relationship between the scene displayed on the screen and the one that is happening inside the hotel room is made evident when Paula refuses to be subjected to anal penetration and shouts in despair, "I am not a whore!"[13]

If we question who these characters are and what kind of family surrounds them, we can easily surmise that they are orphans, that they have no family or home. The fall (or lack) of the father figure as a social and symbolic construct, along with the values that somehow sustained such construct, shows its devastating effects from the time of the economic collapse that Argentina suffered. It is one of the film's main projects to comment on the new relations within the family, whose body suffered the effects of the economic crisis. Among the three films selected for this analysis, a family appears only in *Un día de suerte*; it sustains a dialogue based on parameters that can be called a "family discourse." The family is organized similarly to that of many others that suddenly found themselves in a new situation: an unemployed father, a mother who cooks food to sell outside the house, and an anarchist grandfather who is still able to remember more hopeful times. Elsa shows her emotions, falls in love, wishes to travel and escape, and tries to garner the necessary money to fulfill her dreams. Walter, Elsa's boyfriend, is supportive of Elsa's desires, and he gives her part of the money she needs to travel. Elsa is the only protagonist whose character is built from the traces of political principles put forward by the older generation and who decides to travel abroad, undoing the route of her immigrant grandfather, in search of happiness. In this regard, she is the only protagonist who is able to follow a dream that will soon crumble as stardust. The Italian grandfather from *Un día de suerte* is the only one who establishes a connection with his grandchild. That connection reestablishes some kind of "geographical" balance with the story of the immigrant grandfather, an Italian anarchist who came to Argentina "to conquer America" (*hacer la América*); the Italian grandfather's territory is the space of evocation and political compromise whose political discourse contaminates, to a certain degree, Elsa's discourse, full of *aporias*.

The other characters, in *Vagón Fumador* and *Hoy y Mañana*, inhabit desolated areas where nobody helps anybody. In Paula's case, her distant father's refusal to help her puts her in a very difficult situation. In Reny's case, she explains, "There is no family; I was born from a jar, the result of a genetic experiment" (*No hay familia; nací de un tubo; soy el resultado de un experimento genético*), and when Andrés asks her, "What about the people from the band?" (*¿Y qué pasa con la gente de la banda?*), she answers, "Test tubes" (*Tubos de ensayo*). The lack of a genealogy and the absence of strong emotional ties show the fragmentation of the postmodern subject, thrown on the map of the city that has different desires for the inscription of bodies and fantasies.

Lost in the big city, lost in a net of social relations, lost in the centre of conflict, the characters of these films are like orphans in search of something that can give an answer to their despair and lack of hope, something "real," as in Reny's case. In some ways, and under different circumstances, these characters recreate the orphans from the novels written at the beginning of the twentieth century, looking for their identity and personal freedom outside of the family, which no longer functioned as a place of safety and truth. The leading characters in these three films have their freedom, but they cannot hold on to it due to the harsh economic environment and the lack of work and stability in their lives.

Gender issues are also very relevant in these characters' behaviour. Female protagonists in these movies are no longer a projection of masculine desire, and they are no longer classified in the binary categories of saint or whore, angel or demon. Instead, women have become the despicable symbol of a decomposing social universe where gender polarities have disappeared, and the street experience dislocates the traditional places linked to feminine identity. Gender roles have been deconstructed in the representation of female subjects. Male figures are necessary but at the same time dispensable. While female bodies function as merchandise that is sold or bought to get money, some male characters are the objects of similar transactions. Each person's price must be known to be able to be enjoyed, and, therefore, according to Andrés, the taxi boy in *Vagón Fumador*, everybody must have a price. On the other hand, Reny, the female protagonist, ignores her price and her relationships with other people and responds to her desire to feel something "real" in her life. Although she refuses to fall in love, she wants to feel; she is searching for something to fill the void in her life.

The young protagonists of the selected films refuse to get emotionally involved with other people, to feel emotions, or to talk about them; that is why laughter and crying are colloquial formulas heard as a form of proto-language.[14] There is no love discourse, nor a discourse about the possibility of love. The furthest the characters go is to offer their bodies to obtain some benefit impossible to reach in any other way. Paula's past methods of getting money to pay her rent are failures; Elsa's trip to Italy is a failure since she does not find the Italian man she met in Argentina; Remy's casual encounters with Andrés are failures because they never develop into a substantial relationship. Grief is the machinery that establishes loneliness in the centre of each scenario, reintroducing some formal aspects that resemble the French Nouvelle Vague of the fifties or some of the protagonists from Argentine films of the sixties, captured in a zone of existential doubts. It should be mentioned that the New Argentine Cinema has often been compared to Italian Neorrealism and the Nouvelle Vague because of its formal characteristics.[15]

These young protagonists desire, in some way, to go far away, and, following their desire, they experiment with limits that were not established in the process of constructing their social ties. If they need to eat and they have no money, they steal from the supermarket or prostitute themselves. They do not establish "relationships." There is no language to speak of pain, love, needs, reality, or of the rage that daily failures provoke in their lives.[16]

Some of the characters, however, evidence a progressive growth in their capacity to feel as their story unfolds and they become aware of their present situation. Paula cries in front of the river after the humiliations that she suffered as a streetwalker; she cries as she could not cry before. She needed to hit bottom, falling to the most degrading situation for a woman, in order to let herself cry for the absence of support and love in her life. In the end, she does not fully accept the contract implied by any commercial or merchandise exchange: she is not a whore, but an actress who plays a whore to survive. Paula has not learned what L. Carpenter emphasizes as an important exchange between the prostitute and the client when she explains,

> The prostitute and the client bring to the prostitution contract certain expectations about the mechanics of the contract and the tasks to be performed. They bring with them their relation to their bodies and to the bodies of the other – each constrained by a historical configuration in and throughout modern liberal democracies. (2000: 112)

Although Paula ignores the contract and does not follow the rules of the game, she still wants her client's money. An example of this is the scene with Raul: the Spaniard pays her twice her normal fee for her to stay the night with him, yet Paula tries to leave the house once they finish having sex.

Not all the characters reach this level of awareness. Elsa ends up throwing a coin into the Trevi Fountain, leaving to chance and fate all that she cannot predict will happen in her life. Andrés continues moving on his roller skates, selling himself to clients. Reny, in a near suicide attempt, sees her own blood in the bathtub of her house. Outside, the city stretches its tentacles "like a monster" (*como un monstruo*), as impassive as the creatures that move around in this dark era of loneliness. There is no good or evil because there is no prohibition or law, nor any father figure or authority. The characters' nature, their urban strolling, has as its main trait a lack of scruples in the face of daily bad actions. Stealing, exchanging sex for money, dealing or using drugs, and working degrading jobs are all part of a survival strategy that seems to give meaning to their lives.[17]

As a conclusion, we could say that this kind of cinema creates an aesthetic of neglect that explores the disenchanted lives of the individuals who were pushed to the margins of social institutions and political discourses and who were excluded from the progressive and mobilizing space of the community or social group. As a consequence, they move alone, hopeless and confused, day and night, searching for some kind of redemption, wandering in the city, surrounded by local conflicts and daily violence. They exhibit in their itineraries a clear representation of the interaction between space and subjects in the context of social and political violence.

WORKS CITED

Aguilar, Gonzalo. 2001. "Renuncia y libertad: Sobre una película de Lisandro Alonso." *Mil Palabras. Letras y Artes en Revista* 2: 11–13.

Aguilar, Roberto. 2000. "La ciudad, esa cloaca inmunda." *El Comercio* (Quito), December 29.

Augé, Marc. 1993. "Espacio y alteridad." *Revista de Occidente* 140: 13–34.

Barky, Sandra Lee. 1990. *Femininity and Domination: Studies in the Phenomenology of Oppression*. New York: Routledge.

Baudrillard, Jean. 2000. "Violencia descarnada. El odio." In *Pantalla total*, 107–11. Barcelona: Anagrama.

Bernardes, Horacio, Diego Lerer, and Sergio Wolf, eds. 2001. *Nuevo cine argentino: Temas, autores y estilos de una renovación*. Buenos Aires: Fipresci Argentina.

Braidotti, Rosi. 2000. *Sujetos nómades*. Buenos Aires: Paidós.

Casey, Edward S. 1996. "How to get from space to place in a fairly short stretch of time: Phenomenological prolegomena." In *Senses of Place*, ed. Steven Feld and Keith H. Basso, 13–52. Santa Fe, New Mexico: School of American Research Advanced Seminar Series.

Careaga, Gabriel. 1981. *Erotismo, violencia y política en el cine*. México: Joaquín Mortiz.

Carpenter, Belinda J. 2000. *Re-thinking Prostitution: Feminism, Sex and the Self*. New York: Peter Lang.

Filc, Judith. 2003. "Textos y fronteras urbanas: Palabra e identidad en la Buenos Aires contemporánea." *Revista Iberoamericana* 69, no. 202: 183–84.

García Canclini, Néstor. 1999. *Imaginarios urbanos*. Buenos Aires: EUDEBA.

Grimson, Alejandro, and Gabriel Kessler. 2005. *On Argentina and the Southern Cone: Neoliberalism and National Imaginations.* New York: Routledge.
Grosz, Elizabeth. 1999. "Bodies-Cities." In *Feminist Theory and the Body: A Reader*, ed. Janet Price and Margrit Shildrick, 381–87. New York: Routledge.
Hatzfeld, Marc. 2007. *La cultura de los suburbios.* Barcelona: Laertes.
Lacan, Jacques. 1999. *Seminario II. Cuatro conceptos fundamentales del psicoanálisis.* Buenos Aires: Paidós.
León, Christian. 2005. *El cine de la marginalidad. Realismo sucio y violencia urbana.* Quito: University Andina Simón Bolívar, Ediciones Abya-Yala y Corporación Editora Nacional.
Lyotard, Jean-François. 1987. *La condición postmoderna.* Madrid: Cátedra.
Monteagudo, Luciano. 2002. "El sexo en la vidriera de los cajeros." *Espectáculos* (13 June):12. http://www.pagina12.com.ar/imprimir/diario/espectaculos/6-6214-2002-06-13.html (accessed July 2007).
Seijas, Rodrigo. 2001. "Un día de suerte." http://cineismo.com/criticas/un-dia-de-suerte-htm (accessed July 2007).
Wolf, Sergio. 2001. "The aesthetics of the new Argentine cinema: The map is the territory." In *Nuevo cine argentino: Temas, autores y estilos de una renovación*, ed. Horacio Bernardes, Diego Lerer, and Sergio Wolf, 29–43. Buenos Aires: Fipresci Argentina.

FILMS

Hoy y mañana (*Today and Tomorrow*). Directed by Alejandro Chomsky. Aldebaran Films, 2004.

Un día de suerte (*A Lucky Day*). Directed by Sandra Gugliotta. Barakacine producciones, 2002.

Vagón fumador (*Smokers Only*). Directed by Verónica Chen. Ezeiza Films, 2001.

NOTES

1 All translations are mine unless reference is made to a published translation.

2 *Un día de suerte* (*A Lucky Day*, 2002) is an Argentine and Italian film directed by Sandra Gugliotta. It was her first feature film. In Argentina, it is also known as *Lo que buscas es amor*. The main star is Valentina Bassi, as Elsa. The context of this docudrama is the economic turmoil and unemployment among the young in Argentina between 1999 and 2002. The film won two awards at the Berlin International Film Festival: The Caligari Film Award and the Don Quixote Award. The story takes place over twenty days during the summer of 1999, when people in the south of the city suffered extended power outages. These outages provoked protests in the streets of Buenos Aires, and the film includes documentary-like scenes of the 2000 riots that seem as though they were shot by a handheld camera.

3 *Vagón Fumador* (*Smokers Only*, 2001) is the first movie directed by Verónica Chen; it lasts ninety-one minutes and the main stars are Cecilia Bengolea (Reny) and Leonardo Brezicki (Andrés) playing a couple who wander through the streets of Buenos Aires trying to find a goal for their lives.

4 *Hoy y mañana* (*Today and Tomorrow*, 2003) features a protagonist named Paula (Antonella Costa) who is trapped in an ever-present cycle of unpaid bills and debts. In order to pay these bills and debts, she calls a friend who mentors her in a new way to make money – streetwalking. The two set out to get Paula's rent money and meet a variety of clients during the night, affording all kinds of unpleasant experiences.

5 According to Aguilar, there is a common setting in several films belonging to this new trend of the nineties: "The settings: the stinking and crowded streets in large Latin American cities, the neighbourhoods that do not appear in tourist flyers, refuge for the wretched and the exiled. The characters: stray youth, dragged along by the urban tide, irredeemably unemployed people who try to survive day by day, hour by hour, living on the fringes of the law" (2000: C14) (Los escenarios: las calles, malolientes y hacinadas de las grandes ciudades latinoamericanas, los barrios que no figuran en los folletos de promoción turística, refugio de miserables y proscritos. Los personajes: jóvenes callejeros arrastrados por esa marea urbana, desempleados irredentos tratando de sobrevivir al día, a la hora, en los límites de la legalidad.)

6 The name "dirty realism" is borrowed from literature. It was used to classify a type of narrative cultivated originally by Raymond Carver and Charles Bukowski.

7 "Frente a la actual pérdida de legitimidad de la sociedad letrada que sostiene la identidad nacional, elabora códigos mestizos que reincorporan elementos de la cultura global de occidente y

de los imaginarios locales. Muestra la cultura callejera como un espacio híbrido donde confluye el efecto desterritorializador del imaginario mediático y la reterritorialización por el mundo marginal a partir de sus códigos subalternos."

8   "La ciudad es un monstruo, te fuerza a comprar cosas, a consumir… ellos no ven al monstruo, la brutalidad, en pedazos, parte por parte."

9   "Los barrios o los clanes de barrio ofrecen, cada cual, especialidades diversas, de modo que, en ese universo un tanto paralelo pero tolerado en gran medida, la clientela enterada sabe adónde dirigirse y a quién para tal producto o servicios. Garajes, apartamentos o parking sirven de talleres, el sistema de tontine hace a menudo de banca pirata y salen de las sombras jerarquías ocultas al nivel de redes."

10 "Hay una apropiación de la ciudad que es muy particular en *Vagón Fumador*…. Difícilmente la elegante Plaza San Martín sea parte del circuito de oferta sexual de Buenos Aires, pero el film la convierte en el lugar de reunión de Andrés y de sus amigos y clientes, un aquelarre de taxi-boys aullando frente al Círculo Militar y alrededor del Monumento al Libertador. Esa vampirización de la ciudad (hay algo profundamente nocturno en el film de Chen) le da un valor de extrañamiento…. Con el acompañamiento de un excelente diseño sonoro de Edgardo Rudnitsky, la cámara – como si se hubiera subido a los rollers de Andrés – va atravesando en ralenti las calles y se detiene en la textura de un rostro o en la dinámica de un gesto, capaces de enriquecer el paisaje de neón."

11 "Lo real puede representarse por el accidente, el ruidito, ese poco-de-realidad que da fe de que no soñamos … esa realidad no es poca cosa, pues nos despierta a otra realidad escondida tras la falta de lo que hace las veces de representación."

12 Judith Filc says the following, referring to the consequences of Menem's politics on Argentine society: "These transformations had as a consequence the fragmentation of the middle class (with the subsequent division between winners and losers) and the identity crisis of the so-called 'new poor.' The identity crisis transcended class differences as well. The precariousness of work conditions affected the construction of identity in the popular sectors, cemented in the past in the rights acquired during the first presidency of Perón. The loss of social rights that in Argentina were traditionally associated with the condition of the worker, the disappearance of gathering spaces linked to the workplace, and the loss of representativeness of traditional institutions are all phenomena that came together to contribute to the weakening of social ties, as described by several authors" (183–84). (Estas transformaciones tuvieron como consecuencia la fragmentación de las clases medias [con la división consiguiente en 'ganadores' y 'perdedores'] y con la crisis de identidad consiguiente para los llamados 'nuevos pobres'. Esta crisis identitaria, asimismo, atravesó

las diferencias de clase. La precarización laboral afectó la construcción de identidad en los sectores populares, cimentada en el pasado en los derechos adquiridos durante el primer gobierno de Perón. La pérdida de los derechos sociales que en la Argentina habían estado asociados tradicionalmente a la condición del 'trabajador', la desaparición de espacios de asociación ligados al lugar de trabajo, la pérdida de representatividad de las instituciones tradicionales, todos estos fenómenos se conjugaron para llevar a lo que los diversos autores describen como el debilitamiento del lazo social.)

13 Jean Baudrillard's explanation of at least two kinds of violence serves to corroborate this interpretation of the scene and explain part of the difference: "Traditional violence is much more enthusiastic and is related to ritual sacrifices. The violence of today is simulated, since it emerges not from passion or instinct, but from the screen and the media that pretend to record and broadcast it. In fact, they precede such violence and stimulate it" (Baudrillard 2000: 107). (La violencia tradicional es mucho más entusiasta y se halla vinculada a los sacrificios rituales. La nuestra es una violencia simulada en el sentido en que, más que de la pasión o del instinto, surge de la pantalla y en los media que fingen grabarla y difundirla, pero que en realidad la preceden y la estimulan.) However, there is another kind of violence beyond the virtual one, which applies perfectly to part of the discursive strategy of the New Latin American Cinema and the New Argentine Cinema in particular. In Baudrillard's words, "We can distinguish a primary form of violence: aggression, oppression, violation, the relationship between forces, humiliation, plundering, the unilateral violence of the strongest. This violence can be responded to with a contradictory violence: historical, critical, negative violence…. These are forms of a particular violence, with a beginning and an end, whose causes and effects can be placed and correspond to something transcendent, be it power, history or meaning" (2000: 108). (Podemos distinguir una forma primaria de violencia: la de la agresión, la opresión, la violación, la relación de fuerzas, la humillación, la expoliación, la violencia unilateral del más fuerte. A la cual puede responderse con una violencia contradictoria: violencia histórica, violencia crítica, violencia de lo negativo…. Son éstas, formas de una violencia determinada, con un origen y un final, cuyas causas y efectos son localizables y corresponden a una trascendencia, ya sea del poder, de la historia o del sentido.) Good examples of this type of violence in Latin American films are *Amores Perros*, *La vendedora de rosas*, *Rodrigo D*, *Mundo Grúa*, *Bolivia*, *El cielito*, and *El bonaerense*.

14 Regarding the dialogue exchange among the characters in *Un día de suerte*, Rodrigo Seijas (2001) believes the following: "The moments of routine and relaxing among friends are the most poignant ones: the nonsensical conversations and jokes, the joint

smoking, the intimate scenes between Mirás and Bassi (regardless of the fact that they attract female and male audiences, respectively). On the other hand, the parts charged with ideology are reminiscent of the old haranguing vices of Argentine cinema" (1). (Son los momentos de rutina y aletargamiento entre amigos los que adquieren mayor vuelo en este film: las conversaciones y bromas sin sentido alguno, la fumata de porros, las escenas íntimas entre Mirás y Bassi (más allá de que los dos atraen al público femenino y masculino respectivamente). En cambio, los tramos con marcada "carga ideológica" recuerdan los antiguos vicios declamatorios del cine argentino.)

15 Gonzalo Aguilar explains, "In the movies, on the contrary, Neorealism not only opposed a series of movies that were too similar to the theatre and too distant from daily life, but also showed the erratic and disjointed nature of events, their resistance to be inscribed within preconceived schemas. A *register* of surfaces (streets, gestures, bodies, movements) in a time when ruination did not allow any conventional or comforting realism" (2001: 12–13). (En el cine, en cambio, el neorrealismo no sólo se opuso a una serie de películas que se parecían demasiado al teatro o que se alejaban de la vida cotidiana, sino que vino a mostrar el carácter inconexo y errático del acontecimiento, su resistencia a ser inscripto en esquemas preconcebidos. Un *registro* de las superficies [las calles, los gestos, los cuerpos, los desplazamientos] en un momento en que las ruinas no autorizaban ningún realismo convencional o consolatorio.)

16 Hatzfeld, in his analysis of the culture of poverty, reminds us, "The retail sale of *cannabis* and the occasional prostitution of poor people are unfortunate resources, but partially accepted because they are dictated by the brass law of survival" (2007: 61). (El comercio minorista de *cannabis*, la prostitución ocasional de personas pobres es un recurso ingrato, pero parcialmente asumido porque así lo dicta la ley de bronce de la supervivencia).

17 For Rosi Braidotti, "The nomad does not only represent the lack of a home or compulsive displacement; it is more a figurative way to refer to the kind of person who has renounced any idea of or desire for established patterns. This figuration expresses the desire of an identity made out of transitions" (2000: 58). (El nómade no representa solamente la falta de un hogar ni el desplazamiento compulsivo; es más bien una figuración del tipo de sujeto que ha renunciado a toda idea, deseo de lo establecido. Esta figuración expresa el deseo de una identidad hecha de transiciones.)

Projecting Buenos Aires Back to the Future: Violence in Argentine Post-Dictatorship Science Fiction Film

VICTORIA RUÉTALO

UNIVERSITY OF ALBERTA

While having antecedents in the fantastic stories of Jorge Luis Borges and Adolfo Bioy Casares, no work contributed more to the development of science fiction in Argentina than the 1950s comic *The Eternaut* (*El eternauta*), the adventures of an eternal traveller.[1] Cartoon images of non-humans ("Cascarudos," "Manos," and "hombres-robots," with "Ellos" controlling the overall attack) invading and vacating the busy streets of Buenos Aires foretold the harsh reality suffered by the nation during the Dirty War (1976–83). As equally shocking as the prediction of the horrors to come was the 1976 disappearance of *The Eternaut*'s author, Héctor German Oesterheld, who was part of the leftist guerrilla group the Montoneros. In the case of *The Eternaut*, science fiction not only represented Argentina's gruesome present and future but ironically projected the very means that would end the author's own life. After the fall of the dictatorship in 1983, as Argentina entered its neoliberal phase, filmmakers began to reclaim the science fiction genre to delve into questions about violence in the recent past, immediate present, and distant future of the nation. Science fiction was historically atypical in Argentine cinema, with the notable exceptions of Hugo Santiago's 1969 film *Invasion* (*Invasión*), co-scripted by Borges, Bioy Casares, and Santiago himself, and two other productions in Emilio Vieyra's series of exploitation films: *Stay Tuned for Terror* (*Extraña invasión*, 1965), a U.S.-funded project made for a foreign audience and shot on location in Buenos Aires in English, and *La venganza del sexo* (1967), re-released as *The Curious Dr. Hump* (1971), becoming Vieyra's most popular film abroad with added sexual extras in the later U.S. version. In these early examples, the culprits of the violent and overpowering invasions were outsiders who wanted to take control of the cities: Buenos Aires and the fictional Aquilea (although impossible to not visually identify it with the port city).

After re-democratization, an unprecedented number of futuristic productions surfaced on the Argentine film scene: *Man Facing Southeast* (*Hombre mirando al sudeste*, 1987), *Times to Come* (*Lo que vendrá*, 1988), *Moebius* (1996), and most recently, perhaps the most faithful to genre specifications, *Sleepwalker* (*La sonámbula*, 1998) and *Condor Crux* (*Cóndor Crux, la leyenda*, 2000), a children's science fiction animation. What all of these films have in common is the sudden shift from a plot about the invasion of alien outsiders on the city to one where the threat derives from within medical, political, or social institutions that were meant to safeguard, protect, or benefit society. This threat, which I argue implies a new authoritarian violence propelled by neoliberal measures, perpetuates state violence from the past and signals a corrupt and conspiratorial system harboured from within new power structures. In all of these recent science fiction films, and particularly in *Moebius*, *Condor Crux*, and

Sleepwalker (all completed near the end of Carlos Menem's term), the city, Buenos Aires (Darwin), can be read as a site and network of a post-dictatorship violence, a period marked by neoliberal politics of the state and a policy of forgetting the past violence to leap into the globalized future (Ludmer 1994: 7). In this article I will argue that science fiction films in Argentina in the 1990s represent an apocalyptic world of social inequalities and vestiges of authoritarianism that reflect both directly and indirectly the present neoliberal and globalized nation.

The dictatorship in Argentina insisted on constructing a viable and prosperous nation vis-à-vis its application of neoliberal economic policies. Following re-democratization and the economically volatile administration of Raul Alfonsín (1983–89), Argentina's national political arena was dominated by the popular Peronist leader Carlos Saúl Menem (1989–99). With politics no longer ideologically motivated but economically inclined, Menem violated cherished Peronist welfare state ideals by continuing to implement harsh neoliberal policies of cutbacks and privatization, a project that had began during the dictatorship years. Internationally, Menem promoted the development of "Mercosur" or the "Common Market of the South," a trade partnership between Argentina, Brazil, Uruguay, and Paraguay. The volume of trade and investment between the four countries grew rapidly during the 1990s. These neoliberal policies served to stabilize Argentina's rampant inflation and brought with it unprecedented economic growth for certain sectors. However, essentially these policies would bring about economic slowdowns in 1994 and 1998, culminating in the crisis of 2001 (see Rock 2002: 54–86). Although the films discussed here were made prior to this final crisis in 2001, they "anticipate" (a term detailed by literature critic Fernando Reati in his book about dystopic novels published between 1985 and 1999) a future collapse (2006: 14–15).

Ironically, when it came to the film industry, this laissez-faire shift from public to private would be somewhat masked but becomes rather clear in the examples discussed here. According to Tamara Falicov during this period, "state intervention was utilized in the private interest while it purported to be acting solely in the public interest" (2007: 94). Paradoxically, under Menem, the industry was aided by policies that would actually boost funding to film production through taxes, laws, and decrees. All of these measures helped to strengthen the industry. Yet, the increase in funding had made access to it for filmmakers more difficult as these new funds were earmarked for "blockbuster" films that would draw spectators to the cinema (Falicov 2007: 75–113). In the case of the science fiction films produced during this period of Menem's administration, only *Sleepwalker* received an *opera prima* prize from the state supported Instituto Nacional de Artes Audiovisuales (INCAA) to help in its production. *Condor Crux* was a co-production between Spain and Argentina funded through private companies Patagonik Film Group (partly owned by Channel 13 or Artear [Grupo Clarín] and by Buena Vista International, or Walt Disney), and Spanish-based Tornasol Films. *Moebius* was funded entirely by the Fundación Universidad del Cine; the first feature-length film produced by this private university, which has since funded a new film every two years. Of the three examples, the first two are more in line with the politics of the "blockbuster" with high production values as described by Falicov. *Condor Crux* was produced by the same company that funded the "blockbusters" (that Falicov speaks of), while *Sleepwalker* was not privy to such support it did cost a total of $2.5 million ("*La sonámbula*"), a budget equal to that of *Comodines* (Jorge Nisco and Daniel Barone, 1997), another example that Falicov draws from (2007: 102). The case of *Moebius* is quite different: as a film entirely made by students, with little technological effects, the production cost of $250,000 ("*Vanished*") would yield a very different product from the other two "blockbusters." All three are clear examples of the shift from state-sponsored public funds to private film funding as little state support aided each one. These films do not only speak of the current problems facing the nation, as will be argued in this article; moreover, they themselves are examples of the shift taking place across different aspects of society. Furthermore, one wonders whether the funding mechanisms producing each film will in the end affect the ways that the present, past, and future are represented. Only a detailed analysis will help to shed more light on this question.

All three films were produced during the effervescence of these globalization policies. For some in Argentina, globalization meant economic stability like never before, meanwhile for others it brought several negative features. According to one study, of Argentina's population of 37 million people, 52 per cent (19 million people) were living below the official poverty line, while 20 per cent (7.5 million) could no longer afford sufficient food (Rock 2002: 56). On the other hand, these films address, not only the economic burden of globalization, but also the interrelation between the economic, political, and social reality of the nation. On the political front, Menem implemented policies that would change the nation's confrontation with the past. Menem's predecessor, Raul Alfonsín, had set out to prosecute officers responsible for violating human rights during the dictatorship, although pressure forced him to introduce a cut-off date for further prosecutions. Following his victory, in October 1989, Menem issued several rounds of pardons in favour of former leaders of the military government, eliminating possibilities for further prosecutions. In the wake of these disappointing policies for those who had hoped for justice for the crimes committed, many films, including the ones discussed here, sought to deal with what this official attempt to "forget" meant to the still scarred nation.

In her analysis of fantastic literature, Rosemary Jackson recognizes the fantastic's connection to society: "The fantastic traces the unsaid and the unseen of culture: that which has been silenced, made invisible, covered over and made 'absent'" (Jackson 1981: 4). As a category, the fantastic has the ability to reproduce a new reality that makes the reader question his/her own context. For J.P. Telotte, Jackson's description of the fantastic in literature is useful for thinking about the science fiction film genre because it demonstrates the difficulties of generic demarcation, and as science fiction is a form that encompasses many film types that share certain characteristics, the category of fantasy gives it more flexibility (Telotte 2001: 31). Since questions about generic definition are complex, it is not my intention to engage in a detailed discussion about these specifics; instead, through an analysis of these films, these categories will self-define. Telotte's and Jackson's descriptions of both science fiction and fantasy, nonetheless, are a key starting point from which to visualize the "invisible" and "absent," the most obvious being violence. In a discussion about *Man Facing Southeast*, a "magical realist science fiction film," film critic Michael Chanan applauds the lack of indulgence in "gratuitous violence and [exclaims] the sex is much more tasteful" than Hollywood (Chanan). While violence may not be gratuitous, it is present nonetheless. The "absent" violence in these science fiction films is "seen" and "said" through the visualization of space, a space that invades the ruins of the past to construct a clear picture of the present apocalyptic situation in Argentina.

German thinker Walter Benjamin's concept of allegory furthermore allows us to think about these visual ruins as allegorical emblems. Benjamin reminds us: "In the process of decay, and in it alone, the events of history shrivel up and become absorbed in the [current] setting" (1977: 179). These science fiction films are allegories of ruined cities that will always be referring to the past and present. "In allegory the observer is confronted with the 'facies hippocratica' of history as a petrified, primordial landscape, everything about history that, from the very beginning, has been untimely, sorrowful, and unsuccessful" (Benjamin 1977: 166). By insisting that death and mourning are what lie at the origin of allegory, Benjamin's work provides for literary scholar Idelber Avelar a way of thinking about post-dictatorship ruins. Avelar suggests that, symptomatically, some of the literature produced in and after the dictatorships in South America work through the fragments and ruins of the present as a way of mourning the trauma of the past (1999: 10). Consequently, those expressions trigger untimely eruptions of the past, ones constantly being erased through commodification of society that purposefully negates memory (Avelar 1999: 2). In the science fiction films produced during the Menem administration (*Sleepwalker*, *Moebius*, and *Condor Crux*), place is not neutral, making visible the "unsaid" and "unseen" of this period. Functioning beyond a pure spectacle, the mise-en-scène in these films is a site/sight of meaning that comments on the current situation in Buenos Aires and the nation. While embedded within the global infrastructure highlighted by the film's spatial constructions, these imagined filmic cities prove unable to embrace the global due to the repression of the traumatic past and offer different solutions for ways of dealing with this past. The repressed social unconscious finally resurfaces through the dystopia envisioned in *Sleepwalker, Condor Crux,* and *Moebius*. As one of the characters of the Hugo Santiago 1969 film *Invasion* observes: "A city is much more than its inhabitants."[2] These three films will spatialize the city's immediate struggle between local and global forces by utilizing science fiction to project Buenos Aires into its spatial configuration in order to expose the mourning effects of an unburied and violent past, and thereby leave questions of the "unseen" or "unheard" state violence from the past that continues in the present as a privatized violence.

In *Sleepwalker*, the once mythical port city of Buenos Aires, model of Latin American modernity and development with its effortless flows of ideas, people, and products, is a city under tyrannical chains. Within the walls of Buenos Aires, a catastrophic silent chemical accident erases the memory of 300,000 people. In the wake of the tragedy, the state marshals the rehabilitation of its citizens back into their forgotten daily routines. Reinserted into unfamiliar work and family environments, the amnesia-stricken victims find it difficult to accept the memories supplied to them by the state. Some find solace in the belief in Gauna, a resistance leader who calls out and encourages the affected to: "Awaken." Gauna, whose name is borrowed from one of Bioy Casares's heroes, continues his plea as he instructs his followers: "Fear is the enemy. Leave. Come to me." A year and a half after the explosion, a woman named Eva appears from nowhere. Her special abilities to foretell events in the future and remember elements of a literally colourful past, images that surpass others in quality and quantity and the capacity of available technology, astounds the rehabilitating doctor who has access to the images she produces in her dreams and memories. These images are in colour;

meanwhile, the present of the film (year 2010) is shot in black and white. Eva will become the paradigmatic saviour who will lead all of the citizens towards Gauna and liberate them from this cyberpunk futuristic black and white Buenos Aires.

Similarly, in *Condor Crux*, an animated film, Phizar reigns over the fictional River Plate city of Darwin in the year 2068. Although a concocted city, Darwin contains specific references to Buenos Aires through the filmic clichéd image of the Obelisk and the distinctive accents and lunfardesque expressions of its characters. By recontextualizing the city into Darwin, the film emphasizes the monstrous current state of the city because of the familiar aspects that still remain (Reati 2006: 124). Under the Gloria Mundi Corporation, the people of Darwin are led to believe that a Great War has obliterated the entire world, except for Darwin, which remained protected within an enclosed dome. Kept in the dark and insulated from the rest of the world, Darwin's population justifies its own isolation by accepting the extinction of surrounding societies. Liberation can only be achieved by establishing links between the outside and Darwin's citizens. Dr. Crux, the resistance leader, hopes to reconnect the satellite and finally open lines of communication severed by the dictator Phizar. Captain Crux, son of Dr. Crux, will join the resistance movement, help to destroy the information lapse, and eventually free the metropolis by breaking through the dome and opening Darwin to the world, a truly globalized world.

The distant futuristic depictions in *Sleepwalker* and *Condor Crux* become an imprecise present/future in *Moebius, Times to Come*, and *Man Facing Southeast*. The science fiction in these films is more subtle and relates to the fantastic elements inserted in the plot. Yet, as I will demonstrate through an analysis of *Moebius*, there are clear characteristics that incorporate these films into the science fiction genre. In *Moebius*, most of the film takes place underground as topologist Daniel Pratt (a clear allusion to Italian comic book artist Hugo Pratt who lived in Buenos Aires for ten years and worked with Oesterheld and others) attempts to unravel the mystery of a lost train that has suddenly disappeared. The plot, loosely based on A.J. Deutsche's short story "A Subway Named Möbius" (1950) about the Boston subway system, has been readapted to Buenos Aires and the historical references that this implies. The allegory of the dictatorship and the current (1996) climate in Argentina is clear in this version where thirty people disappear while travelling the labyrinthine tunnels of the city's complex metro structure. Topology, a fascination for the analysis of the surface, will uncover the mystery of the old and modern subway system built in Buenos Aires in 1913. Subways as symbols of modernization in cities can also be read as allegorical structures for the contradictions of that same modernity. In the film, Pratt needs to solve the mysteries of undetected trains appearing when they are not supposed to, of lane changes even when they are not ordered, and of a lost train that he must explain to the authorities. The authorities (General Director, Chief Engineer, Representative of the Mayor, and a Doctor from the Military Hospital) want 'real' answers to the mystery and will settle for nothing less.

VISIONS OF DYSTOPIC CITIES

In *Postales del porvenir*, Fernando Reati examines a corpus of apocalyptic novels published between 1985 and 1999 to argue that these futuristic imaginaries reflect a critique of the present state of the nation under neoliberalism and globalization (2006: 19). Reati dedicates one section of the book to the depiction of the city because "in its materiality and its symbolism, each city constitutes a text that one can read" (Reati 2006: 88).[3] Reati ponders important questions that we should likewise consider: "What did neoliberalism inscribe in the pages of that text[?] How did that new vocabulary translate into the collective imaginary[?]"(2006: 88).[4]

Similar to the framework in Fritz Lang's classic *Metropolis* (1927), *Sleepwalker* is spatially divided into two vertical levels: the upper and lower cities. The upper city is picture perfect: constant shots of the city with its aerial thoroughfares and bridges intertwining between aspiring vertical, lofty, and modern architecture. Although austere, staunch, and clean in its ideal, unused, and empty state, the only proof that this sector is inhabited by citizens are the flickering lights that change with the daily patterns of its residents. Below this beautifully modern landscape lies garbage, piled up as a sign of the waste of the upper city. The austere desolate streets and roadways of the upper city contrast with the overcrowded interior spaces: buildings, nightclubs, and the underground subway, the only option for movement for the people. "Moving through the city is not easy," as one character notes. Both Eva and Kluge travel underground in the subway, full of alienated people who do not interact with one another. For example, in one shot Eva appears in the subway through the narrow door of the car cut off from the rest of the scene, leaving the spectator with the desire to see the whole scene beyond what is framed. Publicly nobody speaks to each other; conversations only happen inside buildings; that is to say, in private spaces where even the authenticity of such words is questionable as family members do not even remember each other. On the streets, at the base or pedestrian level, the only people roaming are graffiti artists and Gauna supporters attempting to propagate their anti-government message. Space here is clearly demarcated between upper and lower city. Streets are empty and the characters are locked within their own private orbits; individualized traumas overwhelm the public and social worlds of the film. The physical environment of *Sleepwalker* is always already marked by melancholy and mourning of the social body, traumas that the collective has been unsuccessful in burying. The city is an empty graveyard that hints at the past violence, but in this future dystopic Buenos Aires, the strong state has relegated everything to the private realm. This peek into Buenos Aires' future shows the city as an unliveable stagnant place where "everyone survives as best as s/he could" as individuals unconnected to others.

Much in the same way, the urban organization of the animated Darwin, a fictionally invented world directly tied to Buenos Aires, reflects a future nightmare dystopia. A towering statue of Phizar looms over the boundless asphalt jungle consisting of empty highways, large image producing screens, and overflowing skyscrapers. But where are the people? Darwin is at a standstill; its circulation of workers and commodities does not correspond to the modern overdevelopment of its space. Named after Charles Darwin, the city, functions under the social Darwinist law of "the survival of the fittest." Shots of empty streets suggest that survival confines Darwin's citizens to more private spaces. The overpowering city space has literally swallowed up its people, who hide inside modernity's pockets. The film's animated form further contributes to allegorizing the sparse landscape of the penal colony. Produced digitally with three-dimensional technology, the background of the film creates a sophisticated verisimilar aesthetic that amplifies the spatial scenery. In contrast, the flat traditionally animated characters lack in visual authenticity. These caricatures clash against the enticing grasp of the city. The authority, the Gloria Mundi Corporation, whose shadow looms over the city, has reached the top of the food chain, obliging its prey, the citizens, to seclude to hiding.

Moebius is based on the mathematical concept of a möbius strip (discovered by German mathematicians August Ferdinand Möbius and Johann Benedict Listing in 1858), constructed by joining the ends of a strip of paper with a single half twist. A line drawn from the seam down the middle will meet back at the seam but on the other side, and if continued it will go back to the original spot but be double the length of the original piece of paper. This shows that there is only one boundary in a möbius strip, and that if one wants to travel over the surface one can continue forever and at the same time reach different unfathomable dimensions. In the film, it is the subway that functions as a möbius strip and an allegory, as the voiceover of topologist Daniel Pratt explains in the film's opening scene:

> The subway is without a doubt a symbol of our times, a labyrinth where in silence we cross others without knowing who they are or where they are going. Hundreds of platforms, which

we utilize to establish a balance, to reassess the situation, and intend to board more than a train, a change of lifestyle. It's a strange game in which we descend infinite tunnels without realizing that in each transfer we are definitively changing our destiny. With the subway I discovered the most powerful machinery of travel but I would never imagine what in a short time would happen to me.[5]

As these words are spoken, the scene shot in slow motion displays the flow of people entering the subway system. The first shots are angled from below, eliminating people's faces to emphasize the anonymity of the legs moving through the station. A shot of a turnstile revolving follows while people enter the station. As the credits appear topographical maps and plans of the subway network are shown and juxtaposed to close-ups of the machinery and technology of the subway network (lights, exposed pipes): a concern with changes in society brought about by technology defines the science fiction genre (Telotte 2001: 12). As in *Sleepwalker*, most of the film takes place inside buildings or in the underground, scenes that are sifted through a blue filter that gives it a gritty texture, the cold tone of a dystopic and decayed looking place, much in the same way that Ridley Scott uses blue in both *Blade Runner* (1982) and *Alien* (1979) to evoke similar visual waste. Many of these scenes in the underground were shot with a 1926 camera that Mosquera found in an antique shop and rebuilt to push its technology to a new dimension ("*Vanished*"). Technology in the film and in its making is reconfigured to question the very condition of late capitalist alienation as the scene detailed above and the words spoken by Pratt illustrate. It is not technology, however, that leads to newfound realms, it is the belief in the most complex of all machines, "man" himself, as the professor explains at the end of the film.

Throughout the film, Daniel Pratt is seen in the underground or in indoor spaces crossing tunnels, descending and ascending stairs, and walking through hallways. When he goes to the archives to find the plans for the last extension of the subway, he is lost in the many rows and aisles of archives that surround him. Pratt's movement through open and sometimes partitioned spaces by walls and other obstacles conveys a journey through a space that is multifaceted. The characters reiterate the complexity of the task of chasing a missing train. The angles capturing a look from below or above further contribute to giving the space of the film an added dimension. Space is certainly labyrinthine and eternal like the möbius strip. As in the other two films discussed, this labyrinthine space lacks people. Besides the first scene described above, the spaces that Pratt intersects are empty. The absence of the people, the disappearance of the train, and the posters plastered on the subway station walls of the missing passengers all refer to the same thing: thirty in *Moebius* and 300,000 in *Sleepwalker* clearly allude to the "affected" of history, the 30,000 people that disappeared during the Dirty War. The streets in the future/present are emptied because they are not livable spaces. As an allegory, the absence of people in all three films bares a looming presence of a past and present violence.

Physically and spatially *Sleepwalker*, *Moebius*, and *Condor Crux* construct a Buenos Aires–Darwin space literally enclosed in the power-seeking fantasies of their corrupt leaders. As fortified metropolises, these cities struggle to keep their inhabitants inside respective communities rather than provide protection from outside intruders as was the case in early science fiction film and literature. Buenos Aires is surrounded by a wall in *Sleepwalker*, which markedly provides a fence between inside and outside. A dome secures and physically isolates Darwin from the rest of the world. Despite authoritative efforts to encapsulate the city, an outside margin or periphery exists to counteract and reaffirm the oppressive effects of the polis. As suffocating as its alter ego, the barren wasteland beyond the protective shield of Buenos Aires in *Sleepwalker* offers another path. As one of the actors affirms: "There are only two paths [in the city]: inside and out. And there is no direction outside." The windy open road that lies ahead for its voyagers, Eva and Kluge (who wants to help Eva escape), leads to a succession of ruins: lifeless trees, extinct wildlife, and crumbling structures. The travellers come across a wanderer, who like the stray birds, has no specific direction. All are lost in the nightmarish post-nuclear *Mad Max* (1979) landscape; everyone forgets the path. Directly linked to the city; the periphery suffers seclusion. Much like the lower city in Buenos Aires, it is a site of waste and ruin. Yet, on the other hand, only through Eva's search for the outside path can society hope to finally achieve salvation. Although the outskirts are as much an unliveable space as the claustrophobic metropolis, Eva must penetrate the heart of the nation in order to rescue it, and that heart lays in the periphery, not the centre. It is in the periphery, the suburb of Saavedra, that she finds Gauna, who brings an eventual end to the nightmare.

On the other side of Darwin's dome resides, not the imagined apocalyptic ruins of *Sleepwalker*, but instead a place where Latin American legend and history meet. After Captain Crux escapes Darwin, his ship crashes in the Amazon where a community of natives lives untouched by the forces of "civilization." Crux's initiation voyage leads him to an encounter with both the past and the rugged landscape of the continent. From the dreamy mythical city El Dorado, to the heights of the historical Machu Picchu, to a fictional resistance city hidden inside a mountain, Crux remaps a continent already erased by the nefarious despot, Phizar. Consequently, Crux will become the one to break the bubble of the dome, free the minds of Darwin's citizens, and help to construct a more livable space, a new order in New Darwin. Utopia is only reached with the opening up of the city to the world, a truly global order, which is not in the hands of only one corporation. Ironically, this film presents a similar "New World Order" as the one envisioned by Menem where the death of one corporation (the state) leads to the new life of many.

In *Moebius*, there is only one mention of an outside and it happens during the scene when Pratt is asked by the original architect to investigate the problems with the subway. On the roof of a building, in the open air, the architect says that he is tired of the city and its confinement and thus needs to escape it. Moreover, he complains of the heat in the underground subway. The only escape possible is the one that Professor Mistein finds with the discovery and implementation of a real-life möbius strip in the train. Pratt is only able to enter this other realm to meet his professor at Borges station, where a mural with endless levels of buildings adorns the background. Daniel Pratt then realizes that he has stepped back in time to the 4th of March, when the train had disappeared and he runs by the missing souls who are transfixed within their own world to reach the real architect of the experiment. The professor explains to Pratt that he would much rather be left in the "shadows than continue to live in a sea of deafness that is dragging us to become incurably wretched." For him there is no such thing as a disappearance because the traces of the past are still fixed within our souls. This is contradicted at the end when the director finds the lost train. The authorities, present throughout the whole ordeal, impose onto the director "here nothing has happened." The director knows what has happened because he reads Daniel Pratt's notes and finally understands; however, officially he is mandated to forget. Unlike *Sleepwalker* or *Condor Crux*, there is no resolution in *Moebius*: the incident repeats itself, at the very end of the film yet another train has disappeared. Therefore, complete oblivion is not an option.

    Where *Condor Crux* resolves the suppressive control of Phizar by opening communication with Darwin's people, *Sleepwalker* further lures its spectators into its circular inescapable reality. *Condor Crux* re-establishes a new city called New Darwin, where the "natural rights" of the community are respected, and all despite social and racial differences, shall live collectively. *Sleepwalker*, on the other hand, ends in bittersweet colour. The final scene completes the images that repeatedly haunted the spectator through Eva's dreams. Eva awakens to the doorbell in a country mansion. She walks down the stairs, opens the door and sees Kluge, who immediately hugs her, but she does not recognize him. Gauna, Eva's partner, appears, and the spectator finally sees his face; Gauna is the same doctor working for the authoritative state. Gauna still has a discernable mark on one side of this face, the same physical trait that characterized the amnesia-stricken "affected." Unlike the foundation of a newfound order clearly portrayed in *Condor Crux*, understandable for a film marketed towards audiences of children, *Sleepwalker* ends where it begins, with the same images of the present. The hope of salvation eventually leads to another realization: Eva's dystopia is not in the future but in the present repression of the future, which by the end of the film becomes the chronological past. Eva's salvation; therefore, is the fulfillment of the apocalypse: complete amnesia about the future-past. In an earlier scene, the doctor, before he is shot to death, foresees Eva's importance. "The end of the world is a woman who awakens," states the doctor. Ironically, the seemingly progressive narrative falls into the trap of the biblical paradigm of the fallen woman who forsakes the entire nation by leading it to forgetfulness. While all these films come to a conclusion that replicates Menem's global policies, only *Moebius*, the less expensive non-blockbuster of the three, offers no resolution but a repetition, which stresses the very place where the past and present violence remains unforgotten.

WORKS CITED

Avelar, Idelber. 1999. *The Untimely Present: Postdictatorial Latin American Fiction and the Task of Mourning.* Durham, NC: Duke University Press.

Benjamin, Walter. 1977. *The Origin of German Tragic Drama.* Trans. John Osborne. London: NLB.

Chanan, Michael. 1998. "Latin American Cinema in the 90s. Representational Space in Recent Latin American Cinema." In *Estudios Interdisciplinarios de América Latina y el Caribe* 9 (Jan.–June). http://www.tau.ac.il/eial/IX_1/chanan.html.

Falicov, Tamara. 2007. *The Cinematic Tango: Contemporary Argentine Film.* London: Wallflower Press.

Jackson, Rosemary. 1981. *Fantasy the Literature of Subversion.* London: Methuen.

Ludmer, Josefina. 1994. Introduction. In *Las culturas de fin de siglo en América Latina: Coloquio en Yale, 8 y 9 de abril de 1994.* Rosario: Beatriz Viterbo: 7–24.

Reati, Fernando. 2006. "Postales del porvenir." *La literatura de anticipación en la Argentina neoliberal (1985–1999).* Buenos Aires: Editorial Biblos.

Rock, David. 2002. "Racking Argentina." *New Left Review* 17 (Sept./Oct.): 54–86.

"La sonámbula." n.d. In *Enciclopedia AxxónLine de la Ciencia Ficcion y Ficción Argentina.* http://axxon.com.ar/wiki/index.php?title=La_son%C3%Almbula.

Tellotte, J. P. 2001. *Science Fiction Film*. Cambridge: Cambridge University Press.
"Vanished." 1998. In *Metro Active Movies*. http://www.metroactive.com/papers/sonoma/11.12.98/moebius-9845.html.

FILMS

Cóndor Crux, la leyenda [*Condor Cruz, The Legend*]. Directed by Juan Pablo Buscarini, Swan Glecer, and Pablo Holcer. Patagonik Film Group and Tournasol Films S.A., 2000.

Extraña invasión [*Stay Tuned for Terror*]. Directed by Emilio Vieyra. Productores Argentinos Asociados, 1965.

Hombre mirando al sudeste [*Man Facing Southeast*]. Directed by Eliseo Subiela. Cinéquanon Productions and Transeuropa S.A. Cinematográfica, 1986.

Invasión. Directed by Hugo Soto. Proartel S.A., 1969.

Lo que vendrá [*Times to Come*]. Directed by Gustavo Mosquera R. Tripiquicios, 1988.

Moebius. Directed by Gustavo Mosquera R. Fundación Universidad del Cine, 1996.

La sonámbula [*Sleepwalker*]. Directed by Fernando Spiner. Metrovisión, and Gativideo, 1998.

La venganza del sexo. [*The Curious Dr. Hump*]. Directed by Emilio Vieyra. Productores Argentinos Asociados, 1967 and 1971.

NOTES

1. *El eternauta* was first published in *Hora cero suplemento seminal* in 1957 and ran until 1959. The same version was reissued in 1961 in a magazine titled *Eternauta*. In 1969 Héctor Oesterheld published a more politically referential and violent version of the comic in the weekly *Gente*. This version was drawn by the hand of Alberto Breccia, the original one had artwork by Francisco Solano López. *Eternauta II*, published in *Skorpio* in 1975 with artwork by Francisco Solano López, was even more openly critical of the political situation in Argentina. It was written while Oesterheld was in hiding until he disappeared in 1977. Since Oesterheld's disappearance, other versions have appeared: *Eternauta tercera parte*, *El mundo arrepentido*, and *El eternauta, el regreso*.

2. All translations are mine unless reference is made to a published translation.

3. "En su materialidad y su simbolismo cada ciudad constituye un texto que se puede leer."

4. "Qué inscribió el neoliberalismo en las páginas de ese texto, cómo se trasladó ese vocabulario nuevo al imaginario colectivo…"

5. "El subterráneo es sin duda un símbolo de los tiempos que corren, un laberinto donde en silencio nos cruzamos con nuestros semejantes sin saber quiénes son ni adónde van. Cientos de andenes en los que aprovechamos para establecer un balance, rever una situación e intentar abordar más que un tren, un cambio de vida. Es un extraño juego en el que nos sumergimos por infinitos túneles sin darnos cuenta de que en cada transbordo estamos cambiando definitivamente nuestro destino. Con el subte descubrí la más poderosa máquina de enviar pero nunca llegué a imaginar lo que en poco tiempo me iba a ocurrir."

List of Contributors

GABRIELA COPERTARI is Associate Professor of Spanish (Latin American Film and Literature) at Case Western Reserve University. Her areas of research are film, literature, culture, and politics in contemporary Latin America. Her articles on Latin American literature, and on Argentine cinema have appeared in journals such as *Latin American Literary Review*, *Journal of Latin American Cultural Studies* and in *MLN*. She has recently published a book on Argentine cinema: *Desintegración y justicia en el cine argentino contemporáneo* (Tamesis, 2009).

ANA FORCINITO is Associate Professor of Spanish at the University of Minnesota. She specializes in twentieth-century Southern Cone literature and film. Her articles have appeared in *Chasqui*, *Confluencia*, *Crítica Hispánica*, and *Revista de Estudios Hispánicos*. Her current research deals with the testimony of survivors of political prison and clandestine detention camps in Argentina and Uruguay and Latin American film directed by women and (post-)feminist approaches to "New Latin American Cinema."

NATALIA JACOVKIS is an Assistant Professor of Spanish at Xavier University in Cincinnati, Ohio. She holds a PhD from the University of Florida. Her areas of interest are urban representation in contemporary Latin American film and literature, detective fiction, and cultural responses to neoliberal discourse. She has published articles on contemporary Argentine cinema in *Tinta,* on urban representation on contemporary Argentine noir novels in *Ciberletras* and on Mexican literature and film on *Confluencia* and *Revista de Humanidades del Tecnológico de Monterrey.*

IGNACIO LÓPEZ-VICUÑA is Assistant Professor of Spanish at the University of Vermont. He received his PhD in Hispanic Literature and Culture from the University of Pittsburgh and an MA in Comparative Literature from the University of Massachusetts, Amherst. His book project, provisionally titled *After the Metropolis: Urban Cartographies in Contemporary Latin America,* examines representations of urban space in recent literature, film, and cultural critique. His research interests include modern Latin American literature and film, urban studies, and queer theory.

ELIZABETH MONTES GARCÉS is an Associate Professor of Spanish and Head of the Department of French, Italian and Spanish at the University of Calgary. Her research focuses on Latin American women's writing and film. Her book *El cuestionamiento de los mecanismos de representación en la novelística de Fanny Buitrago* was published in 1997. She has since published several articles on Fanny Buitrago, Rosario Sanmiguel, Soledad Acosta de Samper, Minerva Villarreal, María Luisa Puga, Rosario Ferré, Carmen Boullosa, and Laura Restrepo in prestigious journals such as *Texto crítico, Letras Femeninas, Revista Canadiense de Estudios Hispánicos, Anuario de Letras,* and *Revista de Literatura Mexicana Contemporánea.* In 2007 a volume she edited on *Relocating Identities in Latin American Cultures* was released by University of Calgary Press. She is currently working on a book on the relationship between body and text in the works of four Latin American female writers: Ana María Shua, Diamela Eltit, Carmen Boullosa, and Laura Restrepo.

ZULEMA MORET is Associate Professor of Spanish at Grand Valley State University and the director of the Latin American Center. Her research focuses on Latin American Women Writers and the relations between Literature and Art. She has published *Las escrituras de Escombros: artistas de lo que queda* (2006), *Estas chicas cuando crecen, dónde van a parar?* (2008), *La huella liberada. Homenaje a Iris Zavala* (Z. Moret, coord.) (2008). She has also published articles, short stories and poems in *Confluencia, Texto Crítico, Alba de América, Texturas, Chasqui, Inti, Hispamérica, Studies in 20th Century Literature, Studi Spanici*. She has edited *Mujeres Mirando al Sur: Poetas Sudamericanas en USA* and *Intersecciones: Abordajes de lo popular en América Latina* (2008).

MYRIAM OSORIO is Associate Professor of Spanish at Memorial University of Newfoundland, Canada. She is the author of a book on the narrative work of Colombian writer Albalucía Ángel, where she explores the concepts of agency, travel and feminism entitled *Agencia femenina, agencia narrativa: una lectura feminista de la obra en prosa de Albalucía Ángel*. She has also published on *Historia del Rey transparente* by Rosa Montero and a collective dictionary for the reading of *me llamo Rigoberta Menchú y así me nació la conciencia*. Forthcoming articles also with U of Calgary Press include "Subjection and Injury in *El vuelo de la reina* by Tomas Eloy Martinez" and " Bodily Representations: Disease and Rape in Francisco Lombardi's *Ojos que no ven* ", co-authored with Elizabeth Montes. Dr. Osorio is currently working on the representation of the city of Havana in post-revolutionary Cuban film.

FERNANDO REATI is Professor of Spanish and Chair of the Modern Languages department at Georgia State University, Atlanta. He is the author of *Nombrar lo innombrable: Violencia política y novela argentina, 1975–1985* (1992) and *Postales del Porvenir: La literatura de anticipación en la Argentina neoliberal, 1985–1999* (2006). He co-edited with Adriana Bergero *Memoria colectiva y políticas de olvido: Argentina y Uruguay, 1970–1990* (1997) and with Mirian Pino *De centros y periferias en la literatura de Córdoba* (2001). His articles on literature, film, theatre and visual representations have appeared in books and journals in Argentina, United States, Mexico, Italy, Germany, Venezuela, and Spain.

CAROLINA ROCHA is Assistant Professor at Southern Illinois University, Edwardsville. She holds a PhD from the University of Texas and specializes in contemporary Southern Cone literature and film. She is the editor, along with Hugo Hortiguera, of *Argentinian Cultural Production during the Neoliberal Years*. Her articles on Argentine film have appeared in *Revista de Estudios Hispánicos*, *Studies in Latin American Popular Culture*, *Ciberletras*, and *Bulletin of Spanish Studies*. In the summer of 2007, she took part of a National Endowment for the Humanities seminar in Argentina. She is currently working on a manuscript that explores representations of masculinity in contemporary Argentine cinema.

VICTORIA RUÉTALO is Associate Professor of Spanish and Latin American Studies at the University of Alberta, Canada. Her essays on Latin American film and culture have been published in *Studies in Latin American Popular Culture*, *Quarterly Review of Film and Video*, *Journal of Latin American Cultural Studies*, and *Cultural Critique*. She recently co-edited with Dolores Tierney *Latsploitation: Latin American Exploitation Cinemas*.

BEATRIZ URRACA is Associate Professor of Spanish at Widener University. A native of Spain, she has a PhD in Comparative Literature from the University of Michigan. Her research focuses on nineteenth- and twentieth-century Latin American fiction, emphasizing Argentina and the representations of its national identity. She has published on Gorriti, Gorodischer, and Borges. Her two most recent articles involve the films of Trapero and Caetano, and of Verónica Chen, and are part of a larger project entitled *Social Change in Contemporary Argentine Cinema*.

Index

A

Abuelas. See Grandmothers of the Plaza de Mayo
Actis, Munú, 9
  Ese inferon, 88n7
"The Aesthetics of the New Argentine Cinema" (Wolff), 184
Agosti, Orlando Ramón, 87n3
Agozino, Adalberto, xx
Agüero, Felipe, xix
Aguilar, Gonzalo, 199n5, 202n15
Aira, César, 4
Aldini, Cristina, 9, 88n7
Alfonsín, Raúl (administration, 1983-89), 205
  prosecution of human rights abuses, 207
Alfred Bauer award, 127
Alice doesn't (De Lauretis), 69
Alien (1979), 214
allegory, 208
Alonso, Lisandro, 163
Alsop, Rachel, *Theorizing Men and Masculinities,* 36

Alterio, Héctor, 100
Amado, Ana, 164
  "Cine Argento," 181n2
Amalia (1912), xii
Americas Watch, xviii
Amnesty Laws. *See Indulto* (Amnesty Laws)
Los amores de Laurita (Shua), 64n1
Amores perros (2006), 112, 201n13
Ana (fictional character), 100–101, 104–5, 108
Andermann, Jens, xvii
Andrés (fictional character), 185–87, 190, 195–96
Andruetto, María Teresa, *La mujer en cuestión,* 8
Angeleone, Juan Pablo, xix
anti-hero, 128
Anti-Oedipus (Deleuze), 48, 53
"any-space-whatever," 136
apocalyptic novels, 211. *See also* science fiction

Arendt, Hannah, 8
   Eichmann in Jerusalem, 6
Argentina, 97, 164
   crisis (2001), 111, 122, 205
   democracy (*See* redemocratization)
   dominant national narrative (1880-1930), xxii, xxv, 113, 139, 172
   economic decline, 168
   as a «European» nation, 155–56, 169
   historical background, xiii–xvi
   Latin Americanization of, xxvi, 168
   military dictatorship, xi, xii, xix, xxvii, 8, 51, 68, 146, 164, 205
   myth of past and future national grandeur, 169, 172
   neoliberal phase (*See* neoliberal policies)
   official politics of oblivion, 74, 78, 205, 207
   recession 1989, xi
   transformation from welfare state to planning state, xiv
   unspeakable parts of Argentina's past, 135
Argentina (old and new types of violence), xvi–xxi
Argentina as white. *See* Argentina, as a "European" nation
Argentine context (in recent Argentine cinema), 125, 139
Argentine films of the sixties, 195. *See also* New Latin American Cinema
Argentine foundational myths. *See* Argentina, dominant national narrative

Argentine novels of the seventies and eighties
   narrative techniques, xxiii
"Argentine's Blockbuster Movies" (Falicov), 181n1
Argentinian exceptionalism, xxvi
Armed Forces, xix, xxvii. *See also* military government (1976-83)
Armony, Ariel and Victor, 168
Arregui (2001), 124n2
Ashes from Paradise. See Cenizas del paraíso (1997)
Aspects médicaux de la torture chinoise (Elizondo), 11
audience. *See* readers (or audience); spectator
Augé, Marc, 136, 189
El aura (2005), xxvi, xxvii, 126, 134, 142n4
   awards, 127
   civilization and barbarism myth, 125, 137
   hunt as primary motif, 138
   plot of the foiled heist, 128, 131
   protagonist in, 127–32
   psycho-noir drama, 127
   spaces in, 137–38
Auschwitz (Nielsen), xxiii, 3–16
   torture and abuse in, 4–6, 10, 14
authoritarian gaze, 74
authoritarian system, xxiv, 48
   possibility of escape, 57
   writing (or creativity) as means to undermine, 59, 62
authoritarianism, 68, 71, 82, 204–5
Auyero, Javier, xv
Avelar, Idelber, 208

B

bar in *Bolivia*, 147, 150, 164–65, 167, 173, 178
    claustrophobic atmosphere, 175, 177
    as Foucauldian heterotopia, 166–67
    inequalities and relationships of power, 174
    old forms of community bonds, 171
    reproduces xenophobic attitudes of Argentine society, 171, 178
    "sense of belonging," 169
Barbarian Despotic Machine, 53–54
"Barbaric Spectacles" (Rocha), xxvi
barbarism, 97, 107–8, 135. *See also* civilization and barbarism
Barbeito, Alberto, xiii, xiv
Barone, Daniel, 206
Barthes, Roland, 83
Baudrillard, Jean, 201n13
Baudry, Jean-Louis, 87n4, 88n4
Bechis, Marco, 15, 74
Bemberg, María Luisa, 74, 87n2
Benjamin, Walter, 208
Berlin International Film Festival, 137, 199n2
Bernades, Horacio, 115, 124n4
    Nuevo Cine Argentino, 181n2
Berto (fictional character), 4–7, 13–16, 18n5
Besteman, Catherine, xix
    Violence, xvi
Beyond the Pleasure Principle (Freud), 94–95

Bielinsky, Fabián, xxvi, 125, 127–28, 139, 142n4
Billy the Kid, 130–31, 142n5
Bizzio, Sergio, 4
Black, Joel, 134
Blade Runner (1982), 214
blockbuster films, 206
The Blonde Ones. *See Los rubios*
The Bloody Countess. *See La condesa sangrienta* (Pizarnik)
Blumberg, Axel, xviii
Boccanera, Jorge, *Redes de memoria*, 88n7
"Bodies at Risk" (Martins), 110n2
"Bodies-Cities" (Grosz), 186
bodily fragments, 27–28
body-without-organs, 50–51
The Bodyguard. *See El custodio* (2006)
Body's Recollection (Levin), 31
Bogotá Film Festival, 127
Bolivia (2002), xxviii, 87n2, 150, 163–78, 201n13
    anonymity of the characters, 176–77
    bar (*See* bar in *Bolivia*)
    collision among people of same social class, 152
    contesting hegemonic neoliberal discourses, 178
    critique of racism, 157
    cumbia villera in, 158–59
    deconstruction of ethnic/national categories, 152, 157, 173
    documentary effect, 176
    feeling of latent violence, 175–76
    fragmentation, 176
    instability of national boundaries, 146–47

neorealism, 147–54, 176
potential for new forms of solidarity, 178
recalls political films of late sixties, 176
sense of helplessness, 151
underside of transnationalization, 154, 164
violence, 153, 165, 175–76
xenophobia reflects Argentine society, 171, 178
bolivianos, 18n5, 151–52, 156–57, 160
El bonaerense, 201n13
Bonasso, Miguel, *Recuerdo de la muerte*, 88n7
Bonnie and Clyde (1976), 93
Bordón, Sebastián, xviii
Borges, Jorge Luis, 15, 203–4
"El milagro secreto," 3
Boston subway system, 211
Bourdieu, Pierre, 103, 169
Braidotti, Rosi, 202n17
Brandoni, Luis, 100
Brazil, 205
Breccia, Alberto, 220n1
Brédice, Leticia, 101
Bruno (fictional character), 73–74
Buchanan, Rhonda, 47
Buena Vista International, 206
Buenos Aires, xxviii, xxix, xxxii, 71, 100, 112, 114–15, 118, 150, 184
  in *Bolivia*, 165, 168, 177–78
  in Caetano's films, 145
  in *Condor Crux*, 209–10, 213, 215
  in *El custodio*, 126, 136
  in early Argentine science fiction, 204
  in *El cielito*, 117
  in *El eternauta*, 203
  gated neighborhoods and country clubs parallel to impoverishment, 177
  hidden and illegal trends, 188
  human rights violations, xviii
  "invaded" by *mestiza* masses, 156, 170
  invasion of dark-skinned immigrants, 168
  main setting of *Un día de suerte*, *Vagón Fumador*, *Hoy y Mañana*, 185, 187
  modernity eroded by mestizo lower class, 170
  in *Moebius*, 209–11, 215
  in *La muerte como efecto secundario*, 48, 53
  orphanhood, 119, 183, 193
  peripheral neighbourhoods, 184, 188–89
  in *Pizza, birra, faso*, 147
  post-national space, 160
  poverty, 155, 177
  site of post-dictatorship violence, 205
  in *Sleepwalker*, 209–10, 212, 215–16
  transnational city, 155
  2000 riots, 199n2
  as white, modern, civilized, 168, 170
Bukowski, Charles, 199n6
Butler, Judith, xxiv, 25–26, 30
  Precarious Life, 110n7
  The Psychic Life of Power, 25, 27, 34
  on subjection and injury, 24, 38

C

Caballos Salvajes (Piñeyro), 110n3
cabecitas negras, 156
Cabezas, José Luis, xviii
Cabras, mujeres y mulas (Shua), 64n1
cacerolazos (potbanging), xv, xx
Cadillac (fictional character), 114–15, 117, 119
Caetano, Adrián, xxviii, 85, 87n2, 89n13, 112, 128, 134, 145–60, 163–78
  use of music, 147, 158–59
Calabrese, Elisa T., "Historia y ficción," 42n2
Caligari Film Award, 199n2
Calveiro, Pilar, 70
  Poder y desaparición, 9
Cámara Argentina de la Industria Cinematográfica, 87n2
La cámara oscura (2007), 124n2
Camargo (fictional character), xxiv, 25–27, 32–33, 45n33
  archetype of an abuser, 24, 29, 33
  impunity, 39
  lonely, motherless youth, 37–38
  misogynist discourse, 30
  power to influence public opinion, 37
  self-concept, 34–36
  unattainable ideals of masculinity, 35
Camila, 74, 82, 87n2
campo, 83
Canclini, Néstor García, xxi
capitalism, 48
  codification of desire, 49
  desire and, 62
  late capitalist alienation, 214
  male-dominated, xxviii
Capitalist Machine, 61
  at expense of Argentinian people, 56
  impact on women, 60
Carpenter, L., 196
Carri, Albertina, xxiv, xxv, 16, 68, 75–83, 85
Carri, Roberto, 75, 77
  Isidro Velázquez, 76, 87n1
Cartagena film festival, 127
Carter, Angela, 12–13
Caruso, Ana María, 75, 77
Carver, Raymond, 199n6
Casa de Geishas (Shua), 64n1
Casares, Adolfo Bioy, 203–4, 209
Casey, Edward, 184
Cavallo, Domingo, 56, 65n14
Cayetano, Saint, 119, 121
Cenizas del paraíso (1997), xxvi, 100, 103
  crisis of masculinity, 101, 105, 107
  state's inability to sanction violence, 99, 108
censorship, xii, 68
centre/periphery relationship, 184–85, 188
Cerruti, Gabriela, 78–79
Cesares, Bioy, 204
Chanan, Michael, 208
Chango (fictional character), 114, 117–21
Chávez, Julio, 127–28, 136, 139, 142n4
Chen, Verónica, xxix, 184, 190, 199n3
children of detainees and *desaparecidos*, 79. *See also* HIJ@S
Chomski, Alejandro, xxix, 184

Index   229

El cielito (2004), xxvi, 84, 111–22, 201n13
    Bernades' review of, 124n4
    disintegrated world, 122
    inverted image of a national identity narrative, 113
    Joanna Page's reading of, 124n6
    religious images in the film's *mise-en-scène*, 114, 119
    representation of violence in, 112
La ciénaga, 84, 87n2
"Cine Argento" (Amado), 181n2
cinema of the seer, 149
Citizens of Fear (Rotker), xxi
citizenship, xx
    citizens as consumers, xxi, 97
    devaluation, xv
    privatization, 68
city, the, 186, 209. *See also* Buenos Aires
    city under siege, 187
    El dorado (mythical city of), 216
    life in the big city, 184
    social violence in, 112, 191
    vampirization, 190
city wanderers (protagonists of *Un día de suerte*, *Vagón fumador*, *Hoy y mañana*), 185
civil resistance, xix, xx
civilian population
    ethical and moral responsibility (*See* collective responsibility)
civilization, 95, 106, 135–36
civilization and barbarism, xii, xxvi, xxvii, xxviii, 94, 97, 107–8, 126, 128, 138, 147
    in *El aura*, 125, 137

    in *Bolivia*, 164
    in *El custodio*, 125
    importance in nation-building, 170
Civilization and Its Discontents (Freud), 94–95
Civilización y barbarie en el cine argentino y latinoamericano (Lusnich), xxii
Civilized Capitalist Machine, 53–54, 56, 60–61
civilized societies
    violent action demands response from authorities, 96 (*See also* state)
The Civilizing Process (Elias), 94
A Clockwork Orange (1971), 93
collective responsibility, 7, 10. *See also* complicity
collective trauma, 15
collective violence, xv
Comodines (1997), 206
complicity, 75. *See also* collective responsibility
La comtesse sanglante (Penrose), 11
CONADEP, 6, 72
concentration camp survivors. *See* detention camp survivors
concentration of income, xxi, 177. *See also* inequality; poverty; wealthy people
La condesa sangrienta (Pizarnik), xxiii, 11
Condor Crux (2000)
    Buenos Aires (Darwin) in, 209–10, 213, 215
    funding, 206
    new city called New Darwin, 217
    newfound order in, 217
    place in, 208

Cóndor Crux (2000), xxix, 204
Constantini, Humberto, xxiii
consumption, 169
    identities shaped by, xxi
contemporary Argentine cultural production. *See* New Argentine Cinema
Copertarí, Gabriela, xxvi, 221
Cordobés (fictional character), 146, 165, 167, 174
corruption, xv, 21n26, 23, 34, 37, 99–100, 107, 139, 174, 184
Couceyro, Analía, 76–77, 79–80, 85
Crane World (1999), 136
Creole (criolla) society, 117
Crime and Violence in Latin America (Frühling), xxii
crime as only alternative, 118, 146, 157
    legal / illegal activities combined, 113, 147, 188, 199n5
criminality, xxi. *See also* law-breaking without sanctions
    embrace of crime, 146
    "laburitos" (little jobs), 117, 119
crisis (2001). *See under* Argentina
crisis of masculinity, 35, 97–98, 102–3, 105, 107
    risk to civilization, 106
The Crisis of Masculinity and the Politics of Identity (Heartfield), 45n31
La crítica de las armas (Feinmann), xxiii, 8
A Critique of Weapons. See La crítica de las armas (Feinmann)
Crónica de una fuga (2006), 85
    military dictatorship period, 146

Crux, Captain (fictional character), 210, 216
cumbia villera, 147, 158–59
The Curious Dr. Hump (1971), 204
El custodio (2006), xxvi, xxvii
    awards, 127
    civilization and barbarism myth, 125
    protagonist in, 127–29, 132–35
    unexpected ending, 128

D

Darín, Ricardo, 127, 134, 137, 139
Darwin (Buenos Aires). *See* Buenos Aires
De Lauretis, Teresa, 88n6
    Alice doesn't, 69
Death as a Side Effect. See La muerte como efecto secundario (Shua)
death instinct, 95, 98
Deleuze, Gilles, xxiv, 48–49, 54, 58–59, 62, 148, 157, 167
    Anti-Oedipus, 48, 53
    "any-space-whatever," 136
Demare, Lucas, xii
democracy as impunity, 82
democratic continuity (1990s), xx
democratic continuity (2003), xvi
democratic government (1983-1989), xii, xiii, 67
democratic societies
    (in)equality in, 110n7
democratic transition, 82
desaparecidos, 70, 72, 75, 88n5
    children of, 79
Desaparecidos Project, 88n9

desire, 50–53, 57
  in Capitalist Machine, 54, 60–62
  Deleuze and Guattari's conception of, 48–49, 58, 62
  social context and, 48
desiring-machine, 49, 52, 58
detention camp survivors, xxv, 9–10, 70, 72. *See also* disappearance and survival; survival mechanisms
Deutsche, A.J., "A Subway Named Möbius," 211
Un día de suerte (2002), xxix, 184, 188, 192, 201n14
  awards, 199n2
  camera work in, 199n2
  city under siege, 187
  "family discourse" in, 193
  urban dwellers of Buenos Aires (protagonists), 185
Diana, Marta, *Mujeres guerrilleras*, xxvii
El diario, 28–29, 37, 39, 44n27, 45n33
Días de pesca (Shua), 64n1
Díaz del Moral, Juan, 76
dictatorship in Argentina. *See* military government (1976-83)
"dirty realism" *(realismo sucio)*, 184, 199n6
Dirty War (1976-83), xxii, xxvii, 51, 203, 215
disappearance and survival, xxv, 10, 68–70, 75
disappeared, xvii, xix, 81–83, 100, 203, 211, 215
disappeared, theme of, 70
disappeared, untold stories of, xxv

Discipline and Punish (Foucault), xxiv, 25
discourse of modernity, xxviii, 164
Disney, Walt, 206
disorientation, 189
"docile body," 27, 43n13
documentaries, 68, 76, 80
  fictionalization, 77
Don Enrique (fictional character), 149–53, 166–67, 169, 171–72, 174–75
Don Quixote Award, 199n2
Dorrego's Execution. See El fusilamiento de Dorrego (1908)
Due Obedience, decree of, xvii, xxvii, 87n3
Duhalde, Eduardo, xvi
dystopia, 209, 212, 218
dystopic novels, 205

E

eccentric gaze, 72, 74
Echeverría, Esteban, xxxiiin1
economic slowdowns in 1994 and 1998, 205
economy of survival, 117
  crime as only alternative, 118, 146–47
  legal / illegal combination, 113, 188
  prostitution, 192
education, xiii, xxv
Eichmann in Jerusalem (Arendt), 6
Eldorado (mythical city of), 216
Elias, Norbert, xxvi, 95
  The Civilizing Process, 94

Elizondo, Salvador
  Aspects médicaux de la torture chinoise, 11
  Farabeuf, 10
Elsa (fictional character), 185, 187–88, 191–93
emasculation, xxvi, 108
emotional involvement (lack of), 195
employment, 194
employment as foundation for social identity, 113. *See also* unemployment; working class
Ernesto (fictional character), xxiv, 51–52, 55, 57, 60
  liberation from fixed idea of possessive love, 58
  lines-of-flight, 58
  perfect schizophrenic, 59, 61
  use of writing and creativity, 48, 59, 62
escraches, xx, 15, 21n26
Ese infierno (Actis), 88n7
Ese infierno (That Hell), 9
ESMA concentration camp, 9, 13
Los espíritus patrióticos (1989), 124n2
Etchecolatz, Miguel, xix
El eternauta, 220n1
  Buenos Aires in, 203
ethics of defiance, 147
ethics of representation, 83–84
Eva (fictional character), 209–10, 212, 215–18
evil, banality of, 6, 14
evil, how society legitimizes, 13
evil, magic of naming, 3–4, 15
evil within selves, xxiii, 14–16

"exclusionary modernization," xiv
"exclusionary" society, xx
eyes (covered or uncovered)
  in postdictatorship cinema, 74

F

Fajardo, Diógenes, "Procesos de (des)mitificación en *La novela de Perón y Santa Evita*," 42n2
Falicov, Tamara, 205–6
  "Argentine's Blockbuster Movies," 181n1
family, xxix, 107. *See also* father-son relationship; orphans
  in city (in *El cielito*), 116–17
  in country (in *El cielito*), 116
  effects of social exclusion, 114, 117
  effects of uncontrolled violence, 101
  employment (effects of unemployment), 113
  fall (or lack) of the father figure as a social and symbolic construct, 105, 108, 116, 193–94
  masculinity in crisis and, 98, 102, 104–5
  in *La muerte como efecto secundario*, 47–48
  new relations within, 193
  with no authority figures, 117
  nuclear family, 54
  patriarchal family, 112, 116
  protective parent, 120–21
fantasy, 207–8
Farabeuf (Elizondo), 10
father-son relationship, 54–57, 100–102, 105–6, 109

man / baby relationship, 111, 118–20
fathers / judges
   victimized by violence, 105
fault-lines metaphor, xix
Feinmann, José, *La crítica de las armas,* xxiii, 8
Félix (fictional character), 113–17, 119
   flashbacks, 114, 120–21
   "migration" to Buenos Aires, 118
   saviour father to Chango, 111, 118–20
female abuse, 34, 134, 138. *See also* women
female bodies as merchandise, 194. *See also* prostitution
femicide, 44n29
Fernández, Guillermo, 85
Fernández L'Hoeste, Héctor D., 166, 173
Festival del Cine y la Mujer, 87n2
"Ficción y realidad en *La novela de Perón* de Tomás Eloy Martínez" (Parodi), 42n2
Filc, Judith, 200n12
Fitzimmons, Annette, 36
Flaubert, Gustave, 15
The Flight. See El vuelo (1995)
Flori, Mónica, 47–48, 64n3
Florianópolis Festival, 70
Forcinito, Ana, xxiv, 221
foreign gaze, 71–73
foreign investment, xiii, xiv, 56
"former life" (in New Argentine Cinema), 130
   flashbacks, 114, 120–21, 135

Fortier, Anne-Marie, 165–66
Foster, David W., *Violence in Argentine Literature,* xxii
Foucauldian heterotopia, 166–67
Foucauldian prisoner, 26
Foucauldian terms, 27
Foucault, Michel, xxvii, 23, 43n13
   Discipline and Punish, xxiv, 25
foundational national narratives. *See* Argentina, dominant national narrative
"fourthspace," xxvii, xxviii, xxix, xxx
The Fragile Male (Greenstein), 36
fragmentation of postmodern subject, 194
"fragmented and corroded body," xxiv
Franco, Jean, 171, 177
Freddy (fictional character), 149–54, 157–59, 165, 167, 171, 173–74, 176
   strategies of resistance, 175
Freddy (fictional character) / Rosa relationship
   potential for new forms of solidarity, 178
Fresán, Rodrigo, 4
Freud, Sigmund, xxvi, 48–49, 96–97
   Beyond the Pleasure Principle, 94–95
   Civilization and Its Discontents, 94–95
Friedman, Milton, 56, 65n14
Frühling, Hugo, xxi
   Crime and Violence in Latin America, xxii
Fuentealba, Carlos, xviii
Full Stop, decree of, xvii, xxvii, 87n3
Fundación Universidad del Cine, 206

La furia (1997), xxvi, 98–99, 102
   crisis of masculinity, 101, 105–7
   state's inability to sanction violence, 108
El fusilamiento de Dorrego (1908), xii

G

Gallo, Mario, xii
Ganduglia, Silvia, "La representación de la historia en *La novela de Perón*," 42n2
Garage Olimpo (1999), 15, 74
Gardella, Liliana, 9, 88n7
The Gaucho War. See La guerra gaucha (1942)
gauchos, 147
Gauna (fictional character), 209–10, 212, 216–17
Gaviria, Víctor, 191
gaze, 67–68, 70
   camera / gaze relationship, xxviii, 87n4
   complicit voyeuristic gaze of the audience, 190
   Don Enrique's, 174
   in Félix's flashbacks, 120
   male gaze, 25
   multiple gazes, 74
   in *Un muro de silencio*, 88n4
   privatization, 68
   in reconstruction of meaning after the military regime, 74
   revisioning of the nonauthoritarian gaze, 68
   in *Los rubios*, 75
   totalitarian gaze, 67
   transgressive gaze, 69

gaze and the camera relationship, xxviii, 87n4
Gazzera, Carlos, 18n5
gender roles, xii, 194
   changed by breakdown of social order, 96
   impact of social exclusion on, 112, 114
German experience of Nazism, 13, 19n13
Getino, Octavio, 176
Giardinelli, Mempo, xxiii
Giles, James R., xxvii, xxviii
Girard, René, 142n7
Glauber Rocha Prize, 70
globalization, xxviii, 164, 171, 211
   poverty and, 207
globalized urban culture, 184
Gloria Mundi Corporation (fictional body), 213
The Godfather (1972), 93
Gorelik, Adrián, xxxii, 177
Grandmothers of the Plaza de Mayo, 78–79
Grant, Catherine, 71
Greenstein, Ben, *The Fragile Male*, 36
Gregorio (fictional character), xxiv, 48, 51–54, 62
   hinge mechanism, 54
   repressive means to control his children, 55–57
   victim and authoritarian father figure, 54–55
grief, 195
Grimson, Alejandro, 97, 112–13, 155–56
Grosz, Elizabeth, "Bodies-Cities," 186

Guano, Emanuela, 170
Guattari, Félix, xxiv, 48–49, 53–54, 58–59, 62
Guebel, Daniel, 4
La guerra gaucha (1942), xii
Gugliotta, Sandra, xxix, 184
Gundermann, Christian, 148, 165, 178
Gusmán, Luis, *Villa*, xxiii, 8

H

Hatzfeld, Marc, 188, 202n16
Havana Festival, 70, 127
Heartfield, James, 35
    The Crisis of Masculinity and the Politics of Identity, 45n31
Heridas urbanas (Isla), xxii
heterotopia, 166–67
H.I.J.O.S., 15, 21n26
HIJ@S, 78–79
hinge mechanism, 54, 56
"Historia, memoria y testimonio" (Salem), 42n2
La historia oficial (1985), 15, 67, 82
"Historia y ficción" (Calabrese), 42n2
Hitchcock, Alfred, 42n8
Holland, Eugene, 48–49, 54, 59
Hollywood films, 93, 126, 208
Hombre mirando al sudeste (1987), 204, 208, 210
Hombres y mujeres del PRT-ERP (Mattini), xvii
homophobia, 13
La hora de los hornos (1973), xii, 176
The Hour of the Furnaces. See La hora de los hornos (1973)
Hoy y mañana (2003), xxix, 184, 190, 192, 199n4

desolated areas where nobody helps anybody, 194
urban dwellers of Buenos Aires, 185
human rights, 15, 67, 71, 74
Human Rights Award, 70
human rights violations, xviii, xix, xx, xxvii, 6, 68, 82, 87n3
    collective responsibility for, 7, 10
    prosecution of, 207
Human Rights Watch, 44n29
hunt as motif, 138
hyperinflation, 56

I

Ianni, Octavio, 174
identity, xxi
    social identity, 113
identity crises, 184
"Ideological Effects of the Basic Cinematographic Apparatus" (Metz), 87n4
"The Imaginary Signifier" (Metz), 87n4
IMF, 56, 62
immigrants, xxv
    blamed for Argentina's economic troubles, 153, 155, 172–73 (*See also* xenophobia)
    cumbia villera, 159
    dark-skinned immigrants, 168
    European immigrants, 169
    «foreign» in age of globalization, 157
    illegal immigrants, 151
    taking «Argentine» jobs, 149
    undocumented immigrants, 150, 155

immigration/migration as path of work and progress, 113, 116–18
impunity, xviii, 21n26, 34, 39, 69–70, 79, 99, 104, 108
    as condition for consolidation of democracy, 70
    culture of, xxiv
impunity laws, 71, 82, 84, 87n3. *See also Indulto* (Amnesty Laws)
indigenous population as "barbaric," 169
individual / society tension, 94–95
individualism, 169, 171
Indulto (Amnesty Laws), 71, 74, 82, 87n3. *See also* pardon
inequality, xiii, 174, 205. *See also* social classes
    in Latin American cities, 166
    unequal status of men, 97
(in)equality in democratic societies, 110n7
injury, 24, 38
injustice, 108
    social injustice, 154
    vigilante justice, 115, 122
Instituto Nacional de Artes Audiovisuales (INCAA), 206
interpellation, 38, 44n22, 46n37
interrelation between economic, political, and social reality, 207
Invasión (1969), 204, 209
Isidro Velázquez (Carri), 76, 87n1
Isla, Alejandro, *Heridas urbanas,* xxii
Italian Neorrealism, 195

J

Jackson, Rosemary, 207–8
Jacovkis, Natalia, xxviii, 221
Jahamanne, Laleen, 148
Jara, Rene, 73
Jasper, Karl, 19n13
Jelin, Elizabeth, 15, 75
job insecurity as cause of structural violence, xix. *See also* unemployment
Johnson, Peter, 167
journalist's role, 45n33
judiciary (judges), 100
    crisis of masculinity, 103, 106–7
    failure as fathers, 105
    victimized by violence, 98, 105
Juicio a las juntas, 84
Junta Trials, 6, 71–72, 87n3
justice, absence of. *See* injustice

K

Kamchatka (2002), 16
Kate Benson (fictional character), 71, 73–74
    foreign gaze, 72
Kessler, Gabriel, xxi, 97, 112–13, 155–56
kidnapping scenes, 76, 81, 83–84
killers' psychological development (in *El aura* and *El custodio*), 126
Kirchner, Néstor, xvi
Klein, Naomi, 56
    The Shock Doctrine, 65n14
Kluge (fictional character), 212, 215, 217
Kohan, Martin, 76, 79, 81

L

labour, world of. *See also* employment
 replaced by world of crime, 118
"laburitos" (little jobs), 117, 119
Lacan, Jacques, 191
Lang, Fritz, *Metropolis*, 211
Laughton, Charles, 46n36
Lavalle Street, 185, 187
law-breaking without sanctions, 96–97. *See also* impunity
Lefebvre, Henri, 170
 The Production of Space, xxvii
legal / illegal activities combined, 113, 188
 living on the fringes of the law, 147, 199n5
Lennon, Kathleen, 36
León, Christian, 185, 191
Lerer, Diego, 181n2
Lerman, Diego, 87n2
Levin, David, *Body's Recollection*, 31
Lewin, Miriam, 9, 88n7
El libro de los recuerdos (Shua), 64n1
Listing, Johann Benedict, 213
Little Heaven. *See El cielito*
The Little Mermaid, 43n20
Lo que vendrá (1988), 204, 210
Lo Vuolo, Rubén, xiv
Lombardi, Judge (fictional character), 100–102
 crisis of masculinity, 103, 106–7
loneliness, 190, 195–96
lootings. *See* civil resistance
López, Fernando, 99
López, Francisco Solano, 220n1
López, Jorge Julio, xix

López-Vicuña, Ignacio, xxviii, 178, 222
 "Postnational Boundaries in *Bolivia*," xxviii
lower classes, xiv, xv, xx, 97. *See also* working class
 resistance to bourgeois norms, 147
A Lucky Day. See Un día de suerte (2002)
Ludmer, Josefina, 142n5
Lusnich, Ana Laura, *Civilización y barbarie en el cine argentino y latinoamericano*, xxii

M

Mad Max (1979) landscape, 216
magic of naming evil, xxiii, 3–4, 15
Makantasis, Judge (fictional character), 100–101, 103–4, 108
 crisis of masculinity, 107
 failure as a father, 105
male attempt to dominate and construct the female, 23–25. *See also* misogynist ideology
male characters as merchandise, 194
male gaze, 25
male power, 32
Man Facing Southeast. *See Hombre mirando al sudeste* (1987)
Marcelo (fictional character), 165, 167, 169, 171–72, 174–75
Marcos Lombardi (fictional character), 99–103, 106–7
marginality, 184, 197
marginalized youth, 112–13, 115, 164
El marido argentino promedio (Shua), 64n1

Mármol, José, xii
Marrale, Jorge, 103
Martel, Lucrecia, 87n2, 89n13, 163
Martínez, Tomás Eloy, xxiv, 42n2
   ambivalence, 46n33
   narrative strategies, 23
   La novela de Perón, 23
   Santa Evita, 23
   El vuelo de la reina, xxiii, 23–39
Martins, Laura, "Bodies at Risk," 110n2
Martorell, Elvira, 81
Marx, Karl, 49
masculine middle class. *See* middle-class men
masculinity
   crisis of, 35, 97–98, 102–3, 105–7
   diminished by unequal status of men, 97
   macho pride, 13
   "man is a wolf to man," 96, 138
   traditional notion of, 36
Masetto, Antonio Dal, xxiii
Masiello, Francine, 125, 137
Massera, Emilio, 87n3
El matadero (1839), xxxiin1
Mattini, Luis, *Hombres y mujeres del PRT-ERP*, xvii
Mcduffe, Keith, "La novela de Perón," 42n2
Medical Aspects of Chinese Torture. See Aspects médicaux de la torture chinoise (Elizondo)
memory, 70, 78
   blurred memory, 81
   childhood memories, 81
   fictionality in, 80
   intergenerational transmission of, 15
   official politics of oblivion, 74, 78, 208
Menem, Carlos, xi, xiv, xvi, 47, 59, 155, 216
   decrees of Full Stop and Due Obedience, xvii, xxvii
   film industry under, 206
   first term (1989-95), xiii, 56
   hinge mechanism, 56
   manipulated Argentina's desire, 62
   neoliberal policies, 56
   neoliberal policies of cutbacks and privatization, 56, 205
   pardons, 82, 207
   second term (1995-2000), xv, 56
menemismo, 169–70
Menemista government, 163
   neoliberal policies, xxix
Menis, María Victoria, xxvi, 111–22, 124n2
Mercado (fictional character), 172
Mercedes (fictional character), 114, 116, 118–19
Mercosur (Common Market of the South), 205
mestizo, 116–17, 156
Metropolis (Lang), 211
Metz, Christian
   "Ideological Effects of the Basic Cinematographic Apparatus," 87n4
   "The Imaginary Signifier," 87n4
middle class, xiv, xxv, xxvi, 10, 168
   descent into poverty, xx, xxv, 170
   disillusioned middle-class young people, 164

fragmentation of, 200n12
middle class, 173
"new poor," xx
potbanging, xv, xx (*See also* civil resistance)
strategies of differentiation and exclusion, 173
middle-class men, 97–98
victimization, xxvi, 99, 101
Miguez, Daniel, xxii
"El milagro secreto" (Borges), 3
military government (1976-83), xii, xix, 51
censorship during, 68
films related to, 67, 146, 164
neoliberal economic policies, 205
practices inherited from, xix
state-sponsored political violence, xi, xxvii (*See also* disappeared; violence)
Vezzetti's study of, 68
"mirror-screen," 88n4
mirror stage in visual studies, 87n4
misogynist authoritarianism, xxii, 30
misogynist ideology, xxii, 30–31, 34, 45n31, 46n36
Miss Mary, 87n2
mobile borders, 146, 149, 184–85, 188
Möbius, August Ferdinand, 213
modernity, discourse of, xxviii, 164
Moebius (1996), xxix, 204, 206
allegory of dictatorship and current climate in Argentina, 211
Buenos Aires in, 210–11, 215
camera work in, 214
disappearances in, 211, 215
funding, 206

no resolution, 217–18
place in, 208
subway in, 213–14, 216
Molloy, Sylvia, 124n3
Momentos, 87n2
monopoly over violence, 96
replaced by monopoly over tax revenues, 97
Monteagudo, Luciano, 189
Montes Garcés, Elizabeth, xxiv, 222
Montoneros (leftist guerilla group), 204
Moreira, Juan, 142n5
Moreno, Rodrigo, xxvi, 125, 127–28, 135–36, 139, 142n4
Moret, Zulema, xxviii, xxix, 223
Mosquera, Gustavo, 214
La muerte como efecto secundario (Shua), xxiv, 47–62, 64n1
La mujer (the woman), 25–26, 31
bodily fragments, 27–28
a body waiting to be regulated, 28
La mujer en cuestión (Andruetto), 8
Mujeres guerrilleras (Diana), xxvii
multiple gazes, 74
Mundo Grúa, 87n2, 201n13
murder of women by controlling lovers, 33–34, 38–39, 44n27, 44n29. *See also* male attempt to dominate and construct the female
Muro, Francisco (fictional character), 103–4, 107–8
Un muro del silencio (1993), xxv, 68–75, 83
awards, 70
disappearance and survival in, 68, 70, 75

gaze, 70, 88n4
theme of foreignness, 71
Murúa, Lautaro, 71

N

Naming the Unnamable. See *Nombrar lo innombrable* (Reati)
narrative inevitability, 146
narrative of victimization, 170–72
narrative techniques
    novels of 1970s and 1980s, xxiii
nation as the *mise-en-scène* in *Bolivia*, 173
"The nation as the *mise-en-scène* of filmmaking in Argentina" (Page), 181n4
national borders, uncertainty of, 152. *See also* mobile borders
National Cinema Institute (Instituto Nacional de Cine y Artes Audiovisuales), 77
National Commission on the Disappearance of Persons. *See* CONADEP
national myths. *See* Argentina, dominant national narrative
national-populist economic programs, xiv. *See also* welfare state
"natural rights," 217
negro, 151–52, 154, 156, 160
Negroni, María, 12
neo-realism, xxviii, 147–54, 157
"neogauchesca" aesthetic, 147
neogauchesca defiance against narrative of national identity, 158
neoliberal discourse, 164–65
    effect on urban planning, 177
neoliberal globalization, 160

neoliberal paradigm
    worth measured by ability to consume, 169
neoliberal policies, xxvi, xxix, 47–48, 53, 62, 65n14, 94, 97, 173, 205, 211
    contradictions of, 145
    crisis (2001), 111, 122, 205
    de-nationalization as result of, xxviii, 146–47
    "end of geography," 174
    impact on Argentine society, 112, 153
    impact on working class men, 153, 156
    injustice, 146
    intolerance and violence, 146
    New Argentine Cinema's treatment of, 164–65
    new forms of violence, xxii, 69, 204
neorealism, 202n15
New Argentine Cinema, xxviii, 74, 112, 128, 136, 139, 181n2, 195
    antecedents, 165
    Argentine context in, 125, 139
    collapse of the *menemista* dream, 163
    "dirty realism" in, 184
    neorealism, 176
    popularity in international film festivals, 163
    "preceded by a former life we did not see," 130
    representation of violence in, 68, 93–94, 125, 201n13
    subversion of neoliberal discourse, 164–65

visual treatment of space, 184
youth as marginalized segment, 164
new generation of Argentine cinema (late 1990s), 83
New Independent Cinema, 87n2, 89n13
New Latin American Cinema, 68, 82, 184
"new" New Cinema, 87n2
Nielsen, Gustavo, xxiv, 12, 16
   Auschwitz, xxiii, 3–16
   magic of naming evil, 15
The Night of the Hunter (1955), 46n36
Nine Queens (2000), 127
Nisco, Jorge, 206
no-places *(no-lugares),* 189–90
La noche de los lápices, 82, 84
Nombrar lo innombrable (Reati), xxii, xxiii
"non-places of supermodernity," 136, 139
Noriego, Gustavo, 175–76
Nouvelle Vague, 195
La novela de Perón (Martínez), 23
«La novela de Perón» (Mcduffe), 42n2
«La novela es un acto de libertad» (Pla), 42n2
Novoa, Laura, 100
Nuevo Cine Argentino (Bernades), 181n2
Nunca más (Never Again), 6–7, 71

O

Oedipus complex, 48
Oesterheld, Héctor German, 203, 210, 220n1
official politics of oblivion, 74, 78, 205, 207
The Official Story. See La historia oficial (1985)
orphanhood in Buenos Aires, 119, 183, 193
orphans, 26, 117, 120–21, 190, 193–94. *See also* family
Oso (fictional character), 146–47, 149–51, 153, 157–58, 165, 167, 169, 171–72
Un oso rojo (2002), 87n2, 128, 134, 142n4, 145–46, 152, 157
   Buenos Aires in, 145
   embrace of crime, 146, 160
   "neogauchesca" aesthetic, 147
   use of *cumbia villera* (music), 147, 158
Osorio, Myriam, xxiv, 223
"other," 126, 131, 139, 170, 172, 190
outsiders as culprits (in early Argentine science fiction), 204
Oviedo, José Miguel, 47

P

Page, Joanna, 124n6, 173
   "The nation as the *mise-en-scène* of filmmaking in Argentina," 181n4
"paradise lost," xxvi, 121
Paraguay, 205
paraguayos, 151–52, 156, 160
pardon, 82, 207. *See also* Due Obedience, decree of; Full Stop, decree of; *Indulto* (Amnesty Laws)

Parodi, Cristina, "Ficción y realidad en *La novela de Perón* de Tomás Eloy Martínez," 42n2
Pasado y presente (Vezzetti), xxiii, 10
Patagonik Film Group, 206
patriarchal family, 112, 116
patriarchal laws, 34
patriarchal power, 39
patriarchy, 45n31
Paula (fictional character), 100, 103, 185, 190, 193–94
　growth in ability to feel, 195–96
　prostitution only work she can find, 192
pauperization. *See* poverty
Penrose, Valentine, *La comtesse sanglante*, 11
peripheral neighbourhoods, 188–89
Perón, Eva, 42n1
Perón, Juan Domingo, 42n1, 56, 156
Peronist redistribution policies, 170
Peronist welfare state, 205
Peruzzotti, Enrique, xviii
Phizar (fictional character), 210, 212, 216–17
Piña, Cristina, 12
Piñeyro, Marcelo, xxvi, 16
　Caballos salvajes, 110n3
piqueteros (picketers), xx, 118, 187, 192
Pizarnik, Alejandra, 12
　La condesa sangrienta, xxiii, 11
Pizza, birra, faso (1998), 89n13, 146, 152, 157
　Buenos Aieres in, 145
　crime as only way to protect family, 146
　irreverence towards national discourse, 147

　use of *cumbia villera*, 147
　use of music, 147, 158
　violence of social exclusion, 112, 122
Pla, Valeria Grinberg, "La novela es un acto de libertad," 42n2
place, 209. *See also* spaces
　no-places *(no-lugares)*, 189–90
　"non-places of supermodernity," 136, 139
　places that are void of life, 190
"Los placeres de la necrofilia" (Llosa), 42n2
Plan Jefas y Jefes, xvi
Plaza San Martín, 185
Poder y desaparición (Calveiro), 9
police, xv, 114–15, 151, 154, 175, 177
　human rights abuses, xviii–xix
pope, 187–88
post-national community, 159
post-national era of globalization, xvi
post-national space, 146, 160
Postales del porvenir (Reati), 211
postdictatorship cinema. *See* New Argentine Cinema; science fiction film (post-dictatorship)
postmodern subject, 194
"Postnational Boundaries in *Bolivia*" (López-Vicuña), xxviii
potbangings, xv, xx
poverty, xv, 56, 169–70, 184, 207
　culture of, 202n16
　external and foreign, 156–57
　'new poor,' identity crisis of, 200n12
　"structural violence" of, xix, xx
　threat to neoliberal narrative, 155

power
- abuse of, xviii
- ordinary individuals as powerless and devoid of freedom of choice, 139
- patriarchal power, 39
- political power, 13
- regimes of power, 23
- relations, 24
- social operation of power, 30
- state monopoly of physical power, xvi

Power and Disappearance. See Poder y desaparición (Calveiro)
powerful, law of, xxvi
Pratt, Daniel (fictional character), 213–17
Pratt, Hugo, 210
Precarious Life (Butler), 110n7
Primitive Territorial Machine, 53
private film funding, 206
privatization of social life, xxi
privatization of state-owned companies, xiv, 56, 65n14
privatized violence, 209
Proceso de Reorganización Nacional, 82
"Procesos de (des)mitificación en *La novela de Perón y Santa Evita*" (Fajardo), 42n2
The Production of Space (Lefebvre), xxvii
property rights, xiii
prostitution, 185, 190, 196, 199n4. *See also* survival mechanisms
protection and shelter, fantasy of, 122
protective parent, 120–21
protests and demonstrations. *See* civil resistance

The Psychic Life of Power (Butler), 25, 27, 34, 38
psycho-noir drama, 127
psychoanalytic theory, 87n4
El pueblo de los tontos (Shua), 64n1
Puenzo, Luis, 15
punishment, 23–24, 29, 31–32, 38, 55, 96, 98, 104, 108

R

racism, 13, 146, 151, 173, 175. *See also* xenophobia
radical dependency, 26–28
Ramus, Susana Jorgelina, *Sueños sobrevientes de una montonera*, 88n7
Rapado (1996), 89n13
rape, 5–6, 32–34, 44n24, 103
re-representation, 68
readers (or audience), xxv, xxix, 190. *See also* spectator
- moral responsibilities, xxii
- as unwilling confidant, 31
- voyeurism, xxiii, 11–13
Réage, Pauline, *The Story of O*, 43n21
"real," 191, 194–95
"realimagined," xxvii
'reality,' 165
Rear Window, 42n8
Reati, Fernando, xxv, xxvii, 205, 223
- *Nombrar lo innombrable*, xxii, xxiii
- *Postales del porvenir*, 211
- "Torture and Abuse as a National Art Form," xxiii
Recuerdo de la muerte (Bonasso), 88n7
A Red Bear. See Un oso rojo (2002)

redemocratization (1986-90), xviii, 70–72, 76, 88n5, 205
   haunted by violence of the past, 69
redemocratization process, 83–84
   impunity and, 70
Redes de memoria (Boccanera), 88n7
Redgrave, Vanessa, 71
Reguillo, Rossana, 174
Reimis, Reina (fictional character), xxiv, 24, 27, 30, 36
   attempts to avoid subjection, 38
   docile body that can be raped and murdered, 34
   murder, 33, 38–39
   radical dependency, 26–28
   rape, 32–33
   representing the body politic, 42n6
   as successful journalist, 29
   symbolically made to stand for Camargo's mother, 38–39
   warning for other women, 34
Reinoso, Gilou García, 82
Rejtman, Martín, 89n13
Remedi, Gustavo, 147, 158
Reny (fictional character), 185–87, 190–91, 194–95
"La representación de la historia en *La novela de Perón*" (Ganduglia), 42n2
representation, 71, 82
   ethics of, 83–84
   legitimacy of, 69
   process of, 76
   of survival, 70
   of violence, xii, 83–84, 112
revelation, 67
revolutionary process, 60
Rich, Adrenne, 69

Rich, Ruby, 82
Riches, David, xii
Roberto (fictional character), 114, 116–19
Robin, Regine, 78
Rocha, Carolina, 224
   «Barbaric Spectacles,» xxvi
Rodrigo D, 201n13
Rosa (fictional character), 150, 154, 158–59, 165, 167, 171, 173–74, 178
   strategies of resistance, 175
Rose, Jacqueline, *The Psychic Life of Power*, 38
Roth, Cecilia, 108
Rotker, Susana, *Citizens of Fear*, xxi
Rúa, Fernando de la (term of office (2000-2001)), xv, xvi
Rubén (fictional character), xxvii, 127–28, 132–37, 142n4
Los rubios (2003), xxv, 16, 68, 75–82, 84
   blurring documentary and fiction, 75
   campo, 83
   Carri's presence as the subject of gaze (and voice), 79
   as documentary film, 76
   exploration of memory in, 78
   fictionality of memory, 80–81
   fictionality of the Carri character, 77
   fragmentation and opacity of representation, 82
   generational conflict in, 77
   Kohan's analysis of, 79, 81
Rudnitsky, Edgardo, 190
Ruétalo, Victoria, xxix, 224

rule of law, 94, 96, 99, 105, 107. *See also* criminality
rural past as lost paradise, 120
rural violence *vs.* urban violence, 112–13, 115, 118

S

Sade, Marquis de, 12
Salem, Diana, "Historia, memoria y testimonio," 42n2
San Martín, José de (the "Father of the Land"), 187, 190
Sánchez-Prado, Ignacio M., 112
Santa Cruz, xviii
Santa Evita (Martínez), 23
Santiago, Hugo, 204, 209
Sarmiento, Domingo F., xxvi, 94, 125, 127, 135, 170
Sarmiento's dichotomy, 110n3, 139
Scavo, Carlos, 173
schizoanalysis, xxiv, 48, 59, 61
science fiction film (post-dictatorship), xxix, 203–18. *See also* New Argentine Cinema
 "absent" violence in, 208
 allegories of ruined cities, 208
 apocalyptic world of social inequalities, 205
 on economic burden of globalization, 207
 funding for, 206
Scilingo, Adolfo, xxvii
 El vuelo, xvii
Scott, Ridley, 214
Seijas, Rodrigo, 201n14
Señora de nadie, 87n2
September 11, 2001, 110n7
Seré, Mansión, 85

sexual exchanges (or encounters), 185, 189. *See also* prostitution
sexual violence and pornography in works of Marquis de Sade political significance, 12
The Shock Doctrine (Klein), 65n14
Shua, Ana María, xxiv
 Los amores de Laurita, 64n1
 Cabras, mujeres y mulas, 64n1
 Casa de Geishas, 64n1
 Días de pesca, 64n1
 El libro de los recuerdos, 64n1
 El marido argentino promedio, 64n1
 La muerte como efecto secundario, xxiv, 47–62, 64n1
 El pueblo de los tontos, 64n1
 El sol y yo, 64n1
 Soy paciente, 64n1
 La sueñera, 64n1
 Viajando se conoce la gente, 64n1
silence about the past, 82
silence that impunity represents, 71
Silverman, Kaja, 99
Silvia Cassini (fictional character), 72, 74–75, 85
site/sight of meaning
 as mise-en-scène (of science fiction films), 209
«sky» In *El cielito,* 121
Sleeping Beauty, 43n20
Sleepwalker. See La sonámbula (1998)
Slotkin, Richard, 138
Smoking Car. See Vagón fumador (2001)
smuggling as way of surviving, 188
Smulovitz, Catalina, xviii
Snow White, 43n20

social adaptation to overwhelming military power, 9
social classes (structural differences), xii, xv. *See also* inequality
　criticism of (60s and 70s), xii
　lower classes, xiv, xv, xx, 97, 147
　middle class, xiv, xv, xx, xxv, xxvi, 10, 164, 168, 170, 200n12
　middle-class, xxvi, 97–99, 101
　upper classes, xiv
　working class, 113, 146, 152–53, 170
social decadence in Argentine society, 47
social exclusion and violence, 112, 114, 149
social gaze, 70
social identity, 113
social memory, xxv, 7, 68, 74, 85
social mobility, xxv, 153, 172
social orphanhood, 119
social production, 49, 53
social unrest, xv, xvi. *See also* civil resistance
Soja, Edward W., 166
　Thirdspace, xxvii
El sol y yo (Shua), 64n1
Una sola muerte numerosa (Strejelevich), 88n7
Solanas, Fernando, xii, 125, 139
Solanas, Pino, 176
"solidarity camera," 71
La sonámbula (1998), xxix, 204
　Buenos Aires in, 205, 209–10, 212, 215–16
　disappearances in, 215
　ending, 217–18
　"New World Order," 216

opera prima prize, 206
　place in, 208
　subway in, 212
　upper and lower cities in, 211–12
Sontag, Susan, 83–84
Soy paciente (Shua), 64n1
spaces, 137–38, 185. *See also* place
　"any-space-whatever," 136
　"fourthspace," xxvii, xxviii, xxix, xxx
　as frame through which violence of site can be perceived, 184
　lesser known, 184, 188–89
　post-national, 146, 160
　visual treatment of space, 184
　visualization in science fiction film, 208
spectator. *See also* readers (or audience)
　identification with the camera, 87n4
　possible complicities, 70, 75
Stagnaro, Juan Bautista, 89n13, 112
　La furia, xxvi
standard of living, xv, xix, xx, xxvi. *See also* poverty
Stantic, Lita, xxiv, xxv, 68–75, 78, 82, 85, 87n1
　role in Argentine cinema, 87n2
Stark, Jeffrey, xix
state, xii, 97. *See also* welfare state
　absence of protector or benefactor state, 119
　as arbiter among social classes, xiv, xxvi
　control of social production, 53
　downsizing of state, xvi
　embodiment of civilization, 94
　erosion of, 164

failure to provide justice and punish criminal acts, 99, 108
intervention in private interest, 205
legacy of repression, xxii, 8
legitimacy of, 96
reduced role, xxi
weakened state, 98
state-run system of hospitals and nursing homes, 52, 54
   bodies of elderly as bodies-without-organs, 50
   comparison to torture chambers, 51
   microcosm of nation under neoliberalism, 53
   profit from diseases of wealthy elderly, 48
   violence against the bodies of patients, 50, 54, 62
state-sponsored violence, xi, xvii, xxvii, 67
   monopoly over violence, 96–97
   neoliberal measures as, 204
   "unseen" or "unheard," 209
state terror, 15, 82
Stay Tuned for Terror (Extraña invasión) (1965), 204
The Story of O (Réage), 43n21
street theater, 15
Strejelevich, Nora, *Una sola muerte numerosa*, 88n7
structural economic changes. *See* neoliberal policies
"structural violence" of poverty, xix, xx
subemployment, xx
subjectivation, xxiv, 24, 28, 30–31, 34
   Butler's concept of, 24–27, 38

"A Subway Named Möbius" (Deutsche), 211
subways, 211–14, 216
La sueñera (Shua), 64n1
Sueños sobrevientes de una montonera (Ramus), 88n7
surveillance, 24–25, 33
survival mechanisms, 9. *See also* disappearance and survival
survival strategy (stealing, dealing drugs, etc.), 196
survivor's gaze, 72
Svampa, Maristella, xx, 97, 135
Szir, Pable, 87n1

T

Tamburini, Claudio, 85, 88n7
Tan de repente, 87n2
Taylor, Bonnie, 16
Tealdi, Bruno (fictional character), 71–72
Telotte, J.P., 207–8
testimonial narratives, 68, 72–73, 76, 80, 85, 88n7
Theorizing Men and Masculinities (Alsop), 36
Thirdspace (Soja), xxvii
thriller/drama genre, 99–100
time-image, 148
Times to Come. *See Lo que vendrá* (1988)
Today and Tomorrow. *See Hoy y Mañana* (2003)
Tokar, Elisa, 9, 88n7
Tornasol Films, 206
Torres, Diego, 99
Torres, Juan Carlos, xx

torture, xxiii, 42n5, 64n5
   aestheticization of, 10
torture and abuse, 11–12
   in *Auschwitz*, 4–6, 10, 14
"Torture and Abuse as a National Art Form" (Reati), xxiii
torture chambers, 51
totalitarian gaze, 67
totalitarian narrative, 82
transgressive gaze, 69
transnational flows, 164
transnational interests, 174
transnationalization, 154–55, 164
Trapero, Pablo, 87n2, 89n13, 136, 163
Triquell, Ximena, 88n5
Tulchin, Joseph, xxi
"two demons" theory, 8

U

undocumented immigrants, 150, 155
unemployment, xv, xix, xx, 56, 113, 155, 157, 192
   family disintegration, 117
   political protest against, 118
unilateral power, 26, 38
unions, xiv, 97
unsettling of borders. *See* mobile borders
upper classes, xiv
urban poor turned into "foreign" elements, 156
urban strolling, 196
Urban Wounds. See Heridas urbanas (Isla)
urban youth. *See* marginalized youth
Urraca, Beatriz, xxvi, xxvii, 224

Urso, Norberto, 88n7
Uruguay, 205

V

Vagón Fumador (2001), xxix, 184, 186, 195, 199n3
   camera in, 189–90
   city of fragments, 187–88
   desolated areas where nobody helps anybody, 194
   extreme loneliness, 190
   no-places *(no-lugares)*, 189
   soundtrack, 190
   urban dwellers of Buenos Aires (protagonists), 185
Vanished, 206, 214
Vargas Llosa, Mario, "Los placeres de la necrofilia," 42n2
Los Velazquez, 87n1
La vendedora de rosas, 201n13
La venganza del sexo (1967), 204
verbalization of atrocities
   as way to prevent them, xxiii, 3–4, 15
Verbitsky, Horacio, xvii, xxvii
Vezzetti, Hugo, 68, 71–72
   Pasado y presente, xxiii, 10
Viajando se conoce la gente (Shua), 64n1
Videla, Jorge Rafael, 87n3
Vieyra, Emilio, 204
vigilante justice, 115, 122
Villa (Gusmán), xxiii, 8
violence, xiii, xxv, 24, 111, 175, 183–84. *See also* torture
   as an economic, political, and social phenomenon, 112
   against the bodies of the elderly, xxiv, 53–54

from crumbling institutions (family and workplace), xxix, 94
demands response from authorities (in civilized societies), 96
devoid of freedom of choice, 128
dissident armed groups, xvi, xvii
in Hollywood films, 93, 126, 208
of interpretation, 69
legitimate use of, xvi, xvii, 96
monopoly over, 96–97
as "natural" and "aesthetic," 112
overflow of accumulated violence, 142n7
policy of forgetting past violence, 74, 78, 205, 207
representation of, xii, 83–84, 93, 112
result of weakened state, 98
rural violence *vs.* urban violence, 112–13, 115, 118
of site, 184, 191
of social exclusion, 112, 114, 122, 149, 170
state-sponsored, xi, xvii, xxvii, 67 (*See also* military government (1976-83))
structural violence of poverty, xix, xx
triggered by neoliberal reforms, 47, 112, 122, 164, 204
victimizer as impersonal, mediocre bureaucrat, 8
violence, gender, and social class association, 185
Violence (Besteman), xvi
Violence in Argentine Literature (Foster), xxii
voyeurism, xxiii, 12–13, 190
reader/spectator's act of, 11
El vuelo (1995), xvii
El vuelo de la reina (Martínez), xxiii, 23–39
male desire for control and punishment, 24
narrative strategies, 25–31, 33, 37, 44n22
power relations, 24, 32
regimes of power, 23
surveillance, 24–25

W

"wall of silence," 82
A Wall of Silence. See Un muro del silencio (1993)
Wang, Diana, 13
Washington Consensus, xiii
wealthy people, xxi, 48, 55. *See also* concentration of income; inequality
chance to survive, 52
welfare programs
Plan Jefas and Jefes, xvi
welfare state, xiii, xiv, xxv, 170, 205
Wenz, Steven, 122
wilderness, 126–27, 135, 138
Williams, Gareth, 159, 168
Wolf, Sergio, 130, 181n2
"The Aesthetics of the New Argentine Cinema," 184
The Woman in Question. See La mujer en cuestión (Andruetto)

women, xxiv, 36. *See also* female abuse; misogynist ideology; La mujer (the woman)
    murder by controlling lovers, 33–34, 38–39, 44n27, 44n29
    torture, 42n5
Women Fighters. See Mujeres guerrilleras (Diana)
women's sexuality, 27–28, 31, 174–75
working class, 113, 152, 170
    impact of neoliberal policies, 146, 153
workplace, xxix
World Bank, 56

X
xenophobia, 13, 146, 151–54, 171–73, 175

Y
Yo la peor de todas, 87n2
Young, Richard, 47–48

www.ingramcontent.com/pod-product-compliance
Lightning Source LLC
Chambersburg PA
CBHW052058300426
44117CB00013B/2178